INTRODUCTION TO COMPUTER SCIENCE

ABOUT THE AUTHOR

Vladimir Zwass received his Ph.D. in computer science from Columbia University in 1975. He is currently an associate professor and chairman of the Computer Science Committee at Fairleigh Dickinson University. He was previously a member of the professional staff of the International Atomic Energy Agency in Vienna, Austria. As a consultant, he has advised, among other companies, Citibank and the Metropolitan Life Insurance Company.

Professor Zwass is the author of *Programming in FORTRAN,* a companion volume in the Barnes & Noble Outline Series and has contributed to professional journals. He is a member of the Association for Computing Machinery, the Institute of Electrical and Electronics Engineers, Sigma Xi and Eta Kappa Nu.

INTRODUCTION
to

Vladimir Zwass

COMPUTER SCIENCE

BARNES & NOBLE BOOKS
A DIVISION OF HARPER & ROW, PUBLISHERS
New York, Cambridge, Philadelphia, San Francisco
London, Mexico City, São Paulo, Sydney

Designed by Charlotte Staub

Library of Congress Cataloging in Publication Data

Zwass, Vladimir.
  Introduction to computer science.
  (College outline series ; Co/193)
  Bibliography: p.
  Includes index.
  1. Electronic data processing. 2. Electronic digital computers. I. Title.
QA76.Z82   001.64   80-7762
ISBN 0-06-460193-5 (pbk.)

84 9 8 7

To my parents,
Adam and Friderike Zwass,
and to my wife, Alicia

CONTENTS

PREFACE

This book introduces and explains the fundamental concepts of computer science. It is designed to be used in a number of ways: as a textbook, as a textbook supplement, as a review book, as a reference manual, and as an introduction to the field of computing. No previous knowledge of computer science is assumed.

As a college textbook, this volume is intended for a one-semester introduction to computer science course. Together with a textbook on programming in a specific higher level language, it may serve in a two-semester introductory course. Thus, it may be used for the courses designated CS1 and CS2 in the Association for Computing Machinery Curriculum '78.

A companion book in such a course, also in the Barnes & Noble Outline Series, is the author's *Programming in FORTRAN: Structured Programming with FORTRAN IV and FORTRAN 77*.

The present book will also supplement other textbooks for the core curriculum of the Association for Computing Machinery by explaining and illustrating the underlying concepts of computer science.

Since the field of computer science encompasses both the practical and the theoretical aspects of the use and design of computers, its scope is very broad. This is reflected in the structure of the book.

Part One discusses the programming of computers in a manner independent of any specific programming language. Such treatment permits the reader to learn algorithm design, structured design and programming, and the essential constructs of programming languages, without incurring the burden of the details and the bias of a given language. The discussion makes it quite clear that the tools of algorithm design and those of program writing are the same basic programming constructs.

Part Two, supplemented by the appendixes, may be studied independently of Part One. It presents the organization of the three resources of computer systems: hardware, software, and data. The last chapter of this part, together with Appendix C, introduces the essential theoretical concepts of computer science.

Readers who wish to familiarize themselves with the field of computing without making a deeper study of computer science will further their goals by reading the Introduction and Part Two. A rather exhaustive index will help put this book to encyclopedic use. Additional literature is recommended throughout.

I wish to thank my colleagues—computer scientists and practitioners—and my students, for their part in providing the insights needed to develop this presentation of a complex and fast-growing field. I would also like to thank Jeanne Flagg of Barnes & Noble for her expert editorial assistance and Janet Goldstein for her superb job in seeing the book through production.

Vladimir Zwass

INTRODUCTION TO COMPUTER SCIENCE

Introduction
COMPUTERS AND THEIR
USE IN PROBLEM SOLVING

Electronic digital computers emerged in the 1940s and have since entered most fields of human activity as tools for the storage and processing of information.

A computer is not an independent problem solver. However, owing to the speed with which it can retrieve and manipulate large volumes of data, the computer is an essential aid in the problem-solving process. The solution procedure is presented to a computer in the form of a program—a list of the actions required to arrive at the results.

This introduction discusses basic elements of computers and their application as well as the phases of computer program design and implementation.

A. WHAT IS A COMPUTER?

A *computer* is a data-processing machine or, in other words, a machine for the manipulation of symbols. These symbols represent *information* of various kinds, for example, a number or a name.

The word "computer" is used today as an abbreviation for *general-purpose stored-program electronic digital computer*. These attributes refer to the following properties.

General-purpose computers may be applied to solve any solvable problem. The computer is directed by a *program,* that is, a sequence of instructions that determine the operations to be carried out by the machine. Programs are written by humans. One program may be easily replaced by another, thus changing the use of the machine. A machine of more limited capabilities, designed for a particular task, is called a *special-purpose computer.*

All modern computers have their programs stored along with the data in a *memory* (called also *storage*). These *stored-program* computers have been developed from calculating devices in which the sequence of steps to be followed during the calculation is established by means of a plugboard or a "control" punched tape.

The data-processing units of computers are built of *electronic* components, which permit speeds approaching a million elementary operations per second for some machines, and even higher speeds for others. A *computer system* comprises not only data-processing elements, but also *input/output devices,* used to transfer programs and data from the memory of the computer to the outside world and vice-versa. These devices, most frequently electromechanical, are consequently slower.

Digital computers have overshadowed *analog* machines. In analog computers, a physical process (usually the flow of electric current) is used to imitate the computation. The results are obtained by measuring the parameters of the process. Digital computers use symbols as such for computation, without reference to underlying physical phenomena.

B. COMPUTER HARDWARE AND SOFTWARE

In programming, a computer user does not have to deal directly with the physical devices (*hardware*) of the computer system. Instead, special service programs, stored in the computer memory, provide an interface between the user and the bare machine. These programs, called *systems software,* simplify the task of the programmer and the application software written by him or by her and control the use of the hardware.

1. HARDWARE

A computer system includes a number of functionally separate devices that constitute its *hardware:* the *central processor* to which the instructions are directed, the memory system where data and instructions are stored, and input/output devices for communication with the environment of the system.

Computers execute programs; that is, they carry out self-contained sequences of instructions. The central processor (called also CPU, for central processing unit) of the computer is designed to comprehend elementary instructions. Three examples of elementary instructions are (1) add two numbers; (2) compare two numbers and indicate the larger one; (3) carry out next the instruction from a given memory location. These instructions are encoded as sequences of 0's and 1's, to simplify hardware implementation. This code constitutes the *machine language* of a computer. Machine language varies in different computers.

2. SOFTWARE

The intermediary between computer users and hardware is *systems software,* a set of programs that belongs to the configuration of a given computer system and facilitates its use. The programs written by the computer users to obtain solutions to their problems are called *application software.* Often the systems software is referred to in brief as software.

A user of the computer, during the process of program design and implementation which is called *programming,* must specify the operations to be performed. *Natural languages* like English, used for human communication, are not fit for programming because of their ambiguity and lack of precision. On the other hand, programming in a machine language would be exceedingly tedious and would limit the applicability of the programs, since they are not easily transferable to different computers in such form.

Computer users, therefore, program in *programming languages.* The most commonly used are *higher level languages* (such as FORTRAN, COBOL, or PL/I) that combine precision of expression with a certain closeness to natural languages on the one hand and the problem to be solved on the other. Programs written in such languages are largely independent of the characteristics of a particular computer; they are easily *portable* from one machine to another. *Assembly languages,* the other type of programming notations, are much closer to the machine language of a given computer.

A means of translations is required. Programs known as *translators* convert *source programs* (written in a higher level language or in an assembly language, for which the translator has been designed) into *object programs,* expressed in the machine language of the particular computer.

Software also includes *utility programs* (for example, sorting routines) that have been written by *systems programmers,* rather than users, and are stored in the memory of the computer system.

Further, in order to assign the needed resources to a program and to mediate between the demands made by various users in a shared system, a special program is required. This program, which manages all of the system resources, including the users' programs, is called a *supervisor, executive,* or *operating system.*

Extensive programs are required to manage data stores in some computer systems and to facilitate remote communication between a user and the system or, frequently, among distantly located computers.

The operating system, along with the language translators, programs for data management and communication, and utilities programs, constitute the essential software of the computer. User programs (application programs) may be simpler due to the presence of the systems software.

3. INTERDEPENDENCE BETWEEN HARDWARE AND SOFTWARE

From the above description we can conclude that the following functional separation exists between hardware and software of the computer. Hardware is capable of performing elementary operations, specified in the *in-*

struction set of the given computer. Software further extends these capabilities and enables the user:

(a) to specify the program in a manner closer to her or his thinking processes;

(b) to call upon programs resulting from work done by other users or by system programmers to perform part of the task of his or her program;

(c) to rely on automatic resource allocation by the system itself.

C. BRIEF HISTORY OF COMPUTERS

This brief review of the history of computing is designed to give a perspective on the development of electronic digital computers and to show how recently they have emerged.

1. BEFORE THE ERA OF ELECTRICITY

Computational tools emerged in antiquity. The *abacus,* the earliest calculating device, was invented, probably in the Orient, thousands of years ago. By moving beads that have different positional significance on the rods of the abacus, addition and subtraction can be performed. The device is still used in some countries today!

Following a long hiatus, the great 17th-century mathematicians Blaise Pascal and Gottfried Leibniz constructed *mechanical calculators* built around pegged wheels. Pascal's calculator performed only subtraction and addition; Leibniz was able to extend this design for multiplication and division.

Surprisingly, the invention of an *automatic weaving loom* in 1801 by Joseph Jacquard had a strong influence on the future of computing. This tool used *punched cards* to control weaving patterns; that is, a card contained the "program" for the loom's task.

The idea was utilized by Charles Babbage, the creator of the first *general-purpose computer*. He began his work on a card-programmed mechanical "analytical engine" (never completed) in 1833.

Punched-card tabulators were first introduced by Herman Hollerith for the 1890 United States census.

2. EMERGENCE OF MODERN COMPUTERS

In the 1930s the concept of the general-purpose computer became an idea whose time had come. The growing complexity of human society on the one hand, and the new technological possibilities on the other, led to the practical use of the thought of talented people. The English mathematician Alan

Turing made a theoretical analysis of the possibilities of a general-purpose computing device in 1937. The immediate impulse for its implementation was provided by World War II and the computational needs of the military.

In 1944 the first *general-purpose electromechanical* computer, Mark I, became operational at Harvard University. Mechanical computing was slow and unreliable. In 1946 the first *general-purpose electronic computer,* EN-IAC, was completed at the University of Pennslyvania. Its designers, J. Presper Eckert and John W. Mauchly, utilized and expanded the ideas developed by another American scientist, John V. Atanasoff, who first employed electronic devices in the construction of a computer (never completed). The Mark I "program" was located on paper tape, while ENIAC required panel wiring. Under these circumstances, entering a new program into the machine was a major undertaking.

In 1945 John von Neumann of the Institute for Advanced Study introduced the concept of the *stored-program computer.* The first such machine, EDSAC, was completed at Cambridge University in England in 1949.

The era of *mass production* dawned for computers in 1951 when a general-purpose stored-program electronic digital computer, UNIVAC I, was delivered commercially as the first such machine built on an assembly line.

Subsequently, three (or four, according to some views) consecutive *generations* of computers have arisen, distinguished by, among other features, the technology of their electronic devices. The first-generation computers were vacuum-tube machines. The second generation, built on individually packaged transistors, was introduced commercially in 1958. The third generation appeared in 1966 and comprises machines using integrated circuits, that is, logic circuits consisting of many transistors and other electronic devices embedded into a tiny piece (called a *chip*) of semiconductor material of this size: ☐ . The fourth generation of computers is sometimes distinguished by use of large scale integration (LSI), with thousands of transistors on a chip.

In 1965 was installed the first commercial *minicomputer,* a small and relatively inexpensive computer of somewhat limited hardware and software resources. It is often used for a single application rather than for a wide range of applications, as the larger, so-called *mainframe* computers are.

Large scale integration technology resulted, in 1971, in the development of the *microprocessor,* a central processing unit on a single chip. Such a device, when assembled with a few chips for the remaining functions (e.g., memory), constitutes a *microcomputer.*

Mini- and microcomputers, due to their low cost and small size, resulted in a wide distribution of computing. Their capabilities keep growing impressively.

The history of systems software is much briefer, as it originated with the invention of stored-program computers. Initially, the programmers used machine language. Higher level languages began to be introduced in the mid-1950s, with perhaps the most influential of these, FORTRAN, presented in its original form in 1957. Operating systems, initially quite simple in their functions, were also born in the mid-1950s. The 1970s brought sophisticated software for the management of large volumes of interrelated data and remote communications between computers.

D. ESSENTIAL USES OF COMPUTERS

A computer is a tool used by humans in problems-solving processes, rather than a problem-solver in itself. Computers extend human capabilities due to the following attributes: speed of operation, memory capacity, reliability, and cost-effectiveness in many applications.

1. CATEGORIES OF COMPUTER APPLICATIONS

Typical categories of computer applications in which the machine aids the human intellect and senses or relieves people for creative occupations include

(a) tasks that require the management of large volumes of data, such as census analysis or identification of elementary particles;

(b) tasks for which high-speed computation is imperative; these are represented by

(1) *real-time systems* that require a controlling response faster than can be provided by humans, such as rocket guidance or physical process control;

(2) areas where no real-time response is required but where the number of computations involved is so large that the results would be obtained too late to be useful unless a computer was used. Weather forecasting is a good example;

(c) operation in environments inaccessible to humans: these applications included unmanned space flights or operation in the presence of radiation hazards;

(d) routine tasks of a repetitive nature, such as report printing or maintenance of accounts.

The ultimate criterion for the professional use of a computer for a given task is usually cost-effectiveness. In many cases, convenience and just plain satisfaction derived by the user also contribute. Home computing has developed into a significant trend.

2. AREAS OF COMPUTER UTILIZATION

Today almost every area of human endeavor involves the use of computer.
The following computer uses, often appearing jointly, have evolved:

- Numerical computations (the earliest application)
- Information storage and retrieval: the maintenance of a collection of symbolic data, called a *file* (for example, a payroll file), including the programs needed to *access* any item or class of items
- Manipulation of collections of data, including sorting and reduction
- Process control: in a manufacturing process or any other physical process, a computer may be connected to measuring devices on the one hand and controls on the other. The machine analyzes measured data and adjusts the controls in accordance with program instructions
- Communications: handling of messages in communication networks
- Word processing: manipulation of text, most often for printing
- Computer graphics: input, manipulation, and output of pictorial representations, reflecting the real world or created by a human and/or the computer
- System simulation: in order to analyze the behavior of a system, a computer program is used as a model
- Artificial intelligence: a selective trial-and-error search for answers to problems that are believed to require human intelligence because their solution procedure cannot be precisely stated. Examples are theorem-proving and the translation of natural languages, which has so far eluded computerized approaches.

Rapid development of computing is constatly expanding this list.

The costs of computer hardware have been steadily decreasing due to technological progress, whereas the costs of human labor have been on the increase. This combination results in an ever broader use of computers.

E. PROBLEM SOLVING WITH COMPUTERS

As already stressed, the solution of a given problem is up to us. If we choose to incorporate a computer in this work, the following stages may be distinguished in the problem-solving process.

(1) problem definition: The solution we are seeking usually has to apply to a class of problems rather than to a single case. To define this class, assumptions have to be made concerning the information that will be available (the *inputs* to the program to be designed). The nature of the desired results must also be established (the *outputs* from the program for all possible classes of inputs).

(2) problem analysis: The most effective and efficient approach to the solution of the problem must be determined. It may be possible to break up the problem into subproblems. The possibility of incorporating already existing programs should be investigated.

(3) design of the data structure: The composition of the data to be ma-

nipulated by the program is to be determined. This is done in conjunction with the next step.

(4) design of the algorithm: The *algorithm*, or solution procedure for the problem, should be described with the use of an *algorithmic notation*. These notations, avoiding details contained in programs, allow the problem-solver to concentrate on the problem itself.

(5) coding: An appropriate programming language should be selected. A readable program with clear structure should be written.

(6) program implementation: The programmer should be convinced, using the computer and representative sample input data, that the program performs as desired. The behavior of the program in response to all possible input data variations revealed during the problem definition and analysis stages should be investigated.

(7) program documentation: A description of program operation, its data structure, and its input and output specifications must be provided.

(8) program use and possible modification: The program is run, in many cases periodically, to obtain the needed results. It remains a tool and will probably be improved.

F. BASICS OF COMPUTER SYSTEM STRUCTURE

In order to program in a higher level language, it is necessary to understand the elements of computer system organization. A description designed to support such programming is offered here and will be expanded in Chapter 8.

1. FLOW OF INFORMATION IN COMPUTER SYSTEMS

The description of a computer system given in Section B above calls for the basic organization shown in Fig. Introduction–1. This block diagram represents the flow of information (instructions and data) necessary to execute a program.

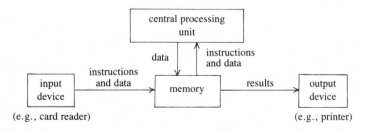

FIGURE INTRODUCTION–1.   Information flow in computers

An *input device* receives the information and places it in the *memory* (also called *storage*). If the instructions are not expressed in the machine language, the software translator is called upon. During the translation and subsequent execution, the *central processing unit* (CPU) fetches the instructions from the memory. During translation, these will, of course, be the instructions of the translator. The CPU also fetches from the memory the necessary data items and applies to them these instructions. The intermediate and final results are also stored in the memory. As the execution of the program is progressing, the results may be communicated the outside world via an *output device*. They may also be stored in memory until the program has been executed and then presented all at once. Programs and/or data may be stored in the memory for extensive perods of time in order to avoid introducing them repeatedly via an input device.

All this information handled by the computer system is encoded as a string of 0's and 1's, that is, in a binary code.

In order to support the described operation of the computer system, extensions to the basic scheme of Fig. Introduction–1 are required. A more detailed picture of the computer system organization is presented in Fig. Introduction–2.

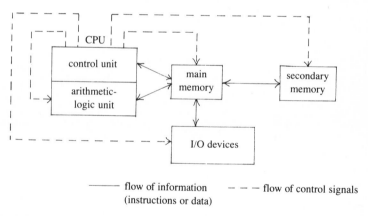

———— flow of information   – – – flow of control signals
(instructions or data)

FIGURE INTRODUCTION–2. The organization of computer systems

2. CENTRAL PROCESSING UNIT

The central processing unit of a computer consists of two functionally distinct parts: the control unit and the arithmetic-logic unit.

The *control unit* directs the actions of the system by carrying out the instructions and establishing their sequence according to the program.

The *arithmetic-logic unit (ALU)* contains the circuitry needed to perform the basic arithmetic operations as well as the logical ones (for example, a comparison). The ALU also contains a certain number of *registers*, or fast-storage elements. Each register can hold a single operand (data item). When in registers, the operands can be added, compared, shifted, or otherwise manipulated.

3. MEMORY

The *main memory* of the computer consists of a number of locations, called *words*, which contain instructions or data items. Every word, consisting of a uniform number of *bits* (each equal 1 or 0), has a unique *address*, its number in the memory. The CPU identifies or *addresses* a given word in order either to *write* into this location, storing new contents in it, or to *read* from it, fetching the contents of the word without erasing them. In this manner, the CPU can obtain the instructions and data for the program and subsequently store the results in the memory.

In order to extend the capacity of the main memory at a reasonable cost, computer systems usually have a *secondary (auxiliary) memory*, selected from cheaper and slower types of storage than the main one. Software and data that are not expected to be needed soon are stored there. The items contained in the secondary storage are usually accessible to the CPU only following their transfer to the main memory.

4. INPUT/OUTPUT DEVICES

A number of *input/output (I/O) devices* serve the need of the computer system for communication with the environment.

The most widely used input devices include card readers and the keyboards attached to display or printing terminals. Output is most often displayed on a cathode ray tube (CRT) screen, similar to a television tube, or printed by a line printer.

Often devices for telecommunication are also included.

SUGGESTIONS FOR FURTHER READING

USES OF COMPUTERS

Slotnick, D. L., and Slotnick, J. K.: *Computers, Their Structure, Use, and Influence*, Prentice-Hall, Englewood Cliffs, N.J., 1979.
This extensive work discusses many aspects of computer application; includes an introduction to computer system organization and BASIC programming.

Dorf, R. C.: *Computer and Man*, Boyd and Fraser, San Francisco, 1974.
In some aspects complementary to the Slotnicks' book, this work includes the discussion of computers in the arts.

Sanders, D. H.: *Computers in Society*, 2nd ed., McGraw-Hill, New York, 1977.
Positive and negative impacts of computers are analyzed.

Adams, J. M., and Haden, D. H.: *Social Effects of Computer Use and Misuse*, Wiley, New York, 1976.

Includes several important papers, documents, and reflections; gives a perspective on the issue of artificial intelligence.

HISTORY OF COMPUTERS

Harmon, M.: *Stretching Man's Mind: A History of Data Processing*, Mason/ Charter, New York, 1975.

From the beginnings.

Goldstine, H. H.: *The Computer: From Pascal to von Neumann,* Princeton University Press, Princeton, N.J., 1974

The author, a collaborator of von Neumann, emphasizes the explosive developments following World War II.

Eames, C., and Eames, R.: *A Computer Perspective*, Harvard University Press, Cambridge, Mass., 1974.

A richly illustrated publication.

Rosen, S., ed.: *Programming Systems and Languages*, McGraw-Hill, New York, 1967.

This collection of seminal papers that appeared in the years 1957-65 contains an introductory historical survey of software and programming languages.

Part One

FUNDAMENTALS OF PROGRAMMING

TO SOLVE A PROBLEM with the use of a computer, a programmer needs to design an algorithm, an unambiguous procedure specifying a finite number of steps to be taken. Every algorithm operates on certain data describing the real-world objects the problem concerns. The steps of the algorithm manipulate these data.

The use of data of appropriate type, organized, when possible, into data structures that reflect the relationships among the particular data items, results in clearer and simpler algorithms. After the algorithm and the data structures used by it have been designed, a program in the selected programming language may be created.

Algorithms consist of steps that manipulate data and of control structures that specify the sequence in which these steps are to be carried out. The essential data manipulation steps are the assignment of value to a data item with variable values, and the input and output of data. These steps may be carried out sequentially, repetitively, or conditionally, as directed by the control structures.

Subalgorithms or subprograms may be called upon to perform a particular subtask in the overall task of the problem solution. Thus, an algorithm and the program that arises from it may be built of several modules. Modular programming makes it possible to design complex systems in a disciplined fashion, with a high degree of reliability and clarity.

To specify algorithms, pseudocode or flowcharts may be employed. When using pseudocode, the programmer specifies the steps of the algorithm using essentially natural language with superimposed control structures. Subsequently, more precision is introduced into this specification. Flowcharts are a traditional graphical tool with standardized symbols.

Both these tools may be used to specify an algorithm in a top-down fashion via the technique of stepwise refinement. Thus, the programmer refines an initial idea of the problem solution into more and more specific terms while identifying the modules that will perform particular subtasks. At the same time the data definition becomes more specific. The last refinement of the algorithm will be coded for computer execution.

The essential programming statements introduced here may be used to express algorithms. They are also, in various form, incorporated in the general-purpose higher level programming languages. Thus, this part of the book also describes the essential facilities of these languages.

ALGORITHMS AND THEIR EXPRESSION

The crucial stage of problem solving with a computer is the design of algorithm and underlying data structure. An algorithm is a precisely expressed procedure for obtaining the problem solution, which is subsequently presented to a computer in the selected programming language. Algorithms are presented in a manner convenient for a human reader, while programs serve the needs of computers.

It is important to remember while designing an algorithm that a computer only follows instructions and cannot take any action that has not been explicitly ordered. The problem solver should, therefore, provide for every facet of the problem in the algorithm itself.

This chapter specifies the properties that procedures for problem solution must have if they are to be algorithms. These are finiteness, absence of ambiguity, sequence definition, input and output definition, effectiveness, and scope definition. Flowcharts are presented as a tool for the expression of algorithms. Subsequent chapters introduce another, frequently more helpful, tool for this task: pseudocode.

A. DEFINITION OF ALGORITHMS

All the tasks that can be carried out by a computer can be stated as algorithms. Once an algorithm has been designed, it is coded in a programming language, and the program is executed by a computer.

An *algorithm* is a finite set of instructions that specify a sequence of operations to be carried out in order to solve a specific problem or class of problems. In other words, an algorithm is a recipe for solving the problem.

An algorithm may be presented on several levels of detail. The hardware of a computer can only obey instructions if they are expressed in the machine language of the computer. The algorithm designer would find it difficult to think in terms of these instructions, as the details would obscure the essence of the procedure. Even the higher level programming languages, which are understood by the software translators of computers, are not a convenient tool for the expression of algorithms. Programs with thousands of higher level language instructions occur frequently. It is impossible to present such programs immediately in their final form; the designer must start with a much more concise representation.

EXAMPLE 1–1

A simple algorithm is presented here as a list of English-language instructions.

Problem

Determine the largest of any three integers.

Algorithm: Initial Description

1. Compare the first and second integers and establish which is the larger one.
2. Compare the latter with the third integer. The larger is the result.

Algorithm: Refinement

1. Obtain (input) the first number; call it NUM1.
2. Obtain (input) the second number; call it NUM2.
3. Compare NUM1 with NUM2 and select the larger; if the two integers are equal, select NUM1. Call this number LARGE.
4. Obtain (input) the third number, call it NUM3.
5. Compare LARGE with NUM3 and select the larger; if the two integers are equal, select LARGE. Call this number LARGE.
6. Present (output) LARGE.
7. Stop.

Notes

Note that certain decisions in the design of an algorithm are made at the discretion of the designer (for example, step 4 may precede step 3; if two integers are equal in step 3, either may be selected). Other steps, however, cannot be changed without impairing the integrity of the algorithm (for example, step 4 has to precede step 5).

EXAMPLE 1–2

A problem somewhat more complex than that of the preceding example is presented here.

Problem

Determine the largest of N integers, where $N > 2$.

Analysis

Since the algorithm has to apply to any $N > 2$, N should be a parameter. Therefore, it will be one of the inputs to the program, along with the integers themselves.

Algorithm

1. Input N.
2. Input first integer; call it NUM1.

3. Input second integer; call it LARGE.
4. Set up a counter of integers that have been read in, call it COUNT; set COUNT to equal 2.
5. Compare NUM1 with LARGE; if NUM1 is greater than LARGE, set LARGE to equal NUM1. If COUNT equals N, output LARGE and stop; else increment COUNT by 1, input next integer, and call it NUM1, then perform this step (step 5) again.

Notes

1. Note that it is not the intention of the problem to save the numbers in memory. Think about the way the numbers are called and the reason for this.
2. Follow through the algorithm with a few integers of your choice and convince yourself in its correctness.

B. PROPERTIES OF ALGORITHMS

A procedure that does not have the properties outlined below is not an algorithm and will not in general give the desired result when a program based on it is presented to a computer.

1. FINITENESS

The execution of a programmed algorithm must be completed after a finite number of operations have been performed. Otherwise, we cannot claim that the execution produces a solution.

It is obvious that the solution procedure outlined in Example 1–1 has this property, since every step is performed once. In Example 1–2, step 5 will be repeated $N-1$ times. Since N is finite, we can conclude that the execution of this procedure will be completed after a finite number of steps.

The following should be noted:

(a) The actual number of steps depends on the granularity (degree of detail) of the presentation of an algorithm.

In Example 1–2, step 5 may be broken up into several steps; steps 1 and 2 may be merged.

Ultimately, the number of steps is the number of machine instructions executed. This, however, also depends on the model of the computer utilized.

(b) The number of operations performed is rarely equal to the number of steps in the description of the algorithm (or the number of instructions in the program). The number of steps actually performed during the execution of a program depends on the input data and may not always be ascertained beforehand.

(c) An algorithm leading to a program due to terminate in 100 years is hardly useful.

The essence of the algorithmic method consists in the repetition of the same step or steps, possibly with some modifications, many times during the execution of a program based on a given algorithm. The length of the program is, therefore, a poor indicator of the execution time.

In Example 1–2 a single step, step 5, is performed $N-1$ times.

2. ABSENCE OF AMBIGUITY

The representation of every step of an algorithm should have a unique interpretation although a representation for a computer may differ from that for a human. It is convenient for humans to deal with algorithms presented in a notation with sparse detail (for example, by a pseudocode or a flowchart), while the computer requires the algorithm to be coded into a program.

This condition means that every time an algorithm is presented for execution with the same input data, the same results are obtained.

3. SEQUENCE DEFINITION

The sequence in which the steps of the algorithm are to be carried out should be unambiguously specified. An algorithm ought to have a unique initial instruction, and every instruction must have a unique successor for given input data.

In algorithmic specifications, including programs, the instructions are performed from top to bottom (the implicit successor of an instruction is the physically consecutive one), unless the instructions themselves otherwise specify.

In Example 1–2, step 5 may be performed more than once, depending on N.

4. INPUT AND OUTPUT DEFINITION

Inputs are the data items presented to the algorithm. An algorithm has either no inputs or a predetermined number of them. The inputs must be of the type for which the algorithm has been designed.

In Example 1–1, the algorithm has three inputs. In Example 1–2, the algorithm is designed for $N + 1$ inputs.

In both cases the inputs must be integers.

Outputs are the data items presented to the outside world as the result of the execution of a program based on the algorithm. An algorithm ought to produce at least one output (otherwise, what use is it?).

The algorithms of Examples 1–1 and 1–2 have one output each.

5. EFFECTIVENESS

The instructions of an algorithm may order the computer only to perform tasks that it is capable of carrying out. A computer cannot perform an instruction if it has insufficient information or if the result of the execution of the order is inherently undefined.

If in Example 1–2 step 1 were omitted, the algorithm would be ineffective for lack of sufficient information, since in step 5 COUNT could not be compared to N.

If any of an algorithm's instructions ordered division of an integer by 0, the result would be undefined.

6. SCOPE DEFINITION

An algorithm applies to a specific problem or class of problems: the range of the inputs has to be predefined; the range determines the generality of the algorithm.

The scope of the algorithm in Example 1–2 is wider than that of the algorithm in Example 1–1 since the latter is the special case, with $N = 3$, of the former.

C. FLOWCHARTS

Due to the detail required of them, programming languages are not a convenient tool for initial algorithm design. The means of notation widely used for algorithms is a flowchart.

The most significant advantage of flowcharts is a clear presentation of the *flow of control* in the algorithm, i.e., the sequence in which operations are performed.

A *flowchart* is a two-dimensional representation of an algorithm; the predefined graphic symbols of a flowchart are used to indicate the various operations and the flow of control.

A basic set of established flowchart symbols is presented in Fig. 1–1. Six of these symbols are *outlines* (also called boxes) of various shapes. When used in a flowchart, they contain appropriate wording, which is made more precise as the flowchart is developed for a given problem solution. The remaining symbol, the *flowline,* determines the sequencing among the tasks represented by the outlines.

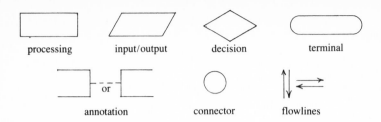

FIGURE 1-1. Flowchart outlines

The symbols have the following meanings:

processing: one or more computational tasks are to be performed sequentially.

input/output: data are to be read into the computer memory from an input device or data are to be passed from the memory to an output device.

decision: two alternative execution paths are possible. The path to be followed is selected during the execution by testing whether or not the condition specified within the outline is fulfilled.

terminal: appears either at the beginning of a flowchart (and contains the word "Start") or at its conclusion (and contains "Stop").

annotation: contains comments that simplify the understanding of the algorithm or the description of data.

connector: makes it possible to separate a flowchart into parts. Identical cross-reference symbols are placed in this outline where the flowline is interrupted and where it resumes.

flowlines: indicate the outline that is to be entered next.

A flowchart for the algorithm of Example 1–2 is presented in Fig. 1–2.

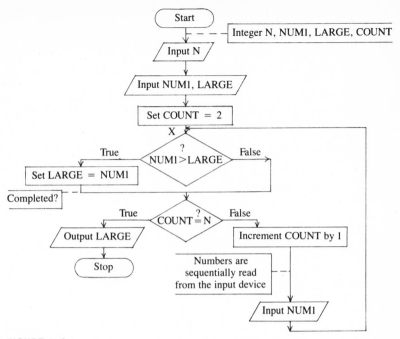

FIGURE 1–2.

If the flowchart were to be separated into two parts at the point marked with X, the connectors would be used as shown in Fig. 1–3.

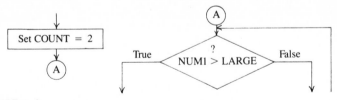

FIGURE 1–3.

Flowcharts allow the reader to follow the logic of the algorithm more easily than would a linear description in English. Since the choice of the level of detail is at the discretion of the algorithm designer, flowcharts are suitable to the top-down method of design (described in Chapter 3), in which the general strategy of an algorithm is established initially and refinements are introduced subsequently. An alternative method algorithm presentation, pseudocode, is also discussed in Chapter 3.

SUGGESTIONS FOR FURTHER READING
FOR CHAPTERS 1–4

Wirth, N.: *Systematic Programming: An Introduction,* Prentice-Hall, Englewood Cliffs, N.J., 1973.

A terse introduction to the design of simple algorithms and to the essential programming constructs. Along the way you will also learn the basics of the programming language Pascal.

Maly, K., and Hanson, A. R.: *Fundamentals of the Computing Sciences,* Prentice-Hall, Englewood Cliffs, N.J.; 1978.

An extensive discussion of algorithm design.

Tremblay, J.-P., and Bunt, R. B.: *An Introduction to Computer Science: Algorithmic Approach,* McGraw-Hill, New York, 1979.

Problem solving in a variety of situations.

Tonge, F. M., and Feldman, J.: *Computing: an Introduction to Procedures and Procedure-Followers,* McGraw-Hill, New York, 1975.

Wirth, N.: *Algorithms + Data Structures = Programs,* Prentice-Hall, Englewood Cliffs, N.J., 1976.

A more advanced book, it may be read as a sequel to *Systematic Programming* by the same author.

Dahl, O.-J., Dijkstra, E. W., and Hoare, C. A. R.: *Structured Programming,* Academic, New York, 1972.

A sophisticated, but clearly presented, discussion of program and data structuring.

2

DATA MANIPULATION
IN PROGRAMMING

General concepts of algorithmic specification in higher level languages are presented in this and the next chapters. These concepts underlie all the general-purpose programming languages and form the basis for learning any of them. At the same time, forms of expression based on these concepts are used for the design of algorithms, before the actual coding. Program components used for the manipulation of data are also discussed in this chapter.

Data items provide information about objects to which the algorithm (or program) refers in general terms. For example, a program that computes a personal income tax needs, among other data, the value of the income of the individual and the values of the tax brackets.

Natural dependencies among the data items, if used to structure the data, result in simpler algorithms. For example, if the tax brackets are arranged in an ordered table, manipulated by the tax computation program, the value of the tax may be determined quite easily, with the brackets easy to modify if necessary.

Various data types and structures are thus employed to represent real-world objects and dependencies between them. Types of simple data items are introduced in this chapter. Arrays, an essential data structure, are also discussed. The discussion of data structures is continued in Chapter 5.

A. STATEMENTS

A *program* is a representation of an algorithm, suitable for computer execution. Since programs are usually not written in machine language, the computer first translates the program and then executes it.

A *statement* is the elementary component of a program. A program statement is analogous to a sentence in a natural language. Statements are either executable or nonexecutable.

Executable statements of a higher level language are orders for an action to be taken by the central processing unit of a computer during the execution of the program. These statements are imperatives. They are translated by software translators into one or (usually) more machine language instructions.

Nonexecutable statements are orders to the language translators or other systems programs and do not produce machine language instructions to be incorporated in the object program. These statements are of descriptive nature. They usually serve to allocate memory space for the data utilized by the program.

Another distinction between programming language statements depends on whether or not they influence the flow of control within a program. Statements are executed sequentially, in the order that they have been presented to the computer, unless there is a *transfer of control*. Some executable statements transfer control to a statement other than the one immediately following. The transfer decision is usually based on fulfillment of a certain condition. Nonexecutable statements and the executable statements that do not transfer control do not influence the sequence of execution, but instead perform tasks of data manipulation.

Data manipulation statements are discussed in this chapter; transfer of control statements, in the following one.

B. SIMPLE DATA TYPES

Algorithms, and programs arising from them, operate on data. The action of an executable statement is reflected as a change of a value of an item of data. Input data are transformed by the program, after intermediate stages, into output data. In the problem-solving process, the design of the data structure is as important as the design of the algorithm and of the program based on it.

Only *simple* (unstructured) *data* are considered here. *Structured data,* discussed in Chapter 5, are collections of simple data items with defined relationships between them. Arrays, structured data with implicitly defined interrelationships, are presented in this chapter.

Data items, as well as program instructions, are represented in the computer memory by one or (usually) more bits.

A *data type* is an interpretation applied to a set of bits representing a given data item. Operations that may be applied to a data item depend on its type. Higher level programming languages usually afford *declarative statements (declarations)* that the programmer uses to specify the type of data items in a program.

The following are the simple data types and the values they may take on:

Integer: a signed number with no fractional part
Real: a signed number with an integer and a fractional part

Both integer and real data types represent numerical data. Additional numerical data types are available in some programming languages (for example, double precision and complex data in FORTRAN).

Logical (or **Boolean**): a data type with only two possible values: **True** and **False** (represented as 1 and 0). Essentially data of this type are used to represent the conditions which underlie decisions as to the flow of control, although they may be utilized to represent any objects with binary values.

Character: an alphabetic character or numerical digit (called together *alphanumeric characters)* or a special symbol (such as $, !, etc.). Characters are usually organized into sequences called *strings* (see Chapter 5). The representations of a number as a numerical data item and as a string differ! This data type extends the power of computers from calculation to general symbolic processing: manipulation of any text.

Most general-purpose languages of today provide these four data types. The availability of various data types makes it easier to design programs in a given language. Certain languages allow the programmer to define his or her own data types in support of the particular application.

In addition, the **Pointer** data type is available in some higher level programming languages. Pointer data identify addresses of other data items. Pointers are used to create data structures (see Chapter 5).

The implementation of various data types with the use of memory words is discussed in Chapter 5.

C. CONSTANTS, VARIABLES, AND ARRAYS

The value of a simple data item in a given algorithm may remain constant or may vary. These items are, therefore, subdivided into constants and variables. The kind of structured data most frequently used is an array.

1. CONSTANTS AND VARIABLES

A *constant* is a data item that remains unchanged throughout the computation based on an algorithm and is, therefore, specified by its value, which is used directly in an algorithm or a program.

A *variable* is a named data item, the value of which may change during the execution of the program.

Constants and variables may be of various types; thus we may have a logical constant or a real variable.

EXAMPLE 2-1

The following simple problem will be used to exemplify several concepts throughout this chapter.

Problem

Add two integers and present the sum.

Algorithm

An initial flowchart of the algorithm is provided in Fig. 2–1.

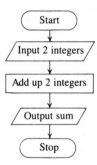

FIGURE 2-1.

In this example, the number of integers is a constant (2); the integers themselves are variables.

Reference to a variable value can be made only via the memory location (or locations) where that value has been stored. The value of the variable is the current content of this named location.

The ability to use variables differentiates computers from rudimentary calculators. Their use makes it possible to postpone presenting actual values until the appropriate point during the program execution.

Memory space is allocated to variables usually as the result of a declarative statement. Subsequently, in order to reference a variable, the address of its location must be used. When using a higher level language, the programmer does not have to be concerned with the actual numerical address. The locations are addressed symbolically. *Symbolic addressing* means that the program refers to the locations by the name of the variable whose value they contain.

Variable names are assigned by the programmer according to the conventions of a given programming language. We will consider them to be a continuous sequence of up to six capital letters and digits, beginning with a letter. Language translators and other systems software associate the variable names used in the program with the numerical memory addresses.

EXAMPLE 2-2

Let us assume that a declarative statement established COUNT as an integer variable. If the location with an address 15555 was assigned to this variable, we have the situation presented in Fig. 2–2(a).

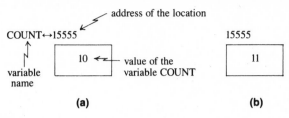

FIGURE 2–2.

The location with the address 15555 contains the value of the variable named COUNT. This value is currently 10. Following the execution of a statement that adds 1 to the COUNT, only the contents of the location will change, as shown in Fig. 2–2(b).

A value may be given to a variable in two essential ways. It may be read in from an input device or assigned during the execution of the program. The kind of value that a variable may acquire depends on its type.

2. ARRAYS

An *array* is a collection of data items of the same type referred to collectively by a single name.

Individual data items, the *array elements,* are ordered by their *subscripts (indexes);* for this reason they are sometimes called *subscripted variables.* The number of subscripts of an array determines its dimensionality. An element of an array is indicated by the array name followed by its subscripts, which appear in parentheses.

Most frequently, arrays with one or two dimensions are used. A one-dimensional array corresponds to a vector; a two-dimensional array to a matrix.

Every element of an array of a given type has two characteristics: its position within the array as determined by its subscripts, and its value.

EXAMPLE 2–3

We have a one-dimensional integer array SCORES. SCORES is thus the name of the array; to refer to the *I*th element of it we would use an index: SCORES(I).

This array, consisting of five elements 17, −3, 2, 4, −5, is shown in Fig. 2–3. It is assumed here that the subscript of the first element is 1 (rather than 0).

An analogy between an array and a table can be clearly seen.

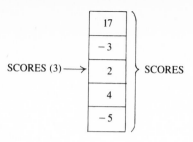

FIGURE 2-3.

EXAMPLE 2-4

To represent sales of a company consisting of three sales regions with four districts per region, a two-dimensional real array SALES may be utilized.

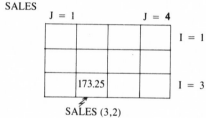

FIGURE 2-4.

A graphical representation of the array is shown in Fig. 2-4. The first subscript of the array corresponds to the row number (which identifies the region), the second subscript to the column number (identifying the district).

It is obvious that subscripts ought to be exclusively integer values, since they denote the positions of array elements.

In many programming languages, arrays have to be declared with the use of a nonexecutable statement.

D. DECLARATIONS

A *declaration* (declarative statement) provides information to the language translator concerning the type of variables and, in the case of structured data, the structure.

Using this information, the translators and other systems software are able to allocate memory space for the data, associate the addresses of the locations reserved for the variables (or arrays) with their names, and select the operations applicable to the data.

Once a variable has been declared in such a statement, it may be subsequently referenced in the program by its name.

In the case of simple data, a declaration has the following general form:

Data type list of variables

Since in Example 2–1 both input variables as well as their sum are integers, they may be declared as

Integer NUM1, NUM2, SUM

They may be subsequently referenced by these names.

In programming languages with *static memory allocation,* such as FORTRAN or COBOL, memory space is allocated to the data by the software translator. In languages with *dynamic memory allocation,* such as ALGOL or PL/I, memory may be assigned to data or released when not needed during the execution of the program.

If the storage is to be allocated during the translation, that is, prior to the program execution, the space required for arrays is to be stated in their declarations.

Thus, to declare an array in the absence of limitations imposed by static memory allocation, it suffices to state its type and dimensionality, for example, as follows:

Integer SALES (1:M, 1:N)

where M and N are integer variables; or, if it is implicit that the subscripts start with 1,

Integer SALES (M, N)

In a language with static memory allocation, the range of subscripts has to be declared in constant terms, for example, as SALES (1:3, 1:5) or SALES (3, 5)

In the description of an algorithm (rather than in a program), it is not generally necessary to delimit the subscript in constant terms.

E. INPUT AND OUTPUT

Input or *output operations* that transfer a single value are elementary operations in higher level programming languages. The details are performed by the systems software.

On input, the value is presented to the computer by the input device (e.g., on a punched card or through a terminal keyboard); on output, it is presented by the computer through the output device (e.g., on a printer or display).

The type of the data presented is usually described by a declarative statement.

The general form of the statements is

Input (device) list of variables
Output (device) list of variables

Instead of **Input**, some languages use **Read** or **Get**; instead of **Output**, **Write** or **Put**.

If the device used as the source or sink of data is implicitly known, it need not be mentioned in these statements. In this case we may regard the input data as coming from the general input file, while the output occurs to the general output file.

From the input device the data are channeled to memory locations of the computer. These locations have been associated with the variable names as a result of the declarations. Subsequently, these data may be symbolically referenced by their names. Constants are, naturally, defined in the program itself, and no input is needed.

When an output statement is executed, a copy of the contents of the locations mentioned in the list of variables is channeled to the output device.

In Example 2–1 we need the following statements:

Input NUM1, NUM2
Output SUM

In order to perform input or output, we frequently desire to specify the layout of the data. Some programming languages include format statements that serve this purpose.

F. ASSIGNMENT

The value of a variable may be established by reading it in from an input device or by using an assignment statement, by which means data manipulation is performed.

1. GENERAL FORM OF ASSIGNMENT STATEMENTS

Assignment is the operation of giving a value to a variable as the result of an assignment statement. In other words, when the assignment is performed, the value is placed in a memory location corresponding to a given variable name.

The general form of an assignment statement is

variable name ← expression

The arrow is the *assignment operator* (some languages use = or := instead of ←). For example,

$$X \leftarrow Y + 2$$

The type of the expression on the right-hand side corresponds to the type of the variable on the left-hand side. The type of variables appearing in the expression must be consistent with the type of the expression. If variables appear on the right-hand side of an assignment, they must have had values assigned to them beforehand.

2. EXPRESSIONS

An *expression* is a formula for obtaining a value. Expressions consist of *operands* (constants or variables) and *operators* (symbols that reflect the rules for transformation of the operand values). Rules of precedence govern the application of operators to operands for a given type of expression. An expression is evaluated from left to right unless the rules of precedence otherwise order.

The following types of expressions may be distinguished:

(a) Arithmetic expressions contain only real and integer variables and constants (in *mixed-mode* expressions). If a given language implementation prohibits such mixed-mode expressions, each expression must consist exclusively of integer or real variables and constants.

These expressions are formed in accordance with the usual rules of arithmetic. *Unary* arithmetic operator for negative values (−) and *binary* arithmetical operators for addition (+), subtraction (−), multiplication (∗), division (/), and exponentiation (↑ or ∗∗), as well as parentheses are generally allowed. Ordinary rules of precedence usually apply.

In the case of integer expressions, an *integer division* operation (÷) is defined. This operation causes the fractional part of the quotient to be discarded.

(b) Logical expressions yield one of the two values **True** and **False**. Among others, logical operators apply; the essential of these are **not**, **and**, **or**, defined by the truth table in Chapter 3–A–3.

The usual application of logical expressions, further discussed in Chapter 3–A, is to express a condition on which the flow of control in a program is to be predicated.

(c) String-manipulation expressions operate on character-valued constants and variables.

The operators for string manipulation include those for concatenation (joining together) of two strings or for selection and possible replacement of a substring. These operations are further discussed in Chapter 5–J.

3. EXECUTION OF AN ASSIGNMENT STATEMENT

An assignment statement produces the following sequence of events:

(a) The expression is evaluated according to the appropriate rules of precedence, and a single value, of a type corresponding to the type of the expression, is obtained.

(b) The value is placed in the location corresponding to the variable name on the left-hand side of the assignment statement.

In Example 2–1, the assignment

SUM ← NUM1 + NUM2

accomplishes the addition.

Constants provide a special case of expressions. To set the value of a variable VAR to 0 we would perform

VAR ← 0

When a location is referenced (i.e., when its contents are read), the value contained in it does not change. The *reading* operation *is nondestructive*.

When a location is assigned a new value (i.e., when it is written into), its previous contents are automatically obliterated. The *writing* operation *is destructive*.

In relation to the assignment statement this means that the original value of the variable whose name appears on the left-hand side is replaced, while the values of the variables referenced on the right-hand side remain unchanged.

Note carefully the following:

(a) When a statement of the form

VAR1 ← VAR2

is executed, the value of VAR2 is *copied* into the location corresponding to VAR1. The value of VAR2 is not changed! The previous value of VAR1 is obliterated.

(b) If the values of two variables, VAR1 and VAR2, have to be exchanged, the use of an intermediate location is necessary:

INTERM ← VAR1
VAR1   ← VAR2
VAR2   ← INTERM

G. COMMENTS

All programming languages offer the possibility of inserting *comments* explaining the data and the logic of the program, along with the statements.

Although comments are listed together with the program statements, they do not influence the execution of programs.

Comments are usually identified by the first character in the line. We will assume that any line starting with an asterisk (*) is a comment. In our description of algorithms, we will also be able to place a comment on a line containing a statement; the comment, surrounded by asterisks, will follow the statement. Judicious use of comments in every program is imperative.

H. REVIEW

The following types of higher-level language statements have been defined:

(1) input/output ⎫
(2) assignment   ⎬ — executable statements
(3) declaration   — nonexecutable statement

These statements do not influence the flow of control within the program, i.e., the sequence in which the program statements are executed. Declaration statements describe data items, while input and assignment statements assign values to them; output statements make these values known to the outside world.

Comments may be inserted anywhere in the program without influencing its execution.

If these statements were the only constituents of programming languages, every statement in a program could only be executed once. Since the algorithmic method is built around repetitive execution of instructions, additional statements are needed to allow for selective repetition and alternative execution. Statements influencing the flow of control are presented in the next chapter.

Every programming language also contains program delimiters to indicate final and, sometimes, initial statements.

As a result of the above discussion, we arrive at the final flowchart for Example 2–1, which is presented in Fig. 2–5.

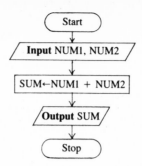

FIGURE 2–5.

3

CONTROL STRUCTURES
IN PROGRAM DESIGN

Basic structures necessary to organize the flow of control in an algorithm or a program are presented in this chapter. Three of these structures: sequence (**begin-end**), decision (**if-then-else**), and loop (**while-do**) constitute the fundamental means of program organization necessary to support a systematic programming process, often called *structured programming*. Additional control structures such as **repeat-until** loop, indexed loop, and multiple choice (**case**) constructs may be employed to simplify this process. A loop may be left prematurely with the execution of an **exit** statement.

While these structures are not available directly in every general-purpose programming language, it is possible to construct them using the statements of a given language. The programmer will find that thinking in terms of these constructs will produce clearly organized programs that are relatively easy to write, read, and modify.

In certain infrequent programming situations, it is expedient, however, to employ an unconditional transfer of control (**goto**).

Two important tools for program design are introduced. Pseudocode, frequently used in preference to flowcharts, serves to arrive at the ready-to-code algorithm in a process of top-down program design, called *stepwise refinement*. Decision tables are employed for systematic consideration of all actions to be taken by the program if certain conditions (or their combinations) exist.

A. CONDITIONS

Two of the basic programming structures, the decision and the loop, make the flow of control in a program dependent on the existence of a specified condition. To specify such conditions, logical expressions are used. In simpler cases, these logical expressions are relations.

1. WHAT A CONDITION IS

A *condition* is an assertion of a value of a variable or of a dependence between the values of two or more variables.

The value of a condition is tested and may be either **True** or **False**. It is, therefore, specified by a logical expression.

> **EXAMPLE 3–1**
>
> We may desire to specify and test conditions concerning values of variables; for example:
> (a) integer variable I equals 0;
> (b) integer variable I is smaller than the doubled value of the integer variable K;
> (c) real variable X is not smaller than real variable Y, and logical variable L has the value **True**.

Conditions are used to provide for the possibility of alternative execution paths in the program (in a decision statement) or to ensure repetitive execution of a group of statements in a loop.

A *simple condition* is a relation; a *compound condition* is a general logical expression that may contain logical variables and relations, with logical operands connecting them.

Since a condition is expressed by a logical expression, its value may be stored in a logical variable as the result of an assignment statement of a form

$$\text{logical variable} \leftarrow \text{logical expression}$$

2. RELATIONS

A *relation* is a logical expression that consists of two arithmetic expressions connected by a *relational operator*, i.e., one of the following

$$< \;\leqslant\; = \;\neq\; \geqslant\; >$$

The general form of a relation is therefore

$$\text{arithmetic expression} \quad \genfrac{}{}{0pt}{}{\text{relational}}{\text{operator}} \quad \text{arithmetic expression}$$

Relations serve to express simple conditions.

> **EXAMPLE 3–2**
>
> Assertions stated in Example 3–1 may be specified with the use of relations as follows:
> (a) $I = 0$
>   Note that this is not an assignment!

(b) $I < 2 * K$

(c) This assertion cannot be specified with a simple condition; a compound condition is required (see below).

The value of the relation is **True** if the condition expressed by it exists; otherwise the value is **False**. Note that the value is not assigned to any location; it is only tested. Note also that this value is of logical type.

In order to test the truth of a relation, its left- and right-hand sides are evaluated, and the question is answered, "does the relational operator express the truth?" If yes, the test gives the value **True**; if not, **False**.

EXAMPLE 3–3

If at the time the relation

$$A * B + C \geqslant D - E$$

is evaluated, the variables, assumed to be of integer type, have the following values:

$$A = 1 \quad B = 2 \quad C = 3 \quad D = 10 \quad E = 5,$$

then when the relation is tested, we have

$$A * B + C = 5; \quad D - E = 5$$

and the relation has the value **True**.

3. COMPOUND CONDITIONS

A compound condition is expressed with the use of any logical expression.

A correct logical expression may contain, in the order of precedence:

(a) arithmetical operators

** (exponentiation operator, sometimes represented as ↑)

* /

+ **−**

These may only join numerical operands.

(b) relational operators

$$< \leqslant = \neq \geqslant >$$

These also may only join numerical data.

(c) logical (Boolean) operators

not

and

or

The action of the Boolean operators is specified by their truth table presented in Table 3–1. The calculus of logical variables, called Boolean algebra, is further discussed in Appendix C.

TABLE 3–1. Truth table for essential operators, where P and Q are logical variables (or relations)

VALUES OF VARIABLES		RESULT OF OPERATION		
P	Q	not P	P and Q	P or Q
False	False	True	False	False
False	True	True	False	True
True	False	False	False	True
True	True	False	True	True

Logical operators operate exclusively on logical-valued entities. These entities may be relations, logical variables, or logical constants (**True** and **False**).

The precedence levels of operations used in logical expressions are brought together in Fig. 3–1.

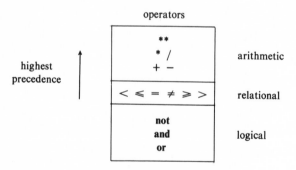

FIGURE 3–1. Operator precedence in logical expressions

Parentheses may be employed to change this order of precedence. Operations of the same order of precedence are performed from left to right.

EXAMPLE 3–4

To specify the assertion of Example 3–1(c), we may use the following compound condition:

$$X \geq Y \text{ and } L$$

The order of evaluation, according to the order of operator precedence and the left-to-right rule, is shown in Fig. 3–2.

FIGURE 3-2.

Note how the second part of the assertion is expressed.

EXAMPLE 3-5

To express the following assertion:

> TOTAL is greater than PART but no greater than the difference between GRAND and PART (where all three are real variables)

this condition may be used:

TOTAL > PART **and** TOTAL ≤ GRAND − PART

EXAMPLE 3-6

Figure 3–3 illustrates the order of evaluation of a compound condition, where BLUE and WIDE are logical variables, and DEPTH and LENGTH are real variables:

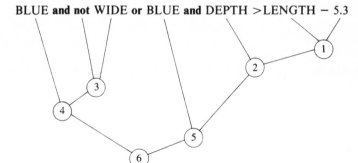

FIGURE 3-3.

Notes
1. Since a relation evaluates to a logical value, it may be joined to another logical operand by a logical operator (as in step 5).
2. Adjacent **and** and **not** (as well as **or** and **not**) do not violate syntax of logical expressions; operators **and** and **or** cannot be legitimately adjacent in a logical expression.

B. DECISION

When the programmer desires to specify two alternative courses of action in an algorithm (or a program), the choice being predicated on the existence of certain conditions, the decision construct is used. In order to select among several alternatives, decisions are nested within one another.

A graphic tool, called a decision table, is helpful in program design when a complex set of conditions and actions has to be considered.

1. DECISION CONSTRUCT

The *decision (branching) statement* is the mechanism for the specification of two alternative statements (or groups of statements), one of which will be chosen for execution as the effect of the given decision statement. This provides the possibility of expressing the following thought: "If a given condition exists, one alternative action should be carried out; otherwise the other alternative action should be taken."

Conditions are specified using logical expressions. The general form of the decision statement is

$$\text{if } C \text{ then } S_1 \text{ else } S_2$$

where S_1 and S_2 are statements (or groups of statements) and C is a condition.

The decision statement is executed as follows:

(a) Condition C is tested and the value **True** or **False** is obtained.
(b) **if** the value is **True,** then S_1 is executed next, **else** (if the value is **False**) S_2 is executed next. Subsequently, the statement following S_2 is executed.

The flowchart of the **if-then-else** construct is shown in Fig. 3–4.

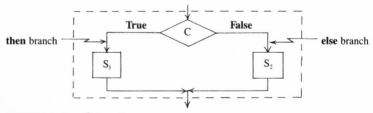

FIGURE 3–4.   **if-then-else** construct

To increase readability of the program, it is a good practice to indent this statement as shown:

$$\textbf{if } C \textbf{ then}$$
$$S_1$$
$$\textbf{else}$$
$$S_2$$

EXAMPLE 3–7

The solution to the following problem will be developed gradually throughout this chapter.

Problem

N integers are to be read in. All the positive integers (including 0's) and all the negative integers are to be separately counted.

Use of Decision Construct

In order to process a given integer, the following statement, initially expressed in English, will be incorporated in the algorithm:

> **if** the integer is greater or equal to 0 **then**
>   increment the counter of positive integers by 1
> **else**
>   increment the counter of negative integers by 1

As will be discussed later in this chapter, expressing an algorithm initially in this form is a helpful method of design.

A special case of the decision statement occurs when the alternative to the statement to be executed conditionally is no action. Such a statement expresses the following thought: "If the given condition exists, execute statement S; otherwise execute the statement following S in the program."

The flowchart of such an **if-then** construct is shown in Fig. 3–5.

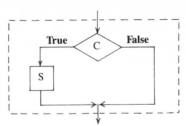

FIGURE 3–5.   **if-then** construct

To avoid ambiguity,† this construct is represented as

$$\textbf{if } C \textbf{ then}$$
$$S$$
$$\textbf{else}$$

where the **else** branch is empty.

---

†The ambiguity arises when an **else** is omitted in a nested decision sequence (see next section). In some programming languages the **else** branch is optional and the **else** always applies to the closest **if** without its own **else**.

2. NESTED DECISIONS

In order to implement a multiway decision (a selection among several alternatives), nested **if-then-else** structure is used. This is built by placing iteratively another decision statement as S_1 or S_2.

For the two-level nesting in both branches we obtain:

> **if** C_1 **then**
>   **if** C_2 **then**
> S_1
>   **else**
> S_2
> **else**
>   **if** C_3 **then**
> S_3
>   **else**
> S_4

The flowchart of this particular structure is shown in Fig. 3–6.

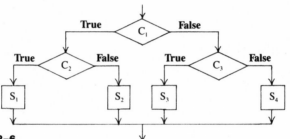

FIGURE 3–6.

It is easier to grasp the algorithm (or program) if no nesting occurs in the **then** branch of the construct. Conditions may be expressed to accomplish this. If such discipline is maintained, a nested **if-then-else** construct has the following general form:

> **if** C_1 **then**
> S_1
> **else**
>   **if** C_2 **then**
> S_2
>   **else** .
>   .
>   .
>   **if** C_n **then**
> S_n
>   **else**
> S_{n+1}

The flowchart of this construct is presented in Fig. 3–7.

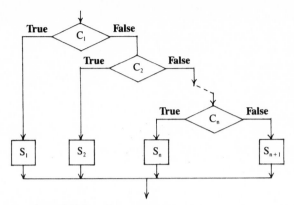

FIGURE 3–7. Nested **if-then-else** constructs

3. DECISION TABLES[†]

When a number of conditions exist that in various combination ought to influence further program execution flow, a graphic tool called a decision table may be used. A *decision table* specifies in tabular form the actions to be taken by the program if a given condition or combination of conditions exist.

Decision tables have the format shown below.

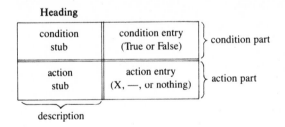

Thus, a table consists of four parts: two, on the left, list all possible conditions and actions, and two, on the right, mark which actions are to take

†This section may be skipped without a loss of continuity.

place when a given combination of conditions exists (the entries of these latter two, considered vertically, are called rules).

A decision table is designed as follows:

(a) List all possible conditions in the condition stub
(b) List all possible actions in the action stub
(c) Provide the number of rules to equal all possible combinations of conditions (2^n for n conditions), excluding obviously impossible or unneeded ones
(d) For every condition entry, mark with X the action entry against the action(s) to be taken
(e) If possible, merge rules differing only in irrelevant conditions.

This is illustrated by the following example.

EXAMPLE 3–8

A decision table for the computation of weekly pay, shown below, expresses the following logic: standard hourly rate applies for 40 or fewer hours worked during the weekdays; weekend work is paid double; names of workers with less than 40 hours worked during the weekdays who worked on the weekend are to be printed out.

Weekly pay	1	2	3	4	5
1. Worked 40 hours in weekdays	F	F	F	T	T
2. Worked less than 40 hours in weekdays	F	T	T	F	F
3. Worked weekends	T	F	T	F	T
1. Compute pay at standard rate		X	X	X	X
2. Compute weekend pay	X		X		X
3. Print out name	X		X		

Note that in this case two combinations of conditions (those involving the two first conditions being true) are impossible and thus omitted from the table. Also the case in which the worker did not work at all has been omitted.

Subsequently, a table may be simplified by introducing so-called don't-care symbols (−), which signify that a certain condition is irrelevant.

Thus, in our example, the simplified table below is obtained by merging rules 2 and 4:

Weekly pay	1	2	3	4
1. Worked 40 hours in weekdays	F	-	F	T
2. Worked less than 40 hours in weekdays	F	-	T	F
3. Worked weekends	T	F	T	T
1. Compute pay at standard rate		X	X	X
2. Compute weekend pay	X		X	X
3. Print out name	X		X	

Thus, if the worker did not work during the weekend, the same processing is applied irrespective of the number of hours put in by him or her during the weekdays.

A decision table may then be directly represented as an **if-then-else** construct. Care has to be taken to encode it in a pleasing fashion.

We will assume that logical variables: FORTY, LESS, and WKND express our three conditions. Then, the last decision table may be encoded as follows:

```
if not WKND then
     compute pay at standard rate
else
     if FORTY then
          compute pay at standard rate;
          compute weekend pay and add to total
     else
          compute weekend pay;
          print out name;
          if LESS then
               compute pay at standard rate and add to total
          else;
```

Note that several attempts may have to be made to arrive at the final construct and that time-saving modifications may be introduced in the actual program.

The use of decision tables forces the programmer to consider systematically all possible conditions and actions and is thus helpful in program design along with such tools as flowchart or pseudocode discussed below.

C. LOOP

The loop mechanism causes repeated execution of a sequence of statements as long as a certain condition is true. When the condition ceases to hold, control is passed to the statement following the last statement of the loop. Such repeated execution is called *iteration*.

If a loop is entered, the execution of the statements included in it (called the *body* of the loop) should, after a finite time, cause the reversal of the condition that caused the entry. Otherwise, an infinite loop would exist, which would represent a programming error and would require the program execution to be stopped by external means.

Every time the body of the loop is executed, the value of at least one variable is changed. Therefore, repeated execution has a cumulative effect.

The general form of the *loop statement* is

while C do S

where C is a condition and S is a statement or a group of statements.

The loop statement is executed as follows:

(a) Condition C is tested.
(b) If the value of C is **True**, S is executed and control is then returned to the **while** statement for the condition to be tested again; otherwise (if the value of C is **False**), the statement following S is executed.

The flowchart of the **while-do** construct is shown in Fig. 3–8.

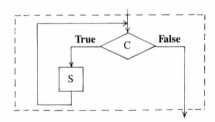

FIGURE 3–8.   **while-do** loop

Indentation of the form

while C do
S

is good practice.

    In Example 3–7 we need:

> **while** we have read in fewer than N integers **do**
>   read in the next integer;
>   increment the appropriate counter by 1;
>   increment the count of integers read so far by 1

Note that if C is **False** immediately before the loop statement is entered,

S will not be executed at all. If C is initially **True** and S is executed, the execution of S should cause C to become **False** after a finite number of repetitions.

D. COMPOUND STATEMENT

As mentioned in Sections B and C of this chapter, it is frequently necessary to place more than one statement in the alternative branches of a decision statement or within a loop. This is made possible by a *compound statement* that encloses a number of other statements within two delimiters **begin** and **end**.

The general form of a compound statement is

$$\textbf{begin } S_1; S_2; \ldots; S_n \textbf{ end}$$

where S_1 is any statement.

This statement causes sequential execution of the enclosed statements S_1, $\ldots, S_n$.

The flowchart of this construct is shown in Fig. 3–9.

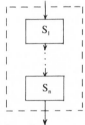

FIGURE 3–9. Sequence (**begin-end**)

If a compound statement is not placed in a single line, the suggested indentation is

$$
\begin{aligned}
&\textbf{begin}\\
&\qquad S_1;\\
&\qquad .\\
&\qquad .\\
&\qquad .\\
&\qquad S_n\\
&\textbf{end}
\end{aligned}
$$

Every program which consists of more than one statement is itself a compound statement.

Every component of a compound statement but the last is delimited from the following one by a semicolon (the last one is delimited by **end**). This makes it possible to place several statements on a line or to have a single statement spanning lines.

Statements that make up a compound statement may be decision or loop statements, as well as assignments and input/output statements. The first two statement types may, in turn, include a compound statement in their branches or as a loop body, respectively.

The following is a solution to the problem posed in Example 3–7, presented in two ways.

A. Algorithm expressed by a flowchart (Fig. 3–10).

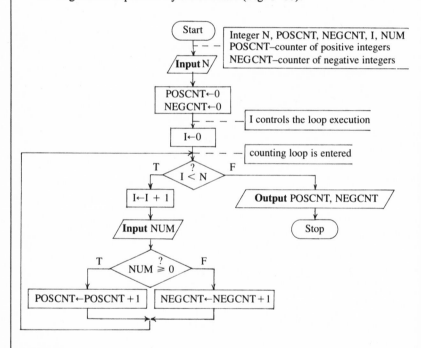

FIGURE 3–10.

Notes
1. While on Fig. 3–10 the comments serve the purpose of explaining the technique, usually they are problem-oriented.
2. A single location, NUM, is used to hold the incoming integers. While this is economic in terms of memory use, only a single (most recent) integer is available in memory at a time.

If our problem required storing the entire array in memory, an array NUM(I) could be used for the purpose.

Note that in our specific case this could be accomplished by textual substitution of NUM(I) for NUM, assuming that a declaration

Integer NUM(N)

would be present in the program.

Follow the logic through.

B. Algorithm expressed by basic programming language constructs.

```
*PROGRAM COUNTS POSITIVE AND NEGATIVE INTEGERS
begin
      Integer N, POSCNT, NEGCNT, I, NUM;
*INITIALIZE
      Input N;
      POSCNT←0;  *COUNT OF POSITIVE INTEGERS*
      NEGCNT←0; *COUNT OF NEGATIVE INTEGERS*
      I← 0;          *COUNT OF INTEGERS READ IN*
*COUNT
      while I < N do
          begin
                I← I + 1;
                Input NUM;
                if NUM ≥ 0 then
                      POSCNT← POSCNT + 1
                else
                      NEGCNT← NEGCNT + 1
          end;
      Output POSCNT, NEGCNT
end
```

E. UNCONDITIONAL TRANSFER OF CONTROL. LABELS

The constructs presented; **if-then-else**, **while-do**, and **begin-end**; are sufficient to express any algorithm. If a program is built using these or similar constructs exclusively, its organization is likely to be clear and well structured.

Sometimes it is, however, difficult to impose these constructs upon a given algorithm. In these cases *unconditional transfer of control* (**goto** statements) may be used. This statement orders the execution of a given statement regardless of its place in the program sequence. The flow of control then proceeds from it.

The unconditional transfer-of-control statement has the general form

goto label

A *label* is the symbolic address of a program statement. Labels are defined within a program by writing them in front of a statement and delimiting them with a special symbol (e.g., a colon). A statement requires a label only if it is to be referenced by another statement, such as a **goto** statement. Labels are generally formed following the same rules as in the case of variable names (although in some languages, such as FORTRAN, labels are numbers). Names created by a programmer, such as variable names and labels, are called *identifiers*.

Since a label identifies a statement, no two statements in a program may have the same label.

EXAMPLE 3–9

A program may include the following statements:

.
.
.

goto THAT;

.
.
.

THAT: FIRST←0;

.
.
.

Following the execution of the **goto** statement, control passes to the statement labeled THAT. The intervening statements are not executed if **goto** is.

The use of a **goto** statement is rarely desirable and should follow a consideration and rejection of other alternatives of expressing the program logic. A disciplined alternative to the **goto,** called an **exit** statement, is available in some programming languages (see Section G-3 of this chapter); in most situations, it may serve to replace the **goto.**

F. DESIGN OF ALGORITHMS. PSEUDOCODE

An algorithm for a problem solution emerges gradually. Thus, the design process results in successive refinements of the algorithm from its original, very general, form to the point when the algorithm may be coded in the chosen programming language. This technique of algorithm (or program) design is known as *stepwise refinement* or *top-down design.* For larger programs, this process includes modular decomposition (see Chapter 4–D).

The number of refinements needed depends on the complexity of the algorithm. Two forms of expression are most frequently used to present algorithms. The first, flowcharts, have been introduced in Chapter 1. An alternative technique, pseudocode, is presented here. *Pseudocode* is a textual presentation of an algorithm, where the actions to be taken by the machine are specified in a manner close to a natural language, with the control structures imposing the logic.

Thus, a final algorithm results from a top-down (from the general to the particular) process of successive refinement of pseudocode. Ultimately, the algorithm may be expressed by the basic statements presented in this and preceding chapters, with the avoidance of detail of a particular programming language (as, for example, the second presentation of the solution in Example 3–7). Extensive use is also made of subprograms, discussed in the next chapter.

The pseudocode of an algorithm becomes a part of the program documentation.

Detailed discussion of the design and presentation of two relatively simple algorithms is presented here. (For the discussion of string processing, see Chapter 5–J.)

EXAMPLE 3–10. Euclid's algorithm

Problem

The greatest common divisor (GCD) of two positive integers is to be determined. (The GCD of two integers is the largest integer by which both of them can be divided exactly.)

Solution

The initial, verbal, solution is subsequently presented in a flowchart form, as well as in the alternative, pseudocode, form.

1. Verbal description of the algorithm: The larger integer is divided by the smaller one. If the remainder is 0, the smaller integer is the required result; otherwise the larger integer is discarded and the smaller integer is treated as the larger one and the remainder as the smaller one, whereupon the procedure is repeated from the beginning.

2. Test: The algorithm is checked for the integers 12 and 46.

   $46 : 12 = 3$, remainder = 10
   $12 : 10 = 1$, remainder = 2
   $10 : 2 \ = 5$, remainder = 0
   GCD = 2

3. Initial flowchart of the algorithm (Fig. 3–11).

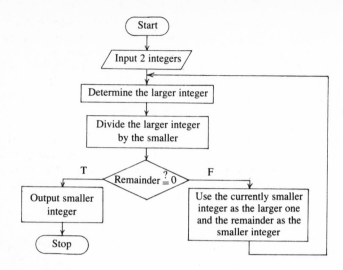

FIGURE 3–11.

4. Refined flowchart (Fig. 3–12);

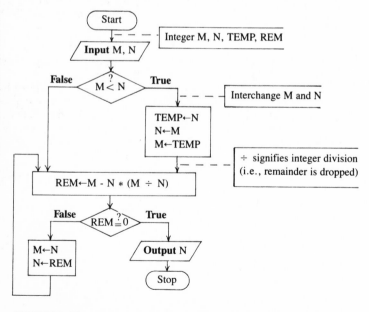

FIGURE 3–12.

5. Algorithm expressed by basic programming structures.

```
*EUCLID'S ALGORITHM FOR FINDING GCD OF TWO POSITIVE
*INTEGERS M AND N
begin
    Integer M, N, TEMP, REM;
    Input M, N;
*DETERMINE THE LARGER INTEGER
    if M < N then
      begin
          TEMP←N;
          N←M;
          M← TEMP
      end
    else;
*COMPUTE REMAINDER
    REM←M − N * (M ÷ N);
*KEEP DIVIDING AND INTERCHANGING UNTIL THE REMAINDER
*BECOMES 0
    while REM ≠ 0 do
      begin
          M←N;
          N←REM;
          REM←M − N * (M ÷ N)
      end;
    Output N
end
```

Notes
1. Note that in order for the **while** statement to be first executed, variable REM ought to have a value. Thus, it is necessary to repeat the statement computing the remainder.
2. Convince yourself that the algorithm works correctly without the initial interchange of variable values if M < N. In this case, the interchange occurs as the first iteration of the loop.

   Do you think, however, that the algorithm is easier to understand as presented? Do you think the algorithm takes longer to execute as presented (count the number of tests and the number of assignments that will be performed in both cases)?

EXAMPLE 3-11. Enhanced bubble sort

Sorting data and searching them are the most common computer applications. There exist, therefore, numerous algorithms to perform these tasks. Presented here is one, a sorting algorithm. Though not very efficient, it is quite simple and thus often used when few items are to be sorted. (A search algorithm is discussed in Example 3-17.)

A set of integer numbers is to be sorted. Ascending order is desired: the larger the number, the higher it should stand in the final list.

Verbal Description of the Algorithm

A bubble sort consists in pairwise comparison of adjacent numbers starting at the one end of the array of numbers. The pair is exchanged if the numbers are in the opposite order to the desired one. One pass through all the numbers does not, in general, suffice. Passes are repeated until, on the last pass, no exchanges are necessary. This confirms that the numbers are in order. Numbers "bubble up" from "the bottom" to take their final place in the array—hence the name of the algorithm. Application of this algorithm to a sample array of numbers is shown below.

i	UNSORTED ARRAY	AFTER PASS 1	AFTER PASS 2	AFTER PASS 3	AFTER PASS 4 (NO EXCHANGES)
7	13	17	17	17	17
6	10	13	13	13	13
5	−10	10	10	10	10
4	17	−10	2	2	2
3	−15	2	−10	−3	−3
2	2	−15	−3	−10	−10
1	−3	−3	−15	−15	−15

Where ⌐ signifies "bubbling". The details of pass 1 are given below, where successive columns indicate the order following the comparison. ⊐ signifies an exchange; ⊐ signifies no exchange.

INITIAL ORDER	1ST	2ND	3RD	4TH	5TH	6TH
				COMPARISONS		
13	13	13	13	13	13	17
10	10	10	10	10	17	13
−10	−10	−10	−10	17	10	10
17	17	17	17	−10	−10	−10
−15	−15	2	2	2	2	2
2	2	−15	−15	−15	−15	−15
−3	−3	−3	−3	−3	−3	−3

It may be observed that the last number moved up during any pass arrives at its final position. An enhanced bubble sort is a bubble sort with a time-saving provision based on this observation: we do not move beyond the number that was moved last at the previous pass; moreover, if the last number was moved into the position second from "the bottom," the sort has been completed and there is no necessity to make an additional pass without any exchanges.

Pseudocode: Initial Description

*BUBBLE SORT
begin
    Input array;
    while exchanges are expected **do**
        perform next pass over the array;
    Output (sorted) array
end

Pseudocode: First Refinement

*ENHANCED BUBBLE SORT IN ASCENDING ORDER
begin
    Input array;
    mark LIMIT; *LIMIT—INDEX OF THE LAST ITEM
                          TO BE COMPARED*
*PERFORM CONSECUTIVE PASSES
    while exchanges expected **do**
        begin
            start at the bottom;
*PERFORM A SINGLE PASS
            while below LIMIT **and** LIMIT $\neq$ 1 **do**
                begin
                    compare pairwise and exchange
                        if necessary;
                    move to next pair
                end;
            mark new LIMIT
        end;
    Output (sorted) array
end

Pseudocode: Second Refinement

*ENHANCED BUBBLE SORT IN ASCENDING ORDER
begin
    Integer A(N), LIMIT, LAST, TEMP, I;
*INPUT ARRAY
    Input N;
    I $\leftarrow$ 1;
    while I $\leq$ N **do**
        begin
            Input A(I);
            I $\leftarrow$ I + 1
        end;

```
*MARK LIMIT—INDEX OF THE LAST ITEM TO BE CONSIDERED
    LIMIT ← N;
*PERFORM CONSECUTIVE PASSES
*IF LIMIT EQUALS 0, THERE WERE NO EXCHANGES DURING
*THE LAST PASS; IF LIMIT EQUALS 1, NUMBERS ARE IN
*ORDER
    while LIMIT > 1 do
        begin
            I ← 1;
*INITIALIZE LAST—INDEX OF THE ITEM MOVED LAST
*DURING THIS PASS
            LAST ← 0;
*PERFORM A SINGLE PASS
            while I < LIMIT do
                begin
*EXCHANGE THE PAIR IF NECESSARY
                    if A(I) > A(I + 1) then
                        begin
                            TEMP ← A(I);
                            A(I) ← A(I + 1);
                            A(I + 1) ← TEMP;
                            LAST ← I
                        end
                    else;
*MOVE TO NEXT PAIR
                    I ← I + 1;
                end;
*MARK NEW LIMIT
            LIMIT ← LAST
        end;
*OUTPUT SORTED ARRAY
    I ← 1;
    while I ≤ N do
        begin
            Output A(I);
            I ← I + 1
        end
end
```

Notes

1. Observe that the algorithm works correctly for special cases ($N = 0$ or $N = 1$).
2. Note the use of variables LAST and LIMIT.
3. Study the modification rendering the refinement of the algorithm from its initial form. The level of detail displayed here in the last refinement is not always required.
4. Apply the algorithm to an array of numbers and trace
   a. consecutive passes over the array;
   b. values of variables LAST and LIMIT.

G. ADDITIONAL CONTROL STRUCTURES

While **begin-end, if-then-else,** and **while-do** constructs suffice to design any algorithm, it is often more natural to resort to different constructs.

Two of these mechanisms are loops: **repeat-until** and indexed loop, and the third is the multiple choice (**case**) statement. Also, an **exit** statement may be used as a more disciplined form of a **goto**.

1. ALTERNATIVE LOOPING CONSTRUCTS

Two alternative looping constructs are sometimes used. In a **repeat-until** loop, the looping condition is tested following the execution of the loop body rather than before it as in the **while-do** loop. An indexed loop construct automatically maintains the variable (loop index) that determines the number of iterations.

A. REPEAT-UNTIL LOOP

In certain programming situations, it is convenient to execute repeatedly a group of statements, with subsequent checking on whether a specified condition has arisen. When this occurs, control passes to the statement following the loop; otherwise, iteration continues.

The general form of such a loop construct is

repeat S **until** C

where S is a statement or group of statements and C is a condition.

This loop is executed as follows:

1. Statement S is executed.
2. Condition C is tested.
3. If C is **False,** the control is returned to the **repeat** statement, whereupon S is executed again; otherwise (C is **True**) the statement following the loop is executed.

It should be noted that the statement (or group of statements) S is executed at least once. If S is then executed again, its repeated execution should change the value of the condition C to **True.**

The flowchart of the **repeat-until** construct is shown in Fig. 3–13.

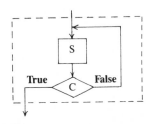

FIGURE 3–13. Repeat-until loop

It is advisable to indent the construct as follows:

repeat
S
until C

The **repeat-until** looping construct may be used in preference to the **while-do** loop when the use of the latter appears artificial.

EXAMPLE 3-12

In Example 3-10 (5), in preference to the **while-do** loop, we could use a **repeat-until** loop. The part of the algorithm following the determination of the larger integer becomes

```
repeat
    begin
        REM←M − N * (M ÷ N);
        M←N;
        N←REM
    end

until REM = 0;

Output M   *DUE TO THE LAST EXCHANGE*
```

Note that the assignment to REM does not have to be included twice.

EXAMPLE 3-13

When a number of data items has to be read in a program, it is desirable to have the computer do the counting. Thus, a sentinel (trailer), a data item outside the range of the actual data, is included as the last item.

Thus, in Example 3-11, if we knew that no element of the array equals 0, the following code fragment could be used to input the array:

```
*ALTERNATIVE INPUT SEQUENCE FOR BUBBLE SORT
I ← 0;
repeat
    begin
        I ← I + 1;
        Input A(I)
    end
until A(I) = 0;
N ← I − 1;
```

Note that some programming languages have an explicit mechanism to test for the end of the input file.

B. INDEXED LOOP

The *indexed loop* (called also *counting loop*) construct provides automatic management of the loop index that determines the number of iterations. The general form of the indexed loop is

for INDEX ← INITIAL-VALUE **until** FINAL-VALUE **by** STEP **do** S

The flowchart of this construct, shown in Fig. 3–14, explains how it is executed.

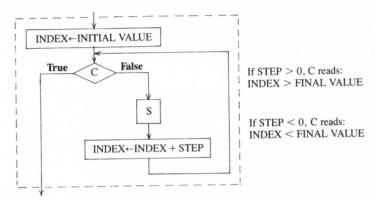

If STEP > 0, C reads:
INDEX > FINAL VALUE

If STEP < 0, C reads:
INDEX < FINAL VALUE

FIGURE 3–14. Indexed loop.

All four variables used in the construct ought to have integer values.

Note that this loop "does more work" than the two other looping constructs: it initializes and maintains the loop index, as well as checks for completion. Thus, it is a terse form of expression, where applicable.

EXAMPLE 3–14
If we want to obtain the sum of the first 50 positive integers, the following indexed loop may be utilized:

```
SUM ← 0;
for I ← 1 until 50 by 1 do
    SUM ← SUM + I;
```

An alternative fragment using a **while-do** loop reads as follows:

```
SUM ←0;
I ← 1;
while I ≤ 50 do
    begin
        SUM ← SUM + I;
        I ← I + 1
    end;
```

2. MULTIPLE CHOICE

When a decision that may have several outcomes is to be made, the **case** construct may be used.

The general form of the **case** statement is

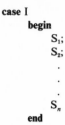

where I is an integer variable with values ranging from 1 to $N > 1$, and S_1, ..., S_n are statements.

A flowchart explaining the execution of this construct is shown in Fig. 3–15 (a nonstandard box is used to show a test with several outcomes).

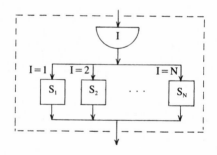

FIGURE 3–15. **case** construct

The **case** statement is executed as follows:

(a) The value of integer variable I is determined.
(b) If this value is j, the statement S_j is executed. Subsequently, the statement following the last textual component of the **case** statement (i.e., following S_n) is executed.

Various multiple-choice alternatives may be easily encoded into a **case** statement. Its use obviates the need for a sometimes deeply nested **if-then-else** construct.

EXAMPLE 3–15

Accounts receivable due from four customers have to be totaled. A single receivable record consists of the customer code (with values from 1 to 4) and the amount due. The end of the input file is marked by the customer code of 0.

```
*TOTALING ACCOUNTS RECEIVABLE
begin
      Integer CODE;
      Real DUE, TOTAL(4);
      for K←1 until 4 by 1 do    *INITIALIZE*
            TOTAL(K) ← 0;
*CLASSIFY AND ADD AMOUNT DUE
      Input CODE, DUE;
      while CODE ≠ 0 do
            begin
                  case CODE
                     begin
                           TOTAL(1) ← TOTAL(1)+DUE;
                           TOTAL(2) ← TOTAL(2)+DUE;
                           TOTAL(3) ← TOTAL(3)+DUE;
                           TOTAL(4) ← TOTAL(4)+DUE
                     end;
                  Input CODE, DUE
            end;
      for K ← 1 until 4 by 1 do
            Output TOTAL (K)
end
```

Notes
1. Note the difference in meaning between the **case** and the compound statement (the first causes sequential, and the second, mutually exclusive, execution of the enclosed statements).
2. Convince yourself that the algorithm works correctly if there are no input data.
3. Design the equivalent nested **if-then-else** construct and compare the two.

3. EXIT

It is sometimes convenient when a certain condition arises to exit from a loop before its completion. This may be, of course, accomplished with the use of a **goto** statement. A more disciplined form of leaving a loop, and, possibly, the constructs that include it, is the **exit** statement.

The general form of this statement is

exit label

where the label identifies the first statement of the construct from which the exit is accomplished. Upon the execution of an **exit** statement control passes to the statement immediately following the construct.

Thus, several levels of nested control constructs may be exited.

EXAMPLE 3–16

The following code fragment may be used to supplant the one shown in Example 3–15.

```
*CLASSIFY AND ADD AMOUNT DUE
CLASS: repeat
            begin
                Input CODE, DUE;
                if CODE = 0 then
                        exit CLASS
                else;
                case CODE
                    begin
                        .
                        .
                        .
                    end
            end
       until CODE = 0
```

Note that we could actually write
    until forever
since the execution of the **repeat-until** loop will always be completed via the **exit** statement.

The **exit** statements are most frequently used to check for special conditions, including errors, concerning the data processed by the loop. The following important example makes use of the **exit** construct.

EXAMPLE 3–17. Binary search

Searching, along with sorting (discussed in Example 3–11), is a most common computer application. It consists in scanning a list of items in order to find the desired item. In practice, the purpose of a search is to obtain the data stored along with the item that identifies it (called the key) and for which the search is performed.

If the list of items is not sorted, a *sequential search* has to be performed: starting with the first item in the list, the list items are compared with the item searched for until the requisite item is found or until the end of the list is reached without success.

Sequential search is inherently slow: a successful search requires on the average $N/2$ comparisons if the list holds N items. Much faster is binary search, one of many algorithms that may be used to search sorted lists.

Binary search resembles a procedure we would use to look up a word in an unfamiliar dictionary. Let us assume the list is sorted in ascending order. First, the middle of the list is checked: if our look-up item is smaller than that in the middle of the list, the search has to continue in the first half of the list; if our item is larger than the middle one, the search will be confined to the second half of the list. We then search the selected half in the same way by checking its middle record, etc. The search may be successfully completed by our finding the requisite item or completed with the discovery that the item is not in the list.

Binary search requires on the average about $\log_2 N$ comparisons to find an item in a list of N items; it is thus much faster than sequential search.

The following is the pseudocode of the algorithm. Note that lowercase comments increase readability in this case.

```
*BINARY SEARCH
*A list KEY(I) consists of N items; we are searching for the
*item called GIVEN; its position INDEX in the list will be
*determined. If the item is not found, the INDEX will be 0.
begin
    Integer KEY(N), GIVEN, INDEX, LOW, HIGH;
    Input N, GIVEN;
    for I←1 until N by 1 do
        Input KEY(I);
    LOW ← 1; *the lowest position in the sublist being searched*
    HIGH ← N; *the highest position in the sublist being searched*
*The position INDEX of the item GIVEN is determined
SRC: while LOW ≤ HIGH do
        begin
            INDEX ← (LOW + HIGH) ÷ 2; *integer division*
            if GIVEN < KEY(INDEX) then
              HIGH ← INDEX − 1 *look in the first half*
            else
              if GIVEN > KEY (INDEX) then
                LOW ← INDEX + 1 *look in the second half*
              else
                exit SRC        *found*
*Value of INDEX is returned
        end;
    if LOW > HIGH then         *not found*
      INDEX ← 0
    else
end
```

Observe the need for the last decision statement. The use of this algorithm is illustrated below.

TABLE 3-2. Steps during binary search: out of nine numbers ($N = 9$) the number 300 is sought (GIVEN = 300).

KEY (I).

BEFORE FIRST COMPARISON	BEFORE SECOND COMPARISON	BEFORE THIRD COMPARISON
5 ←LOW	5	5
21	21	21
73	73	73
124	124	124
INDEX→241	241	241
300	⌐300⌐	→300⌐
450	→450	450
701	701	701
715 ←HIGH	715	715
LOW = 1	LOW = 6	LOW = 6
HIGH = 9	HIGH = 9	HIGH = 6
INDEX = $\left\lfloor \dfrac{1+9}{2} \right\rfloor = 5$	INDEX = $\left\lfloor \dfrac{6+9}{2} \right\rfloor = 7$	INDEX = $\left\lfloor \dfrac{6+6}{2} \right\rfloor = 6$

integer part of

H. CONCLUSION. STATEMENT TYPES IN PROGRAMMING

The following seven statement types are desirable in general-purpose programming languages.

First, there are three control constructs, sufficient to control the execution sequence of any program:

(1) **begin-end;**
(2) **if-then-else;**
(3) **while-do.**

Structural simplicity of an algorithm (or a program) constructed with the exclusive use of these control structures is due to their one-in–one-out property: their flowcharts have a single incoming and a single outcoming flowline. Since any text is written and read from top to bottom, these should be treated as general guidelines for the organization of program flow. Some of these structures are explicitly included in certain programming languages, others may be constructed from the available statements.

In the exceptional cases, when it appears unnatural to express an algorithm using these structures, unconditional transfer of control

(4) **goto;**

may be used.

In addition to the statements controlling program flow, the following data-handling statements (described in Chapter 2) are necessary:

(5) input/output;
(6) assignment;
(7) declarations (nonexecutable).

To explain program logic and the meaning of data, comments should be used.

For the sake of programmer's convenience, many additional statements are offered in higher level programming languages. Important among these are additional control structures, which include:

(1) **repeat-until** loop;
(2) indexed loop;
(3) **case** statement;
(4) **exit** statement.

An extremely important facility of general-purpose languages is subprogram invocation, discussed in the next chapter.

Every language has its rules for naming variables and specifying labels.

4

SUBPROGRAMS AND
MODULAR PROGRAMMING

A computer algorithm of some complexity, and a program arising from it, may be considered a system. To design any system, we need to be able to identify its hierarchical structure and then build it of self-contained but interacting elements—modules. Used for this purpose in programming are subprograms (also called *procedures*): named sequences of statements that perform specific tasks and may be called upon by their names. The presence of subprograms in a program breaks it up into the *main program* that starts the execution and the subprograms that are invoked by the main program or other subprograms during the execution. Collectively, the main program and the subprograms are called *modules* or *program units*.

Two essential types of subprograms exist: functions and, more general, subroutines.

During the invocation (call) of a subprogram, the two modules involved communicate via specified data items. This communication may be accomplished by explicit transmission of data (called *parameter passing*) or through shared memory locations containing the data. The second method of communication, where certain data are considered global to the subprogram and therefore accessible to other program units, is particularly prominent in the so-called block-structured programming languages (such as ALGOL or PL/I).

Recursive use of subprograms, when possible in a programming language, leads in certain cases to simple algorithms.

The design of programs with consistent identification of well-defined tasks and assignment of them to separate modules is called modular programming.

A. DEFINITION AND INVOCATION OF SUBPROGRAMS

The two essential types of subprograms (procedures) are functions and subroutines. Following its execution, a function returns, to the program unit that invoked it, a single value as the value of the function's name. Subroutines are the most general subprograms that may be used to communicate to the calling program unit any number of values. Although a function may be used to pass back a number of values in the manner identical to that of subroutines, this practice is to be avoided.

Subprograms, as self-contained program units, have all the properties of algorithms (see Chapter 1–B), with the possible exception of the lack of output, since another module in the program may be performing that. Subprograms may be independently translated for testing purposes.

Following the invocation and the execution of a subprogram, control returns to the place of invocation in the invoking program unit. No change of control flow in that program unit results.

1. SUBROUTINES

A subroutine is the more general of the two kinds of subprograms. A *subroutine* is a subprogram that may explicitly return an unlimited number of values to the invoking program unit. Subroutine invocation is termed *subroutine call*.

A subroutine call statement has the following general form:

Call subroutine name (list of actual parameters)

A subroutine name is formed in a given programming language like any other identifier, for example, a variable name. It identifies the subroutine among the subprograms contained in a given program.

Parameters (also called *arguments*, see Table 4-1) are data items through which a subroutine *communicates* explicitly with the calling program unit (which may be the main program or another subprogram). Parameters are predefined for a subroutine as to the number and type of every one of them.

Parameters may communicate values to the subroutine (such are sometimes called *input parameters*) or from the subroutine to the calling program unit *(output parameters)*, or may serve both purposes by presenting a value to the subroutine when it is called and subsequently acquiring values as the result of its execution *(input/output parameters)*.

Parameters may constitute single values or arrays of values.

EXAMPLE 4–1

In order to call a subroutine SWAP, which will exchange the values of two integers I and J, the following statement may be used:

Call SWAP(I, J)

In this case, both parameters are of the input/output kind.

One of the purposes of subprograms is their multiple use in a program. Thus, several calls to a given subprogram may be included in various modules of the program (in the programming languages that allow recursion—see Section C of this chapter—also in the subprogram itself). During each call, different values of actual parameters are usually included in the list.

In order for a call to be meaningful, the called subroutine has to be defined and included in the program.

A *subroutine definition* consists of a nonexecutable subroutine heading of the following general form:

> **Subroutine** subroutine name (list of formal parameters)

and the subroutine body, i.e., the statements that constitute the subroutine. Textual appearance of a subroutine body is similar to that of a main program.

Following the execution of the last statement of a subroutine, execution control reverts to the calling program unit, specifically, to the statement textually following the subroutine call. This is the so-called *return* from the subroutine. Subroutine execution is, therefore, a temporary diversion of control from the calling program unit.

The subroutine heading statement lists the formal parameters of the subroutine. These are the variable and array names of the data communicated to the subroutine and/or communicated by it to the calling program unit. The subroutine is written with the use of these names rather than the names used for these data items in the calling program. Thus, the two may be written and translated independently, so long as the lists of formal and actual arguments match. Formal parameters thus constitute place-holders for the actual ones. Formal parameters may acquire values from the actual parameters during the call and may pass values back to the actual parameters during the return. The association between the actual and the formal parameters occurs during the subroutine call and is further discussed in Section B-1 of this chapter.

Different names are used in various programming languages for the formal and actual parameters. The most frequently used names are listed in Table 4–1.

TABLE 4–1. Terminology used for parameter passing

IN CALLING MODULE		IN CALLED MODULE	NAMES USED IN
actual parameter	↔	formal parameter	ALGOL, Pascal
actual argument	↔	dummy argument	FORTRAN
argument	↔	parameter	PL/I

Along with the parameter values, a subroutine may use any number of *local* variables or arrays that are declared and assigned values within it. Their existence is unknown to other program units.

The programmer is free to choose any legal names for the entities (e.g., variable names or labels) local to a program unit. If the names of such entities in two units happen to coincide, they will be treated as referring to different items.

While the formal parameters always have to be variable or array names—(Do you see any sense in employing constants as formal parameters?)—the actual parameters may be expressions (and, in particular, constants, variables, and array elements), as well as arrays.†

An analogy may be drawn between algebraic functions and subprograms in programming in that an algebraic function is written in terms of placeholders for the actual values.

For example, in order to find the hypotenuse of a right triangle with sides x and y, we may use the algebraic function

$$z = \sqrt{x^2 + y^2}$$

Following the substitution of the actual values (e.g., $x = 4$, $y = 3$) for the given case, we find the answer ($z = 5$).

Members of the actual and the formal parameter lists are in one-to-one positional correspondence with one another. The type of parameter in the respective positions in both lists has to be, therefore, the same.

EXAMPLE 4–2

Study the correspondence of parameter lists in this example:

Calling program unit:	Called subprogram:
begin	**Subroutine** WORK(B, D, N)
Integer I, J(100);	**begin**
Real X, Y, Z(50);	**Integer** K(100); M, N;
	Real A, B, C, D(50);
.	
.	.
Call WORK (X, Z, J(I));	.
.	**end**
.	
.	
Call WORK (Z(3), Z, 5);	
.	
.	
.	
end	

---

† Some languages also allow passing of other entities, for example, subprogram names, as parameters.

The following association between actual and formal parameters ensues during each call:

PARAMETER NO.	ACTUAL PARA-ETER DURING 1ST CALL	ACTUAL PARAM-ETER DURING 2ND CALL	FORMAL PARAMETER	NATURE OF THE PARAMETER
1	X	Z(3)	B	a real value
2	Z	Z	D	a real array of 50 elements
3	J(I)	5	N	an integer value

Note that local to the subroutine are the data: array K, variables A, C, M.

All that has to be known to the writer of the calling or of the called program unit is the *interface* between the two: the meaning of every parameter on the list, relative position of the parameters, and their nature. Summing up, a subroutine call is executed as follows:

(1) Parameters are passed, if there are any (the mechanism of parameter passing is discussed further in Section B-1 of this chapter).
(2) The subroutine is executed as if it were an independent program. Output parameters will have values assigned to them; input/output parameters may have their values changed.
(3) Control returns to the statement following the subroutine call in the text of the calling program. This is the return from the subroutine.

Some programming languages have special statements ordering return from a subroutine to the main program (RETURN in FORTRAN or EXIT PROGRAM in COBOL). In a language such as ALGOL, where the subprogram itself (like the main program) constitutes a compound statement, the return occurs when the outermost **end** is reached during the subprogram execution.

Rather than use a parameter to communicate a value, in most programming languages it is possible to share the memory location containing the value among several program units (see Section B-2 of this chapter). Both methods may be used in the design of a subroutine.

The following example presents the definition and use of a simple subroutine.

EXAMPLE 4–3

Problem

A program is to be designed to order any three integers in descending order (i.e., the first is to be the largest).

Solution

```
*ORDERING PROGRAM FOR THREE VALUES
begin
    Integer INT1, INT2, INT3;
    Input INT1, INT2, INT3;
    if INT1 < INT2 then
        Call SWAP(INT1, INT2)
    else;
    if INT1 <INT3 then
        Call SWAP(INT1, INT3)
    else;
    if INT2 < INT3 then
        Call SWAP(INT2, INT3)
    else;
    Output INT1, INT2, INT3
end
*ROUTINE SWAPS VALUES OF TWO INTEGER VARIABLES
Subroutine SWAP(L, M)
begin
    Integer L, M, TEMP;
    TEMP ← L;
    L ← M;
    M ← TEMP
end
```

A subroutine may invoke another subprogram (i.e., another subroutine or a function). A *chain call* results (see Fig. 4–1). Every call is completed with the return to the immediate calling subroutine.

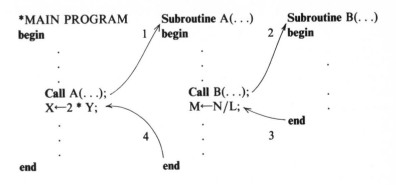

FIGURE 4–1. A chain call. Arrows show the flow of control during the execution; numbers indicate the sequence of events.

EXAMPLE 4-4

If our program that orders three integers is to be used in a more general program that would allow the ordering of multiple triples of positive integers, it may itself be turned into a subroutine:

```
*ORDER TRIPLES OF POSITIVE INTEGERS
begin
     Integer I, J, K;
     Input I, J, K;
*TRAILER DATUM IS −1
          while I ≠ −1 do
               begin
                    Call ORDER(I, J, K);
                    Input I, J, K
               end
end
*ROUTINE ORDERS THREE INTEGERS
Subroutine ORDER(INT1, INT2, INT3)
begin
*ALL STATEMENTS OF THE ORDERING PROGRAM OF
*EXAMPLE 4-3 WITH THE EXCEPTION OF THE
*INPUT STATEMENT
          .
          .
          .

end
*ROUTINE SWAPS VALUES OF TWO VARIABLES
Subroutine SWAP(L, M)
begin
*AS IN EXAMPLE 4-3
          .
          .
          .

end
```

Convince yourself that the routines interact correctly.

Since a subroutine is an independent program unit, which may be used in any program, it has its own flowchart [see Fig. 4-2(a)]. The standard outline used to show a subroutine call in the flowchart of the calling program is presented in Fig. 4-2(b).

The statement in the subroutine where its execution begins following the call is termed its *entry point;* the statement that returns control to the calling program is the *return point* of the subroutine. Most often, these are, respectively, the first and the last statements in the subroutine. Some languages (such as FORTRAN 77, COBOL, or PL/I) allow the programmer to define several entry and return points in a subroutine. Various entry points have their own names and parameter lists.

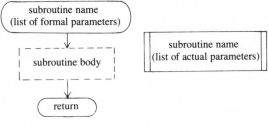

(a) flowchart of a subroutine   (b) outline for a subroutine call

FIGURE 4-2.   Flowcharting of subroutines.

2. FUNCTIONS

A *function* is a subprogram whose name acquires a value as the result of its invocation. Thus a single value is obtained. At the same time, parameter passing and shared memory locations may be used to pass additional values; it is, however, preferable to use a subroutine if several values need to be obtained in the subprogram.

A function is invoked by reference to it, that is, by using its name and the list of actual parameters in any statement where a constant or a variable expected to render a value may be used. The type of the value returned by the function has to be appropriate. Function invocation is therefore called *function reference*. A function reference is, then, a component of a statement and has the general form:

... function name (list of actual parameters) ...

where ellipsis (. . .) stands for the remainder of a meaningful statement. Most frequently, function references are used in an expression of the corresponding type.

> **EXAMPLE 4-5**
> If a function that obtains a square root of a positive real number has been defined, it may be used as follows:
>
> $$X \leftarrow SQRT(Y) - 5 * Z$$
>
> or as follows:
>
> $$\textbf{if } SQRT (X) \leqslant Y \textbf{ then}$$
> $$Y \leftarrow 2 * Z$$
> $$\textbf{else}$$
> $$A \leftarrow Z - SQRT(X)$$

Since the function reference itself is replaced by a value, this value is nameless in the invoking program. There exists, therefore, a certain restriction on the place of function reference within this program. While a subroutine call is an independent statement and may be meaningfully placed where desired, the function reference has to occur where the value delivered by it will be used (note that to circumvent this limitation, temporary variables may be employed).

With these distinctions concerning the invocation, all said about the subroutines in the preceding section applies also to functions.

Function reference is executed as follows:

(1) Parameters are passed, if any (see Section B–1 for details).
(2) The function is executed as if it were an independent program. During the execution, a value of the type corresponding to the type of the function name is assigned to this name.
(3) Return from the function occurs, and the value obtained is substituted for the function reference.
    Other values may be passed back through the parameters or shared memory locations.

A function is defined like a subroutine is. The crucial difference is that the type of the function (i.e., the type of the value that will be substituted for the reference) is to be stated in the function heading. The general form of a *function heading* is

Type Function function name (list of formal parameters)

where the appropriate type is substituted for **Type.**

EXAMPLE 4–6

Problem

Determine the largest number in each of the multiple sets of three positive integers.

Solution

```
*DETERMINE THE LARGEST IN EVERY TRIPLE OF POSITIVE
*INTEGERS
begin
      Integer I, J, K;
      Input I, J, K;
*TRAILER DATUM IS −1
      while I ≠ −1 do
            begin
                  Output I, J, K, MAX(I, J, K);
                  Input I, J, K
            end
end
*THE LARGEST OF THREE INTEGERS IS FOUND
Integer Function MAX(L, M, N)
begin
      Integer L, M, N;
      if L > M then
        MAX ← L
      else
        MAX ← M;
      if N > MAX then
        MAX ← N
      else
end
```

Notes

1. Note that in the function itself, a value is assigned to the function value, without the parameter list.
2. Study the difference between the solution to the problem in Example 4–4 and that in this example.

A function may reference a subroutine; a subroutine may call a function.

Certain widely used programming languages lack the function facility entirely (e.g., COBOL).

In languages that do offer the function facility (such as ALGOL, FORTRAN, or PL/I), there are usually two kinds of functions. *Built-in functions* (also called *intrinsic*) may be referenced without need of their definitions, which have been written by systems programmers and are included by the translator together with the main program. These are commonly used functions, such as square root, logarithm, etc. Sometimes, their code is simply copied by the translator in place of reference (these are so-called *open routines* as opposed to *closed routines,* of which a single copy exists to be invoked). General functions are, however, *programmer-written,* defined by the programmer in order to be referenced.

B. COMMUNICATION WITH A SUBPROGRAM

Data are usually presented to a subprogram being invoked; following a subprogram execution results generally have to be presented to the invoking program unit.

The essential method of communication between the two program units involved in a call (the term will be used in this section to denote both a subroutine call and a function reference) is the passing of parameters. Actual parameters are listed in the invoking statement; and formal parameters, in the subprogram heading.

Another way to communicate is through memory locations defined as accessible to both the calling and the called program units. These locations hold global data accessible to all the subprograms sharing them. The use of global data for communication among program units is of particular importance in the so-called block-structured languages (such as ALGOL or PL/I). This class of programming languages permits modularizing data access in a program as well as modularizing the program itself.

1. PARAMETER PASSING

Through the mechanism of parameter passing, the values of the actual parameters are associated with the corresponding values of the formal parameters in order to transfer data from the calling program unit to the called one and vice-versa.

The association may be performed by three different methods that, in certain cases (i.e., for certain kinds of the actual parameters), may render different results. Usually the method of parameter transfer is beyond the programmer's control since it is defined by the implementation of the language. The understanding of this mechanism enhances, however, the programmer's mastery of the language and averts subtle (and hence hard to locate) errors. Examples 4–7 through 4–9 should be carefully studied.

A. CALL BY REFERENCE

This technique, also known as *call by location* (or *by address)* is used most often. This is the most frequent implementation of subprogram calls in COBOL, FORTRAN, and PL/I.

When a call by reference occurs, the address of the actual parameter is transmitted to the called subprogram. If the actual parameter is an expression, it is first evaluated, and the address of the location holding the value is passed. If the parameter is an array, the address of its first element is passed.

Subsequently, whenever the corresponding formal parameter is referenced in the called subprogram, this address is used to access the location of the actual parameter. Thus, memory locations containing the values of actual parameters are accessible to both the calling and the called program units.

EXAMPLE 4–7

In Fig. 4–3, memory locations pertaining to actual parameters (owned by the calling program unit) and formal parameters (owned by the called program unit) are shown. The following call invokes the following subroutine:

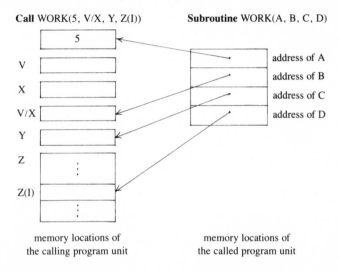

FIGURE 4–3. Call by reference. Arrows represent addresses.

Notes
1. A special location has been created in the memory area of the calling program unit in order to hold the value of the actual parameter V/X.
2. The first two formal parameters, A and B, should not be used to pass values back to the calling program unit. If an assignment is made in the called program unit to the variable A, and if following the return to the calling program unit the constant 5 is utilized there, its value may be different from 5!

B. CALL BY VALUE

This technique of parameter passing may be explicitly specified by an ALGOL or a PL/I programmer.

The value of the actual parameter is passed to the called program unit. This value is placed into the location of the corresponding formal parameter.

Memory locations of the calling program unit are inaccessible to the called one. This method cannot be used, therefore, to pass data back to the calling unit: it is suitable only for the passing of input parameters.

EXAMPLE 4–8

This main program   invokes this subroutine:

begin   **Subroutine** WORK (A, B, C, D)
    Integer I, V, X, Y, Z(100);   **begin**
    .   **Integer** A, B, C, D;
    .   .
    .   .
    V ← 4; X ← 2; Y ← 7; I ← 11;   .
    Z (I) ← 15;   **end**
    Call WORK (5, V/X, Y, Z (I))
    .
    .
    .

end

The relevant memory locations are shown in Fig. 4–4.

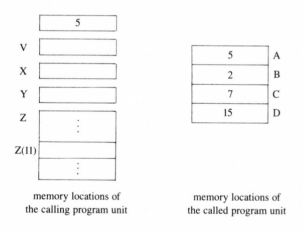

memory locations of   memory locations of
the calling program unit   the called program unit

FIGURE 4–4. Call by value.

An important variation of call by value is *call by value-result*. In this technique, following a call by value and the execution of the called subprogram, the "results," values of the formal parameters, are transferred into the location of the actual ones. This method is sometimes used in FORTRAN implementations.

C. CALL BY NAME

This method, used in ALGOL, is the least obvious in its effects.

The effect of a call by name is specified by the so-called *copy rule:* a formal parameter is replaced textually by the corresponding actual parameter.

EXAMPLE 4–9

This call   invokes this subroutine:

Call WORK (5, V/X, Y, Z (I))   **Subroutine** WORK (A, B, C, D)
                                        begin
                                            .
                                            .
                                            .
                                            $C \leftarrow B - A;$
                                            $D \leftarrow C + A;$
                                            .
                                            .
                                            .
                                        end

All variables are of integer type.

During the execution of the subroutine WORK, the following assignments will be executed in place of these in the subroutine body:

$$Y \leftarrow V/X - 5;$$
$$Z (I) \leftarrow Y + 5;$$

Parentheses are inserted during the textual substitution if necessary to make the resulting statement meaningful.

In the implementation of a call by name, no textual substitution is actually performed. The effect is achieved by invoking a special subprogram, called *thunk*, which is defined by the translating program. The thunk evaluates the actual parameter, whose value is substituted in place of the formal parameter. Call by name is rarely employed to implement programming languages.

D. COMPARISON OF PARAMETER PASSING METHODS

While in most cases the programmer has no control over the way the parameters are passed, in some languages such control exists. For example, in ALGOL, in the same subroutine some parameters may be called by name and others, as specified, by value.

Call by name is the most general method, however complex it is in its implementation. Call by value is not general enough, since no data may be passed back to the calling program (this is remedied in the call by value-result). There is also no point in transferring entire arrays by value, while a single address suffices in a call by reference. Call by reference, however, requires modification when it is desirable to pass to the called program an expression rather than its value.

The following example points out that different calling methods may sometimes have different effects.

EXAMPLE 4–10

We have the following program:

begin	**Subroutine** SUBR (V, X, Y, Z)
Integer A, B, C;	**begin**
A ← 3; B ← 5; C ← 17;	**Integer** V, X, Y, Z;
Call SUBR (A, A, A + B, C);	V ← V + 1;
Output C	Z ← X + Y
end	**end**

The value obtained and displayed for the variable C in the main program depends on the mechanism adopted for parameter passing, as shown below.

1. call by reference: The effect is illustrated in Fig. 4–5.

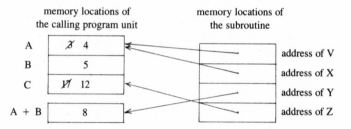

FIGURE 4–5.   Here C = 12.

2. call by value
   (a) pure call by value: C is unchanged, hence C = 17.
   (b) call by value-result: The effect is illustrated in Fig. 4–6.

̶3̶ 4	V
3	X
8	Y
̶1̶7̶ 11	Z

memory locations of the subroutine

FIGURE 4–6.   Here C = 11.

3. call by name: According to the copy rule:

$$A \leftarrow A + 1 \qquad \text{hence } A = 4$$
$$C \leftarrow A + A + B \quad \text{hence } C = 4 + 4 + 5$$
$$C = 13$$

2. SHARED MEMORY LOCATIONS

The alternative method of communication between program units is their sharing of named memory locations holding data. Such shared locations are said to contain global data.

In a specific group of higher level programming languages called block-structured languages (these include ALGOL and PL/I), a facility exists for the modularization of the scope of variables. This means that the sequence of statements over which a variable exists may be arbitrarily delimited by the programmer. In such languages, along with external subprograms, self-contained sequences of statements (discussed in Section A) which may be translated independently, there also exist internal subprograms. These constitute an integral part of the whole that is a program, sharing a number of variables with different parts of it.

A. LOCAL AND GLOBAL DATA

Local data (variables and arrays) exist exclusively in a given subprogram. Their locations are inaccessible to the calling program and therefore they are of only local significance within the subprogram where they are declared. Thus, any valid name may be chosen for them in the program unit.

Global data (variables and arrays) are data items existing in two or more program units to which they are considered global. Memory locations holding these data are shared between these program units: any of them may access their contents and modify them.

Use of global data instead of parameters for communication between program units may be advantageous from the point of view of run-time efficiency when:

- a number of data entities is to be shared among several program units
- arrays are to be shared, and the calls are not implemented by reference.

It should be stressed, however, that explicit parameter passing often contributes to the reliability of the program.

B. GLOBAL DATA IN LANGUAGES WITHOUT BLOCK STRUCTURE

Languages without block structure, such as FORTRAN, use a simple and implicit way of controlling the scope of variables and arrays in a program. In such a language, a variable or array is local to the program unit where it is declared unless declared as common to the units where it is to be global.

Thus, in FORTRAN a COMMON statement is included in all the units which are to share a given data area.

EXAMPLE 4–11

In a language without block structure, we may have the following declarations in a certain program:

main program:

    Global I, ARRAY(100)

subprogram A:

    Global K, SCORES(100)

subprogram B:

    Global M, VALUES(100)

    Thus, variable I is known as K in subprogram A and as M in subprogram B; the array ARRAY, as SCORES and VALUES, respectively.

    Assuming that a subprogram X in this program does not contain the **Global** declaration, it cannot access these locations.

C. BLOCK-STRUCTURED LANGUAGES†

Block-structured languages are higher level programming languages that make it possible to control the *scope* of variables and arrays (i.e., the range of statements where they exist) by allowing for these entities to be declared in their particular compound statements in a program.

    A compound statement **begin-end** with declarations preceding the executable statements contained in it is called a *block*.

    A block is composed of statements and possibly other blocks (said to be nested within it).

    In a program written in one of the block-structured languages (for example, ALGOL or PL/I) a variable may be used only within the scope of its declaration.

    The scope of variables and arrays is defined by the "last-declared" rule as follows. The scope of a variable encompasses the block in which it is declared and all the blocks contained (nested) therein, excluding such blocks where a variable of the same name is declared. This is then a different variable; although the two variables have the same name, they are entirely unrelated.

EXAMPLE 4–12

The scope rule is illustrated in Fig. 4–7. Note that the name B in this program is used for three different variables (denoted on the figure as B_1, B_2, and B_3). The variable F is global to the entire program.

---

† This section and Chapter 4–C may be skipped on the first reading.

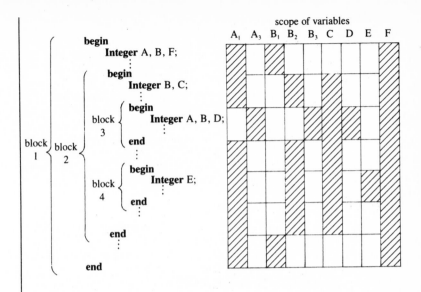

FIGURE 4-7. Scored areas correspond to the parts of the program where a given variable exists.

Block-structured languages are implemented with the use of *dynamic memory allocation:* the memory is assigned to the variables and arrays during the program execution. When a variable is declared, the memory is allocated to it; the memory is released when the scope of this variable is exhausted, since the variable ceases to be known.

On the other hand, in a language without block structure (such as FORTRAN), memory locations are allocated to all the variables and arrays during the translation, before the execution begins. Such an arrangement is called *static memory allocation.*

In a block-structured language, a subprogram may constitute another block in the program. In this case it is termed *internal subprogram.* An internal subprogram shares memory areas with program blocks that contain it and cannot, therefore, be separately translated. All the variables and arrays whose scope encompasses such a subprogram are global to it.

Internal subprograms are the only kind available in ALGOL, while PL/I offers both internal and external subprogram facilities.

Internal subprograms are of essential importance in the block-structured languages. They exist, however, also in such a language, without block structure, as COBOL, in the form of PERFORM-ed paragraphs (code sequences). The internal subprograms share in this case all the data locations with the main program; they cannot, however, be parameterized.

Thus, in block-structured languages, a program may be modularized not only with respect to its statements (i.e., subdivided into subprograms), but also with respect to the data access. In a block, only the data global to it and local within it may be accessed. The rationale behind the block structure is that in a program most of the variables are used only within a certain group of statements. If this group is turned into a block, with local variables declared in it, these variables:

- are inaccessible outside of the block, which results in increased program reliability
- may be independently named
- exist only in this block, and due to the dynamic memory allocation, space economy is possible.

C. RECURSION IN PROGRAMMING

Solutions to certain problems are conveniently expressed partially in terms of themselves. Such solution algorithms are called recursive and use recursive definitions. A *recursive definition* is a computational procedure that consists of:

(1) a general rule (or a set of rules) for obtaining the result for most of the parameters; this rule is defined in terms of itself, with different parameters;
(2) explicit results for some values of the parameters (without these a recursive definition would be circular).

EXAMPLE 4–13

To compute the factorial $N!$ of a positive integer N, it is convenient to use the following recursive definition:

factorial $(0) = 1$
factorial $(N) = N *$ factorial $(N-1)$, $N > 0$

Since the use of recursive definitions is a natural way to present a solution to certain classes of problems, it is desirable to allow for the use of recursion in a programming language.

Recursion in programming signifies that

(1) subprograms may invoke themselves (*direct recursion*);
(2) a chain invocation of subprograms is permitted to result in a closed

circle (e.g., a subroutine A calls a subroutine B, which calls a subroutine C, which calls A); this is *indirect recursion.*

Why do certain languages (notably FORTRAN and COBOL) prohibit recursive invocation of subprograms?

When a subprogram is called, certain locations, called together the *activation record* of the subprogram, are used to hold the values of its local variables and parameters passed to it (or the addresses of the parameters—see Section B–1), as well as the return address. The return address is the address of the statement in the calling program unit that is to be executed following the return from the subprogram.

In a language with static memory allocation, one set of such locations is provided by the translator for a subprogram. If a subprogram is to call itself—obviously before the return to the calling program unit occurs—the contents of these locations will be overwritten.

If a programming language is to allow recursion, dynamic memory allocation is necessary. Such languages as ALGOL and PL/I afford this facility to the programmer. When a subprogram calls itself, a new activation record is created. Since the return has to occur first from the place of the latest call (compare Fig. 4–1 and imagine that multiple copies of subroutine A call one another), the activation records have to be used during the series of returns in the last-in–first-out (LIFO) manner. Activation records are placed, therefore, in memory in the LIFO fashion, thus constituting a data structure called stack (see Chapter 5–G).

When a call occurs, a new activation record is placed on top of the stack; when the returns commence (*recursive descent*), the activation record on top of the stack is used as the source of variable values and the return address. It is subsequently removed from the stack. The last activation record causes the return to the place of initial call of this subprogram.

The following example presents a recursive function FACTOR and the dynamic contents of its run-time stack.

EXAMPLE 4–14

*RECURSIVE COMPUTATION OF FACTORIAL OF $N \geqslant 0$
Integer Function FACTOR(N)
begin
    Integer N;
    if $N = 0$ **then**
        FACTOR $\leftarrow$ 1
    else
        FACTOR $\leftarrow$ N * FACTOR(N – 1)
end

Contents of the stack during the execution of this function for $N = 3$ are shown in Fig. 4–8. Call by value is assumed.

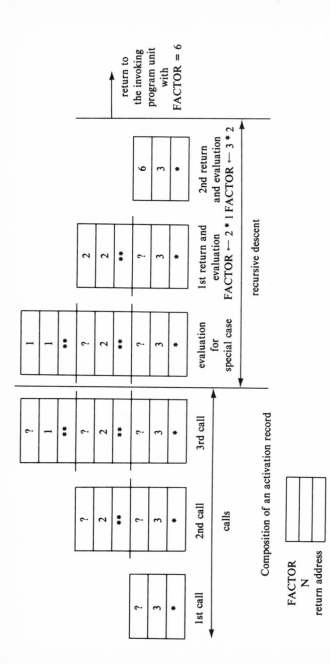

Composition of an activation record

FACTOR
N
return address

?—no value assigned

*—the address of the statement on the calling program to which control is to return

**—the address of the (translated) statement FACTOR ← N * FACTOR(N − 1)

FIGURE 4–8.

The same subprogram may be implemented as a subroutine FACT(N, F), as shown in Fig. 4–9.

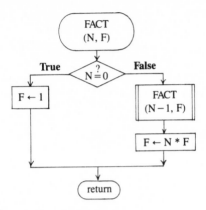

FIGURE 4–9.

Recursive solution to a problem is an alternative to an *iterative solution,* which would deploy a repetitive execution of a sequence of statements with the use of loops. In Example 4–15 a recursive algorithm for obtaining the greatest common divisor of two integers is shown as an alternative to the iterative solution discussed in Example 3–10.

EXAMPLE 4–15

A recursive form of the Euclidean algorithm discussed in Example 3–10 is presented.

```
*RECURSIVE FORM OF EUCLIDEAN ALGORITHM
*IS USED TO DETERMINE GREATEST COMMON DIVISOR
*OF TWO INTEGERS
Integer Function GCD (M, N)
begin
    Integer M, N, REM;
*INTERCHANGE NUMBERS, IF NECESSARY
    if M < N then
        GCD ← GCD (N, M)       *!*
*RECURSIVE DEFINITION
    else
        begin
            REM ← M – N * (M ÷ N);
            if REM = 0 then
                GCD ← N
            else
                GCD ← GCD (N, REM)
        end
end
```

Notes

1. Note how closely this form of expression resembles the verbal description of the algorithm given in Example 3–10.
2. Note the correspondence between the actual and the formal parameters in the case when the interchange occurs:

N corresponds to M; and M to N.

Recursive algorithms are used for their succinctness and ease of expression; they are, however, usually more costly than their iterative equivalents in terms of the execution time and memory space, due to their use of stacks for multiple activation records.

In a programming language without the recursion facility, such as FORTRAN, recursion may be used by including explicit stack manipulation routines into the program itself. The maximum size of the stack has to be known when the program is written, however.

D. MODULAR PROGRAMMING AND ITS ADVANTAGES

External subprograms are independent modules of which large programs may be built. *Modular programming* is a disciplined design of programs through a process of identification, definition, and implementation of modules of which the program is to be constructed. It is best carried out in a *top-down* fashion: by consecutive specification of the program's task in ever finer detail through a series of consecutive refinements of its algorithm.

Thus, during the first steps of the stepwise refinement process (see Section 3–F), the essential modules of the program are identified. While these are, in turn, pseudocoded, lower level modules may be needed, etc. Thus, a *modular decomposition* of the program is accomplished. As can be concluded, a complex program (often called a system) has a hierarchical structure, with the main program at its apex, and with higher level modules invoking lower level ones to perform specific tasks.

It is desirable that every module have a clearly defined single function to perform. The lower the level of the module, the narrower this function. This makes for ease of program implementation and maintenance (if a modification is required, only the modules that perform the affected functions need to be changed).

The top-down modular design process is illustrated by the following example, which introduces two important tools for such design: structure charts and interface tables.

EXAMPLE 4–16

Problem

A program for the periodical maintenance of a master file is to be designed. In other words, the updates to the file collected over a period of time in a so-called transaction file are to be reflected in the master file; thus a new master file is to be generated.

Explanation and Analysis

A master file (for example, the payroll file of an enterprise) consists of a number of records (in the example, one per employee). Each record contains a number of fields (for example, employee name, weekly pay, etc.), with one of these uniquely identifying the record within the file (e.g., the Social Security number). This field is called the key of the file. The master file is sorted on the key.

The records of the transaction file are also identified by the same key. Thus, a transaction file for payroll maintenance may include the record of a new employee with her Social Security number. In general, the transaction file will contain three kinds of updates:

modification of a master file record ("employee's pay was raised");

deletion ("employee was separated");

insertion ("a new employee was hired").

The nature of the update is one of the fields in the corresponding record.

The system to be designed is fairly simple. The small master file may be fully read into the memory. As there are few records in the transaction file, it is not sorted.

Top-Down Modular Decomposition

1. initial description of the algorithm:

*MAINTENANCE OF SORTED MASTER FILE

begin
    Input master file;
    Process all transactions against master file;
    Output new master file
end

2. first refinement of the algorithm:

*MAINTENANCE OF SORTED MASTER FILE

begin
    Input master file;
*PROCESS ALL TRANSACTIONS AGAINST MASTER FILE
    while there are more transactions **do**
        begin
            Input next transaction;
            Search for the master record with the key
                specified by the transaction;

*IF NO SUCH RECORD, THE ONE THAT WOULD PRECEDE IT IS
TO BE LOCATED
    if transaction is Modify **then**
      Modify master record
   else
      if transaction is Delete **then**
        Delete master record
     else
        TRANSACTION IS Insert
        Insert new master record
  end;
 Output new master file
end

At this point we have identified the need for five modules in our program. These modules are shown in the structure chart of Fig. 4–10; during successive refinement steps these may be found to require lower level
modules. Note that the binary search algorithm (see Example 3–17)
may be adapted for the SEARCH module.

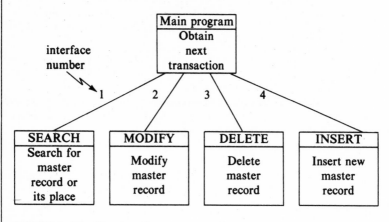

FIGURE 4–10. Structure chart.

As the design progresses, the interfaces between the modules (i.e., the data exchanged as parameters and accessed global blocks) are established. These should be brought together in an interface table of the form shown below.

interface number	input parameters	output parameters	access to global blocks
correspond to these of the structure chart	down the chart	up the chart	names of the blocks

Modular programming has the following advantages as the alternative to straight-line code:

(1) Viewing a program as a hierarchical structure of modules renders the task of its design more easily manageable intellectually.
(2) The product of such design is easier to comprehend and modify.
(3) The organization of the design effort is simplified due to the possibility of its meaningful subdivision.
   If modules communicate through clearly defined interfaces, such an interface is the extent of information about the rest of the program needed by the programmer to implement the module.
(4) A module may be utilized in several places in the same program and, frequently, in several programs. To be thus applicable, modules have to perform well-defined functions.
(5) Modules may be separately translated and tested. This makes for an easier implementation of the program.
(6) If a modular program has to be modified (a frequent occurrence in programming!), only certain modules may need to be changed.

Modular programming results in savings of programmer effort, memory space, and often translation time. It also furthers the reliability of the programming product, because of the multiple use of smaller modules that are easier to test.

   The cost of modularization is most often the increased execution time due to the subprogram invocation.

5

REPRESENTATION OF SIMPLE DATA. INTRODUCTION TO DATA STRUCTURES

The composition of data and the logic of the algorithms that utilize data are closely related.

The representation in computer memory of simple data of the types discussed in Chapter 2 is presented here. A more detailed representation of numerical data, which may be of special interest to an assembly language programmer, is offered in Appendix A.

Simple data items may be organized into data structures that contain information about the relationship among the included items.

Two basic structures are an array, a homogeneous structure consisting of items of the same type; and a record, a heterogeneous structure that may include items of various types. Data structures of higher order, which may be formed from records, include linear lists (in particular, queues and stacks), trees, and graphs.

Judicious use of data structures in programming produces algorithms that are clearer and more concise, and thereby simplify the total program.

A structure that most often appears to a higher level language programmer as an unstructured data item is a character string. Strings are the computer representations of text. Their importance as structures has grown with the computer being used more and more as a processor of general symbolic information. Representation and processing of strings are discussed in the last section of this chapter.

A. SIMPLE DATA

Data of a given type are stored in a variable of the corresponding type. The type of a variable determines the range of values that may be acquired by it during the execution of a program.

Most higher level programming languages require the type of variables used in a program to be declared. Declarations are used to assign memory to these data items as well as to determine what operations are applicable to them.

Certain languages (e.g., ALGOL 68, Pascal, SNOBOL) permit programmers to define their own data types by specifying the set of values that may be assigned to the corresponding variables.

The meaning of a data word is then determined not only by the binary pattern stored in it but also by the type of data it is said to contain.

It should be stressed that although a higher level language programmer is relieved of the details of data representation in most application programming, knowledge of this representation is necessary, however, for a programmer to become entirely proficient in a higher level language or to use an assembly language.

To represent numerical data, almost all languages provide integer and real data types. Some also afford complex and double precision numbers. Most languages allow the programmer to use logical and character data; fewer permit the use of pointers and labels as data types.

Certain languages permit *initialization* of variables, an assignment of initial value in a declaration.

1. INTEGERS

Integers have no fractional part and are usually represented in computer memory as *fixed-point numbers,* i.e., numbers whose radix point is in a fixed position with respect to the digits of the number. A more detailed discussion of fixed-point number representation is contained in Appendix A–4.

Even though in mathematics integers are a subset of real numbers, the two are treated differently in computer arithmetic due to the greater simplicity with which the integers may be represented and manipulated. Since an integer N usually occupies a single word in the memory of a computer model, the range of integers is

$$N \leqslant \mid 2^{n-1} - 1 \mid$$

where n is the number of bits in a word of this computer. This is due to the fact that one bit is reserved for the representation of the sign.

With x bits, 2^x different bit patterns may be specified. For example, if $x = 2$, we have: 00, 01, 10, 11. If we now add a third bit, the number of patterns will double, since for half of them this third bit will equal 0; for the rest it will equal 1.

Applicable operations are the arithmetic operations of addition, subtraction, multiplication, and integer division. The result of integer division is an integer, as the fractional part of it is dropped.

If a result of an arithmetic operation is outside the permissible range for the given computer, *overflow* is said to occur and the result is invalid.

EXAMPLE 5-1

16-bit computers (many minicomputers are of this kind) allow integers in the range from −32,767 to 32,767; 32-bit computers (e.g., IBM System/360–370 machines) have an integer range of ±2,147,483,647.
The range may be extended by programming means.

2. REAL NUMBERS

In programming, when a variable is declared real, the possibility is not excluded of its taking on the value of an integer. The declaration simply implies a different representation of the variable, one designed to increase its range and precision. Real numbers are stored in computer memories by using the *floating-point representation,* which is a version of so-called scientific notation. This representation consists of two parts: the *mantissa* (or *fraction*), which gives the digits contained in the number; and the scaling index, called the *exponent* (or *characteristic*), which determines the place of the radix point with respect to these digits.

EXAMPLE 5-2

In the decimal system,

$123000 = 0.123 * 10^6$

where 0.123 is mantissa and 6 is the exponent;

$0.00151 = 0.151 * 10^{-2}$

where 0.151 is the mantissa and −2 is the exponent.
It is clear that the radix (base) is 10.

In this representation, in general, a number X is represented as:

$$X = M * R^E$$

where M is the mantissa, R is the radix, and E is the exponent.

Since the radix in a floating-point representation is fixed for a given computer (usually it is 8 or 16), is is sufficient to store the mantissa M and the exponent E to describe the number X fully. (See Appendix A-5 for further details of floating-point representation.)

To make the representation of a number unique and to retain the maximum number of digits in the mantissa, *normalization* is usually performed. This means that in the representation of the mantissa, the most significant bit is a digit other than 0. Normalization is accomplished by shifting the radix point, and thereby changing the value of the exponent.

Variables declared as real are stored as *single-precision* numbers, i.e., they occupy a single word. For a given radix, the precision of a number is determined by the number of digits in its representation.

Applicable operations for real numbers are addition, subtraction, multiplication, and (ordinary) division.

In a representation of real numbers in any computer, only a finite set of numbers can be represented. Therefore, an infinite number of real numbers (of higher precision) exists between any two real numbers representable in the memory of a computer. Consequently, the results of any operation should be considered only approximations.

Never test a relation used in an **if** or **while** clause for the exact equality of two real numbers, at least one of which was obtained as a result of an arithmetic operation. In particular, no test of such a number should be made of its equality to 0.0.

Two pitfalls possible in real arithmetic are:

(1) *underflow: cancellation* of two close but unequal numbers of opposite signs as the result of an addition (also called *loss of significance*);
(2) *overflow through division:* caused by a small divisor.

Avoid testing relations such as

$$X/Y < DELTA$$

where DELTA is very small. Instead rephrase this as:

$$X < Y * DELTA$$

In commercial applications, real numbers are sometimes represented in the fixed-point mode. This leaves the control over the radix point with the programmer (and is useful, for example, in representing dollars and cents).

3. MIXED-MODE ARITHMETIC

If mixed-mode arithmetic is permitted in a given programming language implementation, numerical values of different types may be mixed in an expression. In particular, integer and real constants and variables may be used together.

This means that number conversions are performed, when necessary, from the integer to the real mode and vice-versa. These conversions are performed automatically, i.e., at the behest of the supporting software such as translators. With only the change of a representation being involved, a conversion from the integer to the real mode is transparent to the programmer.

Conversion from the real to the integer mode may be performed in two ways:

(1) by *truncation,* i.e., by dropping the fractional part of the real number;
(2) by *rounding* to the closest integer value.

Rounding may be algorithmically expressed as follows:

```
if X>0 then
    begin X← X + 0.5; truncate X end
else
    begin X← X − 0.5; truncate X end
```

Programmers should exercise extreme caution when using mixed-mode arithmetic: They should either perform the conversion themselves or be aware how it is done automatically.

4. COMPLEX NUMBERS

When available as a data type, complex numbers are usually represented in two words containing, separately, the real and the imaginary parts of the number. Each part is a real number, represented in floating-point mode.

5. DOUBLE-PRECISION NUMBERS

Double-precision numbers are available as a data type in some languages and constitute a special case of real numbers.

Two words are used to represent a double-precision number in the floating-point mode. Usually, the second word contains the lower-significant bits of an extended mantissa. This increases the precision of the number without increasing its range.

6. LOGICAL DATA

A logical variable may take on only one of the two values: **True** or **False,** represented as 1 and 0. A logical data item may occupy, therefore, a single bit. In the implementation of most programming languages, however, a single logical data item is placed in its own word.

7. CHARACTER DATA

Characters are components of character strings, an important data structure discussed in the Section J of this chapter.

A *character* as a data item is the internal representation of a printable or control character in computer memory.

The *character set* of a computer usually includes:

(a) 26 Latin upper-case letters;
(b) 26 Latin lower-case letters;
(c) 10 Arabic digits;
(d) special printable characters (arithmetic signs, punctuation marks, etc.);
(e) the blank (space);
(f) control (nonprintable) characters, such as carriage return, line feed, etc.

To represent the character set of a computer, binary codes are used. Two most frequently used codes are

(a) ASCII (American Standard Code for Information Interchange). This is a 7-bit code (see Appendix B-1); hence 128 characters may be represented. An 8-bit variation of the code also exists.
(b) EBCDIC (Extended Binary Coded Decimal Interchange Code). This code, which has gained wide acceptance, was developed by IBM. As an 8-bit code (see Appendix B-2), it makes possible the representation of 256 characters.

The collection of bits, each representing a single character in a given computer, is sometimes called a *byte*. Since most of today's character codes consist of 8 bits, a byte is most frequently 8-bits long. In some computers, such as IBM System/360-370 or PDP-11, bytes have their own addresses and may be accessed independently of the word that contains them.

Binary code determines the ordering of characters by the sequence of numeric values assigned to them. This ordering, called the *collating sequence*, determines the order in which alphanumerical data are sorted when numerical sorting is applied. In EBCDIC, for example, this partial sequence is, in increasing order, blank, alphabetic characters A through Z, and digits 0 through 9.

Character strings are created either by the sequential placement of characters in consecutive memory words or by linking the consecutive characters into a string (see Section J).

8. POINTERS AND LABELS

Certain higher level languages permit the use of addresses as data items.

A *label* is the address of a program instruction, and a *pointer* is the address of another data item.

Pointers are used in the organization of data structures (see Chapter 5–6). The use of labels as variables is treacherous (it leads to self-modifying programs) and is best to avoid.

Usually these addresses are held in single memory words.

B. DATA STRUCTURES

Algorithms operate on data that represent facts about the real world. Algorithm and data, together determining the results of the program execution, are in a symbiotic relation: the more apt the composition of data for the given application, the simpler the algorithm for its processing. To simplify the algorithm, it is therefore often desirable to organize data into logical entities of a higher order than simple variables; these entities are data structures. In other words, a *data structure* is an organized collection of simple data items. It is, therefore, characterized by

(1) the type of items it consists of;
(2) the relationships among these items.

EXAMPLE 5-3

A program is to be designed simulating the operation of a computer center.

Simulation algorithms use data regarding the arrival of jobs to be processed. A number of such data units is generated; each gives the job arrival time, computer resource requirements, etc. Later, the program imitates the processing of these artificially generated jobs by the computer system that is being simulated.

The program will gain in clarity and simplicity if the data pertaining to each job are organized into a single entity, a record. Moreover, it is perspicacious to arrange all such records into a data structure of higher order that lines them up in first-in–first-out fashion according to the arrival time of the job they represent. Such a structure, discussed later in this section, is called a queue.

Certain data structures (such as arrays or strings) are directly available to the programmer in most of the widely used higher level programming languages; others may be constructed using simple variables and available structures.

An array (of one or more dimensions) and a record are basic data structures. An array brings together simple data items of the same type that are referenced by their collective name (the name of the array) and by their subscripts, which identify their positions within the array. Arrays of character strings are also of importance.

A record may consist of simple data items of various types as well as character strings. These data are aggregated into a single entity because they describe attributes of real-world objects described by the record. The given record is usually selected from the higher order structure by the value of one of its items (also called fields).

Simple variables, records, and sometimes arrays may be organized into higher order structures. These structures are often dynamic, which means that during the execution of the programs using them, some of their components may be deleted and some others incorporated; the relationships among the constituents may also change.

Higher order structures include linear lists (and, in particular, their restricted forms such as stacks and queues), trees and binary trees, and graphs (networks).

These structures are utilized to organize the data maintained in the main memory as well as the data kept predominantly in the secondary memory. Data collections residing in secondary storage are organized into self-contained named entities called *files,* often with the use of several higher order structures. File organization is discussed in Chapter 10.

The present chapter introduces the data structures at conceptual level, without devoting space to algorithms for their manipulation.

C. LOGICAL AND PHYSICAL ORGANIZATION OF DATA STRUCTURES

Computer memory consists of words with consecutive addresses. Each word is made up of bits, the number of which in a word is fixed for a given computer model.

Data structures consist of simple data items suitable for the program in which they are used. The relationships among these items (such as sequence, precedence, etc.) form a part of the structure.

If a data structure is directly available in a given programming language (as, for example, arrays are in FORTRAN), the representation of this structure is established by the software translator. If the structure is not available, the programmer has to build it of the available data types.

Since the data structure has to be placed in memory words, every such structure is characterized by its *logical organization* (relationship among its components as required by its application) and its *physical organization* (memory placement).

When simple data items that make up a structure are shorter than memory words, they may be *packed:* several items may be placed into a single word. Since they cannot be directly addressed (only a word or a byte can be), they have to be retrieved by programming means.

EXAMPLE 5–4
An array of logical data (each 1-bit long) may be packed into 16-bit words by placing 16 array elements into a single word.

Two essential methods of memory placement exist for higher order structures such as lists.

When *sequential representation* is used, the components of the data structure are placed into consecutive memory locations. The relationships among these components are implicit in their positions in relation to the others.

The alternative is *linked representation* in which every component of the data structure includes one or more additional data items; these establish its relationship to the surrounding components. Such additional data items are *pointers* (also called *links*), which contain the memory addresses of other items in the structure.

In Fig. 5–1, component A is pointing to component B,

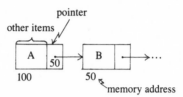

FIGURE 5–1. A pointer.

which means that the value stored in its pointer location is 50, corresponding to the address of the first word of the component B.

Pointers (links) establish the organization of the data structure. Their meaning depends on the structure and is further discussed in the descriptions of various data structures in this chapter.

Sequential representation is rigid since deletions of components from the structure, and insertions into it can be made only at the cost of physical reorganization of the structure in memory. It is applicable, therefore, when the composition of the structure does not change significantly during the program execution.

Linked representation is flexible, in that to effect structural changes it is sufficient to change only a few pointers. It is well suited, therefore, for dynamic data structures. The cost of the flexibility is the memory space and time required to maintain the pointers, which are exclusively structural elements.

When linked allocation is used, the amount of memory available for the data structure is divided into two parts. One holds the structure as it currently exists, and the other (called *available space*) constitutes a pool of "empty" components. When a space is needed for a new component, it is acquired from this pool; when an existing component is no longer required, its space is returned to the pool. Alternatively, unneeded components are gathered periodically for return to the pool.

D. ARRAYS

An *array* is an ordered collection of simple data items of the same type. Logically, an array may have several dimensions, which means that its elements may be identified by several subscripts. (For a broader discussion of the logical organization and use of arrays see Section 2-C-2.)

Physical organization of arrays is usually sequential because their composition rarely changes during program execution. Since arrays are usually available to a higher level language programmer as a "ready" data structure, placement of arrays in memory is performed by systems software.

Two methods of storage placement exist: *row-major order,* used in most languages, when the last subscript changes fastest, and *column-major order,* used in FORTRAN, where the first index changes fastest.

EXAMPLE 5-5

Below is shown a two-dimensional array A(1:3, 1:2) placed in the row-major and column-major orders. To the left of each are hypothetical memory addresses.

	row-major			column-major
100	A(1,1)		100	A(1,1)
101	A(1,2)		101	A(2,1)
102	A(2,1)		102	A(3,1)
103	A(2,2)		103	A(1,2)
104	A(3,1)		104	A(2,2)
105	A(3,2)		105	A(3,2)

row-major order   column-major order

It is assumed that one element is placed per word.

E. RECORDS

A *record* is a collection of data items of various types. These items are frequently called the *fields* of the record and are referred to by their own names. Fields may be composites themselves, having their own subfields. Certain fields of a record may contain character strings that are data structures in their own right (see Section J).

EXAMPLE 5-6

A personnel record of an employee may consist of the fields and subfields shown in Fig. 5-2.

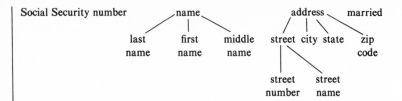

FIGURE 5-2.

In this record, such items as last name or city are character data, while Social Security number or zip code are integers, and "married" is a logical item.

As opposed to records, arrays are homogeneous (they consist of a single type of data) and their elements do not have their own names, being identified by their positions in the array.

A record provides information about various features of the real-world object it describes. Every field describes one of the *attributes* of this object.

A record is usually identified by its *key*, one of the fields selected for the purpose of accessing the information contained in the record. Frequently, records are maintained in an order corresponding to the values of such key; this means they are sorted on the key. If a key is to identify a record, no two records may have the same values of the key.

EXAMPLE 5-7
In a collection of personnel records, the Social Security number of an employee may serve as the key.

In a higher level language in which records may be declared as data structures (such as COBOL or PL/I), indentation is used to specify the record name, its fields, and subfields. The levels of a record are also numbered, as shown in the example below.

EXAMPLE 5-8
The following declaration may be used to declare the record EMPLOYEE of Example 5-6:

```
01 EMPLOYEE
   02 SS-NUMBER
   02 NAME
      03 LAST-NAME
      03 FIRST-NAME
      03 MIDDLE-NAME
```

```
02 ADDRESS
    03 STREET
        04 STREET-NO
        04 STREET-NAME
    03 CITY
    03 STATE
    03 ZIP
02 MARRIED
```

This record would be represented in memory as shown below.

SS-NUMBER	LAST-NAME	FIRST-NAME	MIDDLE-NAME	STREET-NO	STREET-NAME	CITY	STATE	ZIP	MAR-RIED

Note that only the elementary fields and subfields are physically stored. The composite subfields are logical entities.

Physically, record fields are usually stored in consecutive storage locations, frequently in a packed fashion.

Some applications require records of variable length due to the variable length of a field (such as LAST-NAME) or a variable number of fields (such as MIDDLE-NAME).

When records are used as elements of higher order data structures small enough to be kept in the main memory, they are often called the *nodes* of the structure.

Usually the records are organized into *files* that are maintained in the secondary storage and whose parts are introduced into the main memory when required. Files are the essential data organization in volume information processing (see Chapter 10).

F. LINEAR LISTS

A *linear list* is a finite sequence of simple data items or records (for simplicity the elements of the list are called *nodes*). Each of the nodes on a list forming a sequence (except for the first and the last) has a single successor and a single predecessor.

EXAMPLE 5-9

Entries in a telephone directory constitute a linear list. When the nodes of a list are placed in memory in sequential fashion, a *table* is obtained.

If the telephone directory of an enterprise is held in computer memory, it may be stored in a table shown below, where it is assumed that each record occupies 10 memory locations.

MEMORY LOCATION	LAST NAME	FIRST NAME	TELEPHONE EXTENSION
100	ABRAMS	GEORGIA	1234
110	JONES	CAROL	5312
120	SYKES	JOSEPH	0750
130	WILKES	PETER	2312

The alternative physical placement of linear list is a *linked list,* whose general structure is shown in Fig. 5–3.

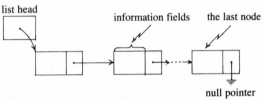

FIGURE 5–3. Linked list (general form)

The first node in the list is pointed to by a special location, called a *list head*, while the last node can be recognized by the fact that its pointer (called a *null pointer*) does not contain a legal address. This is usually shown graphically with the electric "ground" symbol, and the value actually stored may be, for example, − 1.

A list is usually ordered by one of its fields, so that the desired node may be *accessed* (i.e., reached and identified in order to obtain its contents). The order of the sequential list is implicit in the physical placements of the nodes in memory. In a linked list, the order is imposed by pointers.

EXAMPLE 5–10

In the following figure a linked list corresponding to the table in Example 5–9 is shown. It is assumed that the alphabetical order of employees is desired in the list. This order emerged as the result of the movement of personnel in the company.

LIST HEAD	MEMORY LOCATION	LAST NAME	FIRST NAME	TELEPHONE EXTENSION	POINTER (LINK)
110	100	JONES	CAROL	5312	130
	110	ABRAMS	GEORGIA	1234	100
	120	WILKES	PETER	2312	−1
	130	SYKES	JOSEPH	0750	120

Note that the same information is contained in both structures. In the case of the linked list, here, however, the logical structure of the list is not constrained by its physical placement in memory. Thus when employees are hired or fired, no reordering of the list is required, only a change in link values. Note also that an additional field (link) is required in the linked list for maintaining the structural information.

Typical operations performed on a linear list are

(a) insertion or deletion of a node;
(b) joining of two lists or splitting of a single list;
(c) access to an item identified by its key.

Deletion or insertion of a node in a sequential list involves a considerable amount of data movement, while in the case of a linked list it requires a change of only one or two pointers, respectively (see Fig. 5-4). Therein lies the essential advantage of linked structures.

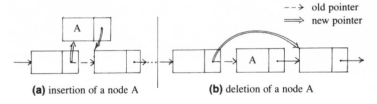

--→ old pointer
⟹ new pointer

(a) insertion of a node A   (b) deletion of a node A

FIGURE 5–4. Management of a linked list

It is also simpler to split a linked list or join two linked lists than to perform similar operations in a sequential list (table). Access to a "random" node is, however, simpler in a sequential list when there is no need for multiple accessing of pointer values in order to "move down the links."

In conclusion, when the composition of a linear list changes considerably during the program execution, linked lists are used.

List entries are often sorted on the values of their keys in order to ensure efficient search for a particular node. Sorting and searching are extremely common operations in data processing and thus many algorithms exist.

These are applicable, with minor modifications, both to sequential and linked lists.

An enhanced bubble sort algorithm is discussed in Example 3–11, and a binary search algorithm, presented as a better alternative to sequential search, in Example 3–17.

Two important variations of the list linking scheme are

(a) *doubly linked list*, whose nodes contain two pointers, the right one pointing to the node's successor, and the left one to its predecessor (Fig. 5–5). It is possible to scan such a list in both directions. Insertion and deletion are also simplified.

(b) *circular list (ring)*, whose last pointer is not null but points to the first node. Any node may be reached from any other in such a list.

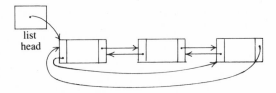

FIGURE 5–5. A doubly linked ring

G. QUEUES AND STACKS

Queues and stacks are restricted linear lists with important applications.

A *queue* is a linear list into which insertions are allowed only at one end (called the rear of the queue) and deletions at the other end (called the front of the queue).

Sequential and linked queues are shown in Fig. 5–6.

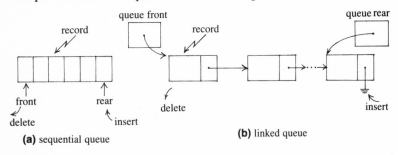

(a) sequential queue

(b) linked queue

FIGURE 5–6. Queue

A queue is used to represent events that are to be considered by the program in the order in which these events occur. It may, for example, be used to simulate the operation of a computer center at which the events are job arrivals (see Example 5–3) or to represent the goods on hand for accounting purposes when a first-in–first-out regimen is used.

A *stack* is a linear list where both the additions and deletions occur at its single end, called the *top* of the stack. Convential representations of the stack are shown in Fig. 5–7.

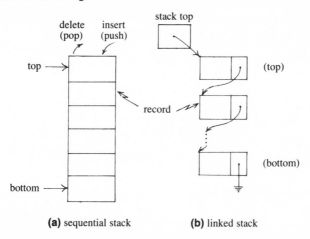

(a) sequential stack   **(b)** linked stack

FIGURE 5–7.   Stack

Stack operations are called *push* and *pop* instead of insert and delete, respectively.

In a stack, items other than the top one are inaccessible. Since the items are always pushed on top of the stack and the last item pushed will be the first one to be popped, a stack is a last-in–first-out data structure.

A stack is used frequently in program design, when during a program execution multiple possibilities arise and all of them have to be followed up. Since only one execution path may be pursued at a time with a single processor, the data representing other paths are pushed on a stack until the time comes to pop them and pursue the execution path these data represent. Stacks are often used in systems programming, particularly to implement recursion (see Chapter 4–C).

H. TREES AND BINARY TREES

A *tree* is a collection of nodes that consists of a special node called the *root*, which has no predecessors, and, possibly, of a finite number of successors of the root. Each of these successors, if severed from the root, is, in turn, the root of another tree.

This recursive definition applies to any of the structures shown in Fig. 5–8, where the nodes of the trees are symbolically shown as circles. Note that "computer" trees are shown with their roots above the branches.

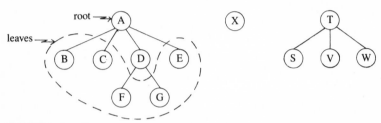

FIGURE 5–8.   Trees

The edges connecting the nodes show the logical organization of the given tree structure.

Whereas a node of a linear list may in general have a single predecessor and a single successor, a node of a tree, other than the root, has one predecessor and any finite number of successors. In a tree structure, a predecessor is called parent; and a successor, child.

Tree structures are used to represent any branching relationship among data items, such as a hierarchical data composition (e.g., an organizational chart of an enterprise or nested sets which consist of smaller sets that in turn may include their own subsets) or decision trees (in particular, game trees).

EXAMPLE 5–11

Computers are often programmed to play board games such as chess or backgammon. In such games, the computer "looks ahead" several moves in order to select its best move against its human opponent. Such a game tree is shown in Fig. 5–9.

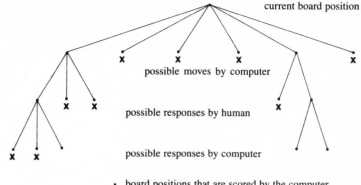

current board position

possible moves by computer

possible responses by human

possible responses by computer

• board positions that are scored by the computer
x moves that are clearly inferior; no further investigation

FIGURE 5–9. A game tree

Such a tree is developed to a desired depth.

General trees, in which a parent may have any finite number of children, are somewhat unwieldy to manipulate. However, they may be easily converted to another data structure, called a binary tree, which may be manipulated more readily.

A *binary tree* is a set of nodes that is either empty or consists of a root and two binary trees coming from it. These two binary trees are called *subtrees* of the root. This recursive definition applies to any of the structures shown in Fig. 5–10.

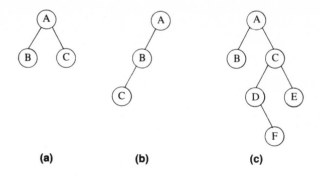

(a)   (b)   (c)

FIGURE 5–10.   Binary trees

Many algorithms require that every node in a binary tree be accessed exactly once; such a scanning procedure is called *tree traversal*.

One of three possible traversal methods is *preorder traversal*, defined recursively as follows: access the root; traverse its left subtree in preorder; traverse the right subtree in preorder.

EXAMPLE 5–12

Nodes of the tree shown in Fig. 5–10(c) will be accessed in the following sequence during preorder traversal:

ABCDFE

Physical representation of trees may be either sequential, in which case nodes are placed in memory in a linear order imposed by a traversal, or linked. In the case of linked allocations, pointers (links) are placed into a parent's node to point to its children. Leaves of a tree have null pointers (see Fig. 5–11, where the linked representation of binary trees of Fig. 5–10 is shown).

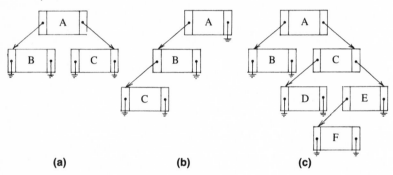

(a)   (b)   (c)

FIGURE 5–11. Binary trees (linked representation). Note that pointers correspond to the edges of the tree.

I. GRAPHS

A *graph* (also called a *network* or a *plex*) is a collection of nodes and edges connecting them. The edges define the relationship among the nodes in the context of a given application.

EXAMPLE 5–13

To represent the data for an inventory program, it may be necessary to maintain the information that relates the parts to the products that use them. Such information may be conveniently maintained in the edges of a graph shown in Fig. 5–12.

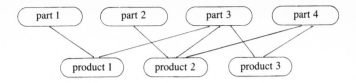

FIGURE 5–12. A graph

Here an edge means: "this part goes into the manufacture of that product."

Some applications require *directed graphs (digraphs)*, in which every edge is directed.

EXAMPLE 5–14

A directed graph may represent a PERT chart, used in project management. In such a digraph the nodes signify events, accomplishments during a project realization; and the edges, the activities that take us from event to event. The edges are labeled according to the duration of these activities; for example, in days (see Fig. 5–13.)

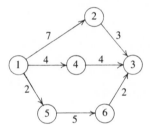

FIGURE 5–13.

Such a graph serves to determine the critical path of the project.

Graphs are used to represent any real-world networks, such as pipelines, telephone networks, or any activity network of which a PERT graph is an example.

A graph is the most general data structure since any node of it may be connected to any other node, or even to itself.

Physical representation of networks in memory is usually linked, with the links corresponding to network edges. Sequential representation is possible by decomposing a network into trees, but duplication of certain nodes is generally unavoidable.

J. CHARACTER STRINGS AND THEIR PROCESSING

Character strings are directly available as a data structure in most general-purpose higher level languages. Processing of text, i.e., character data, as distinct from numerical computing, is an ever-broadening field.

Characters of a string are represented, as discussed in Section A–7, with the use of a binary code, 7 or 8 bits per character. To form a string, these characters are stored as a sequential or a linked data structure, as shown in Fig. 5–14.

The *length* of the string (i.e., the number of characters in it) is most often stored in the preceding word in the case of the sequential representation and in the string head in the linked case.

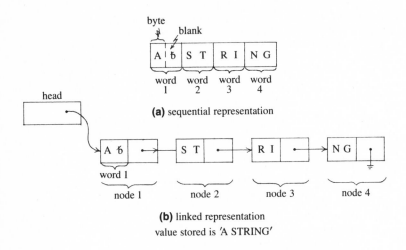

(a) sequential representation

(b) linked representation

value stored is 'A STRING'

FIGURE 5–14. Representation of a string in memory. The value stored is 'A STRING.' It is assumed that a word holds two bytes in this computer.

The additional memory use in the linked representation is compensated for by its processing flexibility. For example, if our string has to be edited into 'A LONGER STRING,' with the attendant insertion of 7 characters (blanks are characters also!), a significant data movement will ensue in a sequentially stored string.

The following are the essentials of string processing.

(1) *A string constant* is enclosed in single quotes; for example

'A STRING'

The quotes are not a part of the string. This is an empty string: ' ', whose use in string processing resembles the use of 0 in numerical manipulation.

(2) *A character-type variable* whose value is a string may be declared as follows:

Character NAME

It is usually also possible to declare arrays and functions whose values are character strings.

In languages with static memory allocation (see Section 4-B-2), the maximum length of every character-type entity has to be declared; if its value is shorter than this length, the locations on the right are padded with blanks. In languages with dynamic memory allocation, the current length of such an entity may be determined by its current value.

(3) *Assignment* is possible of a string (or of a value of a string-valued expression) to a character-type variable; for example,

NAME ← 'V.ZWASS'

(4) The *concatenation* (joining together) of two strings is one of the essential operations in string-valued expressions. Denoted, for example, as // , the operation

string-1 // string-2

appends string-2 to the end of string-1. For example,

NAME ← 'V.' // 'ZWASS'

produces a string 'V.ZWASS' as the value of the variable NAME.

(5) A *substring* (a continuous part of a string) may be extracted from a string by stating the beginning and the end of the desired substring in parentheses following the string name.

The string characters are considered numbered from left (1) to right. Thus in the above example:

NAME(4 : 5) has the value 'WA'
NAME(1 : 1) has the value 'V'

The following assignment

INIT ← NAME(1 : 3) // '.'

produces the value 'V.Z.', as this of the character-type variable INIT.

(6) *Strings may be compared* with the use of the collating sequence of the character code (see Section A-7 of this chapter). All popular codes ensure that the letters of the alphabet are in order $(1 < 2 < \ldots < 9)$, and the blank is smaller than both the letters and the digits.

Thus, considering the values in our running example, during the execution of the statement

if (NAME < 'A.ABRAMS') **then**

.

.

.

else

.

.

.

the **else** branch will be selected.

(7) *Built-in functions* operating on strings are usually available in the higher level languages that afford string processing. Two of the most useful functions are discussed here; both of them operate on any string-valued expressions.

(a) LEN(string) returns the length of the string. Thus, considering the variable NAME above,

LEN(NAME) returns the value 7.

(b) INDEX(subject string, pattern string) determines whether the pattern string is contained as a substring in the subject string. The search for a pattern string in a subject string, performed by this function, is called *pattern matching*. This function returns the value of 0 if the pattern is not found; otherwise, an integer indicating its leftmost ("first") occurrence in the subject is returned. For example,

INDEX(NAME, 'V. Z') returns 0 (watch for those blanks!);
INDEX('TARTAR', 'TAR') returns 1.

Some languages make it possible to replace the pattern string, if found in the subject, by another, called the object string.

A rich complement of string processing facilities is available in the languages specially designed for this purpose, of which the best known is SNO-BOL.

The following example illustrates string processing.

EXAMPLE 5-15

Problem

A name is presented with the full given names; any number of given names is possible. The given names are to be replaced by initials. For example, the input: WYSTAN HUGH AUDEN is to result in the output: W.H.AUDEN.

Solution

```
*ALGORITHM REPLACES GIVEN NAMES BY INITIALS
*FULL—original name
*NEW—name with initials
begin
      Character FULL, NEW;
      Input FULL; Output FULL;
      NEW←' ';                *INITIALIZE AS EMPTY STRING*
*KEEP SEARCHING FOR BLANKS IN THE ORIGINAL NAME*
      I← INDEX(FULL, '  ');
      while (I ≠ 0) do          *ANY BLANKS FOUND?*
        begin
           NEW ← NEW // FULL(1 : 1) // '.' *GET THE INITIAL*
           FULL← FULL(I + 1 : LEN(FULL)); *DROP GIVEN NAME*
           I ← INDEX(FULL, '  ') *FIND NEXT BLANK*
        end;
      NEW← NEW // FULL;   *APPEND THE LAST NAME*
      Output NEW
end
```

Notes

1. Observe that the algorithm works correctly for a name without any given names.
2. Trace the operation of this algorithm on any name.

SUGGESTIONS FOR FURTHER READING

Knuth, D. E.: *Fundamental Algorithms*, 2nd ed. Addison-Wesley, Reading, Mass., 1973.
  A classic, this is the first volume of the planned seven-volume work *The Art of Computer Programming*. Data structures are discussed in the Chapter 2 of the book.

Horowitz, E., and Sahni, S.: *Fundamentals of Data Structures*, Computer Sciences Press, Woodland Hills, Calif., 1976.
  Structured programming is stressed.

Tremblay, J.-P., and Sorenson, P. G.: *An Introduction to Data Structures*, McGraw-Hill, New York, 1976.
  A special stress on applications; among other topics, a fine discussion of the string manipulation.

Gotlieb, C. C., and Gotlieb, L. R.: *Data Types and Structures*, Prentice-Hall, Englewood Cliffs, N.J., 1978.

Part Two

CONCEPTS OF COMPUTER SYSTEMS

COMPUTER SCIENCE IS a study of theoretical and practical aspects of the design and use of computers. With the ever-widening application of computers, this science has been developing and broadening rapidly. In this part of the book, an attempt is made to introduce the key concepts of the field.

Programmers find it convenient to present algorithms to a computer in a higher level language. These languages make it possible to express a problem solution in a manner relatively close to the human way of communication while being precise and unambiguous. A great number of such languages have been introduced, though only a few of them are in predominant use. A program written in such language may be easily transferred to a computer model different from the one employed originally.

When economy of computer resources is required, on the other hand, assembly language is used. Since this language is close to the machine language of the particular computer, the programmer is able to control more directly the use of computer system resources. Assembly language programming is more demanding, however, and the programs are not portable from one computer model (or series) to another.

Neither the programs written in higher level languages nor those in assembly languages are directly executable by the hardware of a computer. Software programs are required to translate them into the native instructions of a given computer, that is, into its machine language, executable directly by its central processing unit. Translators for higher level languages (compilers and interpreters) are significantly more complex than those for assembly languages (assemblers) due to the extensive features afforded to the higher level language programmer.

A computer system comprises a variety of hardware resources; multiple systems are in some cases organized into networks. In order to create an environment amenable to the execution of application programs, extensive software is required. In particular, all the resources of a computer system are managed by a so-called operating system.

Thus, operating systems, translators, and other systems software mediate between the user and the hardware. In some systems, parts of software are permanently stored in special memories (microprogrammed) to become so-called firmware.

While the hardware design of various computer models differs, general principles of computer system organization have emerged. With the exception of the input/output and certain secondary and mass memory devices, functional units of computers are built of electronic devices. The basic components of these are switching circuits with two alternate states. They are often called computer logic.

Along with hardware and software, an increasingly important resource of many computer systems is organized collections of data relating to the applications for which the system is used. This resource is also managed by specialized software programs: file or database management systems.

Like any other scientific discipline, computer science has evolved theoretical foundations. These include the theory of computability (what computers can and cannot do), theory of algorithms and their complexity, theory of formal languages, and the study of algebraic structures leading, among other subjects, to the theory of switching circuits.

6

HIGHER LEVEL LANGUAGES
AND THEIR TRANSLATORS

Today the bulk of programming is done in one of the higher level languages, rather than in an assembly language, particular to the given computer model (see Chapter 7). The programming in a higher level language is easier to learn, and the programs are easier to implement, understand, and modify, since the statements are to an extent self-documenting. Another advantage is the portability of such programs due to the wide use of the main languages.

The ease of higher level language programming is attained at the cost of a relative difficulty of program translation. Translators for higher level languages are significantly more complex than translators for assembly languages, called assemblers. The translation process itself consumes more CPU time and uses more memory than assembly, and the translated code is usually less efficient than a program written in assembly language. Most of the higher level languages are translated by compilers that fully convert the source program into an object program before its execution. Certain languages (often those with complex statements) are translated and executed statement by statement by interpreters. This type of translator does not produce the object code and requires more system resources such as CPU time and main memory, but offers important advantages to the programmer: interactive computing and better error detection.

A survey of the most important higher level languages is presented. This review outlines the areas of application and the specificity of each language.

A. SURVEY OF HIGHER LEVEL LANGUAGES

Languages in wide general use or of importance in a specialized area of computing are included in this survey. The development of these languages started with the advent of FORTRAN, still the language of broadest appeal, in the mid-1950s.

The primary areas of application of these languages are

- general purpose: PL/I, Pascal, ALGOL 68
- business: COBOL, RPG
- science and engineering: FORTRAN, ALGOL, APL
- interactive computing: BASIC, APL, LISP
- symbolic processing: SNOBOL, LISP
- simulation: SIMSCRIPT, GPSS, CSMP
- personal computing: BASIC.

Languages used in the sciences and engineering have extensive facilities for the manipulation of numerical data.

Business-oriented languages are geared to the handling of large volumes of data, stored on secondary memory devices. These languages need, therefore, input/output statements for interaction with such devices and facilities for editing and rearranging data organized into files stored on these devices and for extracting their summaries and printing appropriate reports.

Symbolic processing, ever widening, encompasses the manipulation of free-flowing text and of lists.

Interactive computing requires an interpreted language, with the considerable programming convenience achieved usually at the cost of increased CPU and main memory utilization.

A programmer familiar with the general concepts of programming languages presented in Chapters 1 through 5 and proficient in one of the commonly used languages will find learning another language a relatively simple task.

1. ALGOL

This language, more precisely called ALGOL 60, has had a considerable influence on the development of computer science, even as it has been only of limited practical use in the United States.

Because the language was the first to be precisely defined in a metalanguage [called Backus-Naur form, or BNF notation], it has been extensively used for the description (rather than the implementation) of algorithms.

The data manipulation facilities of ALGOL are similar to those of FORTRAN, since both languages were intended for scientific applications. Thus, both languages allow for a rather simple encoding of computational formulas into assignment statements.

The control structures of ALGOL are, however, more general; the language has block structure and permits recursive use of procedures, these features being supported by dynamic storage allocation (see Chapter 4-B and C).

ALGOL 68, whose design encompasses many theoretical generalizations of ALGOL concepts, is unlikely to supplant ALGOL 60.

2. APL

APL is a powerful language with distinctive features. It is used primarily in the scientific, but also in the business, environment. A scientist or an executive often finds the language easy to learn and simple to use due to its conciseness of expression and interactive nature.

The strength of APL lies in its array manipulation capabilities. Array is the basic data structure of the language, and a number of operations are available for dealing with all of its elements simultaneously. A single operator, for example, counts the number of array elements, another rotates its columns.

APL systems are interpretive and require a special terminal since special symbols and some Greek characters are used to denote the many operators of the language.

Interpretive execution of an APL program is very demanding of CPU time. The use of APL is therefore advantageous where large arrays have to be manipulated with a moderate number of input/output operations, and the resulting program is not to be run on a frequent and regular basis.

The following APL statement computes the average A of a vector (an array of a single dimension) X:

$$A \leftarrow (+/X) \div \rho X$$

where the action of the operators is as follows:

ρX: the number of elements in X
$+/X$: the sum of the elements of X
$\div$: division
$\leftarrow$: assignment.

The parentheses are necessary since the operators are applied in APL from right to left and there is no operator precedence.

3. BASIC

BASIC is an easy to learn interactive language for a broad audience. Even though the language is interpretive, its simplicity leads to low-cost computer use.

BASIC is similar to FORTRAN, but contains fewer control structures and data types and permits no external subprograms.

The advent of personal computing has increased the appeal of BASIC.

4. COBOL

The predominant use in the business environment, due to the extensive file-handling, editing, and report-generating capabilities of COBOL, has made this language the most frequently used of all.

The language was designed to be relatively close to English. A COBOL program is to a large extent self-documenting owing to its system of subdivisions and the use of long identifiers (labels and variable names may contain up to 30 characters).

A COBOL program consists of four divisions:

(1) identification division: identifies the program and the programmer
(2) environment division: ought to contain all the machine-dependent information, such as the names of the computer model, of the devices holding the files, etc.
(3) data division: fully describes all data used by the program and allows them to be structured hierarchically
(4) procedure division: the specification of the algorithm.

The most characteristic of COBOL programs is the data division, an example of which is shown below. The data are structured hierarchically (here, in four levels), with the composition of the actual items described by the PICTURE clause, in this case either as alphanumerical (X) or decimal-numerical (9). A program reference to any data item includes all the data lower in the hierarchy.

An example of data division in a COBOL program is the following:

```
01 SUBSCRIBER-INFORMATION
      02 NAME
            03 FIRST-NAME           PICTURE X(10)
            03 INITIAL              PICTURE X
            03 LAST-NAME            PICTURE X(12)
      02 ADDRESS
            03 STREET
                  04 STREET-NO      PICTURE 9(5)
                  04 STREET-NAME    PICTURE X(20)
            03 TOWN-STATE
                  04 TOWN           PICTURE X(20)
                  04 STATE          PICTURE X(2)
                  04 ZIP-CODE       PICTURE X(5)
      02 SUBSCRIBED-UNTIL
            04 SUB-DAY              PICTURE 9(2)
            04 SUB-MONTH            PICTURE 9(2)
            04 SUB-YEAR             PICTURE 9(2)
```

COBOL is a standardized language; while such standards are voluntary, the facilities provided by various compilers in general coincide. This simplifies the portability of programs from one computer model to another.

5. FORTRAN

The first widely used higher level language, FORTRAN continues to be of great importance in computing. A general-purpose language, its main use is in science and engineering, although it is utilized practically in every environment.

In order to provide for program portability, the language has been standardized. On the basis of the first voluntary standard, the FORTRAN IV version of the language had been developed.

The needs of nonnumeric applications led to the development of a new standard, called FORTRAN 77, based to a large degree on the WATFOR and WATFIV compilers for the language. Facilities for symbolic processing and more sophisticated file handling were provided.

6. LISP

LISP is a specialized language used almost exclusively in modeling human understanding and problem-solving in so-called artificial intelligence applications.

It is designed to manipulate list structures (see Chapter 5–F). In LISP, a list is a sequence of elements of any kind (words, numbers, sentences, etc.). These elements may be lists themselves, this fact implying the inherently recursive nature of LISP.

Presently, LISP is primarily interpreted. Since their data are represented as linked lists, LISP programs require extensive main memory space.

7. PASCAL

Pascal is a tightly designed general-purpose language that implements the control and data structures discussed in Chapters 3 and 5. The language was created to enforce writing of well-structured programs that are easy to implement and modify. The clarity of the language and its extensive error-detection facilities result in fast implementation of programs.

The language is a derivative of ALGOL and has ALGOL's block structure, but provides more data types. Pascal programmers are also able to define their own data types.

While currently used mostly for instructional purposes, Pascal's use is widening, particularly in the programming of microcomputers, and this language is certain to influence computing in the days to come.

Another language based on Pascal, called Ada (after Augusta Ada Lady Lovelace, who collaborated with Charles Babbage as the first "programmer"), has been designed recently at the initiative of the U.S. Department of Defense. With its particular strengths in real-time applications and systems programming, this language is expected to find wide use.

8. PL/I

This very "rich" language combines the features of its predecessors: AL-
GOL, FORTRAN, and COBOL, as well as extensive facilities for symbolic
processing. PL/I can be applied in all areas of computing.

The language has the DECLARE facility, for the description of data
similar to the data division of COBOL. It offers block structure and dynamic storage allocation, which may be controlled by the programmer. Many
data types are included, some to support string and list manipulation.

Due to the versatility of the language, PL/I compilers are very large and
translation is time-consuming, which limits the application of the language.

9. RPG

The acronym RPG stands for Report Program Generator, which indeed expresses the function of this language. It is used to write the precise specification of the problem, rather than the program, which is subsequently generated by the compiler. Languages such as this are known as *declarative*
(rather than procedural).

RPG's use is limited to the generation of reports (summaries) from data
files and to the updating of such files.

Essentially, the compiler modifies a single prepackaged program to
match the given specifications, which include file description as well as input, calculation, and output specifications.

The language is widely used in small data-processing installations.

10. SNOBOL

SNOBOL is a text-processing language. In other words, its essential data
are character strings. The basic operations on these data are assignment,
search for a string pattern (called pattern matching—see Chapter 5-J), and
the replacement of a pattern found.

Consider, for example, this sequence of two statements:

```
TITLE = 'MOBY DICK'
TITLE 'MOBY' = 'GEORGE'
```

The first of these assigns the string 'MOBY DICK' as the value of the
variable TITLE. The second statement is a replacement: the pattern
'MOBY' is compared with the value of TITLE, found, and replaced by
'GEORGE'. The value of TITLE is now 'GEORGE DICK'.

Early SNOBOL implementations were interpretive; now the language is
also compiled, with increased efficiency.

Text-processing applications are growing, as it is becoming economical to
have computers set type, maintain bibliographies and concordances and, in
general, provide printed text where the benefit of human creativity is not
needed.

11. SIMULATION LANGUAGES

A number of special-purpose languages exist to assist in modeling social and physical systems with the use of computers.

Continuous-variable models represent systems that may be described mathematically and in which the system variables change smoothly (for example, current flows in an electrical network). The language frequently used for this purpose is CSMP.

Discrete-event models represent systems in which state changes are discontinuous, steplike. These are often called queueing systems. In such a system, there are a number of "resources," for which the "customers" arrive with a certain regularity; the "customers" are then allocated the "resources" for a certain service time, with the maintenance of a certain queueing discipline. Simulation of such a system is done most frequently and is served by such languages as SIMSCRIPT and GPSS. The languages help to represent the arrivals, the queue, and the departures following the service, as well as to derive the desired statistics.

B. COMPILERS

A *compiler* translates programs written in a given higher level language (source programs) into their machine language equivalents ready for execution (see Fig. 6–1).

FIGURE 6–1. Action of a compiler

Some compilers, however, translate into the assembly language of a given machine, so that subsequent assembly (as described in Chapter 7–G) is required.

The object code obtained as the result of the compilation may be stored and reused repeatedly.

While compilers differ as to their performance objectives and design, they consist of a number of *phases* that consecutively transform the source program. The initial phases of the compiler for a given higher level language are independent of the computer whose machine language is the target; these are lexical analysis, syntactic analysis, and intermediate code generation. The next phase, optimization, depends to an extent on the target machine language in its later stages. The last phase, code generation, is, of course, wholly dependent on it.

1. LEXICAL ANALYSIS

The purpose of the lexical analysis phase is

to prepare the symbol table;
to rid the program of redundancy (comments, blarks, etc.) and encode its
  statements tightly.

The program is scanned statement by statement, while the statement components are recognized. Two kinds of such components are to be distinguished. The first kind are fixed elements of the language, such as keywords, the vocabulary of the language (e.g., GOTO or INTEGER in FORTRAN), and its operators and signs (e.g., *, =, .AND.). The other kind are the *identifiers* (symbolic names) and constants of various types; these are, of course, made up by the programmer.

All such components are called *tokens*. The information concerning the fixed tokens of the language is located in the compiler's permanent tables. The programmer-defined tokens are entered into the *symbol table* that holds their name and attributes. Frequently, separate symbol tables are created for different sets of tokens.

During the scan, the tokens are replaced in every statement by pointers to their entries in the symbol table(s). The output of the phase is the sequence of statements containing such pointers, with no blanks or comments.

EXAMPLE 6–1

In the FORTRAN statement:

A = X * (Y + 10.5)

the following tokens are recognized:

operators and signs: =, *, (, +,)
identifiers: A, X, Y
constant: 10.5

After the programmer-defined tokens have been replaced by pointers to the symbol tables of identifiers and constants, the statement is transformed into, for example,

id-55 = id-77 * (id-125 + cons-2)

(The above statement is, of course, modified here for readability.)

2. SYNTACTIC ANALYSIS

The *parser,* part of the compiler responsible for syntatic analysis, identifies the grammatical structure of the program. This analysis is based on the built-in definition of the source language.

The following tasks† are accomplished:

- The legality of every statement under the language definition is ascertained.
- A *parse tree* is obtained for every statement and for the entire program.

This crucial phase produces the parse tree for the program, appropriately represented in memory. At this point, the compiler "has understood" the program.

The parse tree of Fig. 6–2 will be generated for our statement in Example 6–1 if the common rules of operator precedence are applied:

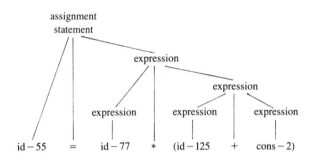

FIGURE 6–2. A parse tree

As a result, the statement is identified as an assignment. The parse tree for the program is constructed from the statement trees.

3. INTERMEDIATE CODE GENERATION

The object code may be generated directly from the parse tree. It is advantageous, however, to convert it first to a selected intermediate form, in which general optimization techniques may be applied to this machine-independent code.

In many compilers this code takes the form of a so-called *three-address code* whose every data-manipulation instruction specifies the operation and the symbolic addresses of the two operands and of the result. There are also unconditional and conditional transfers of control.

When converted to three-address code, our statement of Example 6–1 takes the form of:

† The procedure is similar to grammatical parsing of a natural language text.

TEMP1 ← id-125 + cons-2
id-55 ← id-77 * TEMP1

Note the typical need for a temporary variable.

An alternative representation of intermediate code is the *postfix* (also called *reverse Polish*) notation.

We are used to representing expressions in the *infix notation,* where the operator is placed between the two operands to which it applies. In the postfix notation, an operator follows its operands. The notation does not need parentheses. A postfix expression is evaluated from left to right by applying the operator encountered first to the two operands preceding it, and replacing this triple by the result.

EXAMPLE 6–2

Note the correspondencies between the following expressions:

infix	*postfix*
a + b	a b +
a − b * c	a b c * −
(a − b) * (c + d)	a b − c d + *

Note that the order of operands is the same in both cases; the order of the operators determines the order of evaluation.

We continue Example 6–1, a statement compilation. In the postfix form, our assignment statement is as follows:

id-55   id-77   id-125   cons-2 + * =

Efficient algorithms exist for the conversion from the infix to the postfix form for all types of statements. The primary goal is to convert the arithmetic expressions, which may in turn be quickly converted to the object code with the use of a stack structure (see Chapter 5–G).

4. OPTIMIZATION

This optional phase transforms the intermediate code so as to achieve execution time and memory space economy for the object program.

Some of the strategies applied are moving an invariant statement out of the loop, identifying and computing common subexpressions separately, etc.

5. CODE GENERATION

Most modern compilers generate executable machine code; some, assembly code to be further processed by an assembler.

A code generator carefully allocates the available CPU resources and, in general, attempts to minimize the number of accesses to the main memory.

Assuming that the three-address code originally of Example 6–1 has been generated as the intermediate form and that the code generator will consider every three-address statement separately, the following sequence† of assembly language statements would be generated:

```
LOAD 1, id-125
ADD 1, cons-2
STR 1, TEMP1   (*)
LOAD 1, TEMP1   (**)
MUL 1, id-77
STR 1, id-55
```

Note that the statements (*) and (**) are unnecessary; they will be removed.
(The pointers to the symbol table are at this stage already replaced by the relative addresses of the operands, this not being shown here for simplicity's sake.)

Object code is usually produced in relocatable form; this means that it is subject to loading and linking (see Chapter 7–G).

6. OTHER FUNCTIONS OF A COMPILER

Two additional functions are performed during a compilation:

A. STORAGE ALLOCATION

For a program to be executed, memory space has to be allocated for the program and its data (as well as for some ancillary items). Although the program and the data are actually placed in memory by the loader (see Chapter 7–G), the compiler has to determine memory requirements of a program. This task is performed fully during the compilation process in the case of languages having static memory allocation (such as FORTRAN or COBOL) whose data are fully declared by the programmer and which do not allow recursion. In the case of languages with dynamic memory allocation (see Chapter 4–B–2), such as ALGOL or PL/I, an executing program may require additional memory space or release it. *Run-time support* routines, which perform the additional memory allocation while the program is executing, are therefore needed to accomplish this task.

B. ERROR INDICATION

Lexical and syntactic errors, discovered during the two phases of compilation, are to be indicated to the programmer.

A compiler should display desirable performance characteristics, with the contradictory goals existing. Popular languages have, therefore, two types of compilers:

†You may have to read the next chapter to understand these instructions.

- Fast compilers that perform almost no optimization but offer good error indication. These are used to implement a program.
- Slow optimizing compilers that produce tight object code for multiple production runs.

C. INTERPRETATION AND ITS COMPARISON WITH COMPILATION

Interpreters translate and execute the source program statement by statement. They do not produce object code for the program, although initially most translate the source code into an intermediate code that is then executed interpretively (see Fig. 6–3).

The program execution is, therefore, controlled by the interpreter, which acts as if it were a machine built for the execution of the statements of a given higher level language. Interpretation is a significantly more costly translation method than compilation, since:

(a) as no object code is created, every time a program is run it needs to be interpreted;

(b) in a given program, a statement needs to be interpreted every time before it is executed. This means that if a statement is included in a loop it is translated as many times as the loop body is executed.

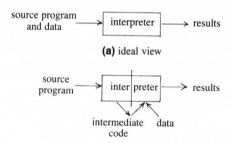

(a) ideal view

(b) most frequent implementation

FIGURE 6–3. Action of an interpreter

The interpreters are used when:

(1) the benefits of interactive execution, such as improved program implementation environment, are desired. Since the statements are executed "out of context," the user input may be accepted at any desired point during the execution in a time-sharing environment. This

practice is supported by the inherently superior error-detection capabilities of interpreters, which can more easily relate an error to the offending statement than compilers.

(2) the language statements are so powerful that their executions takes much longer than their translation (for example, in the case of APL).

SUGGESTIONS FOR FURTHER READING

COMPARATIVE STUDIES OF HIGHER LEVEL PROGRAMMING LANGUAGES

Organick, E. I., Forsythe, A. I., and Plummer, R. P.: *Programming Language Structures,* Academic, New York, 1978.
    A general discussion on an introductory level is followed by the presentation of the essential facilities of ALGOL, FORTRAN, LISP, SNOBOL, and Pascal.

Nicholls, J. E.: *The Structure and Design of Programming Languages,* Addison-Wesley, Reading, Mass., 1975.

Pratt, T. W.: *Programming Languages: Design and Implementation,* Prentice-Hall, Englewood Cliffs, N.J., 1975.

Tucker, A. B.: *Programming Languages,* McGraw-Hill, New York, 1977.
    A comparative discussion of ALGOL, FORTRAN, COBOL, PL/I, RPG, and SNOBOL. The book may serve as an introductory text in any of these languages to a programmer proficient in any procedural higher level language.

SELECTED TEXTS FOR SPECIFIC HIGHER LEVEL LANGUAGES

Rutishauser, H.: *Description of ALGOL 60,* Springer-Verlag, New York, 1967.

Learner, A., and Powell, A. J.: *An Introduction to ALGOL 68 Through Problems,* Macmillan, New York, 1974.

Gilman, L., and Rose, A. J.: *APL—An Interactive Approach,* 2nd ed., Wiley, New York, 1974.

Kemeny, J. G., and Kurtz, T. E.: *BASIC Programming,* 2nd ed. Wiley, New York, 1971.
    By the designers of the language.

McCracken, D. D.: *A Simplified Guide to Structured COBOL Programming,* Wiley, New York 1976.
    An excellent introduction to the language.

Feingold, C.: *Fundamentals of Structured COBOL Programming,* 3rd ed., Brown, Dubuque, Iowa, 1978.
    A thorough guide to the language.

Zwass, V.: *Programming in FORTRAN* (Structured Programming with FORTRAN IV and FORTRAN 77), Harper & Row, New York, 1981.
    Designed to complement the present book.

Hughes, C. E., Pfleeger C. P., and Rose, L. L.: *Advanced Programming Techniques,* Wiley, New York, 1978
    Subtitle of the book: "A Second Course in Programming Using FORTRAN."

Hughes, J.: *PL/I - Structured Programming,* 2nd ed., Wiley, New York, 1979.

Friedman, D.: *The little LISPer,* SRA, Chicago, 1974.

Conway, R., Gries, D., and Zimmerman, E. C.: *A Primer on Pascal,* Winthrop, Cambridge, Mass., 1976.

See also the use of Pascal in the two books by Nicklaus Wirth, the father of the language, referenced in Chapter 1 of the present book.

Myers, S. E.: *RPG: With Business and Accounting Applications,* Reston, Reston, Va., 1974.

Griswold, R. E., Poage, J.F., and Polonsky, I. P.: *The SNOBOL 4 Programming Language,* 2nd ed., Prentice-Hall, Englewood Cliffs, N.J. 1971.

Gordon, G.: *System Simulation,* 2nd ed., Prentice-Hall, Englewood Cliffs, N.J., 1978.

Introduces CSMP, SIMSCRIPT and GPSS.

TRANSLATORS ARE DISCUSSED IN

Aho, A. V., and Ullman, J. D.: *Principles of Compiler Design,* Addison-Wesley, Reading, Mass., 1977.

Gries, D.: *Compiler Construction for Digital Computers,* Wiley, New York, 1971.

7

INTRODUCTION TO
ASSEMBLY LANGUAGES

Every computer model has its own instruction set: a collection of operations executed directly by its central processing unit. These operations, expressed in a binary code, constitute the machine language of the computer. A programmer would find it difficult to instruct a computer in machine language. Programming in a low level language such as this results, however, in an efficient program. Whenever such efficiency is necessary, at the cost of an increased programming effort, assembly language is used. An assembly language instruction is translated into its machine code equivalent by a system program called an assembler, which also provides other aids to the programmer.

That an assembly language is specific to a computer model or a series of models limits the portability of programs written in such a language. Even so, all assembly languages are based on common principles. Such principles are presented in this chapter.

The instruction set of a computer and its input/output capabilities are often referred to as the *computer architecture.*

Appendixes A and B support the presentation in this chapter.

A. REGISTERS, WORDS, AND BYTES

An instruction of a low level language, such as a machine or assembly language, specifies the operation to be carried out by the hardware and the location(s) of the operand(s). The operands, as well as the instructions themselves, are stored in the main memory of the computer. In order to be executed, the instruction and its operands are brought into the central processing unit (CPU).

The CPU of a computer, discussed in greater detail in Chapter 8-A, contains a number of *registers,* units of fast memory. Each register consists of a set of flip-flops, cells where a single bit is stored. The number of bits in a register is known as the *register length*. Every CPU register has a predetermined purpose.

In particular, one or more (typically, 2 to 30, in relation to the power of the computer model) *general-purpose registers* are located in the arithmetic-logic unit (ALU) and are used for data manipulation. An operand may be manipulated (e.g., added to another, shifted, etc.) only while in such a register. The length of the general-purpose registers usually equals that of the memory word of the given computer.

From the programmer's point of view, the main memory consists of a sequence of *words,* with consecutive *addresses* as their identifying numbers (see Fig. 7–1). The contents of a word may be written (with the previously stored information being destroyed) or read (without destruction) during a single memory access. The *word length* (number of bits in it) is fixed for a given computer and lies in the range of 8 to 64 bits for most computers (typically, 16 bits for minicomputers and 32 bits for larger computers). A computer is frequently identified by its word length as say, a, "16-bit computer."

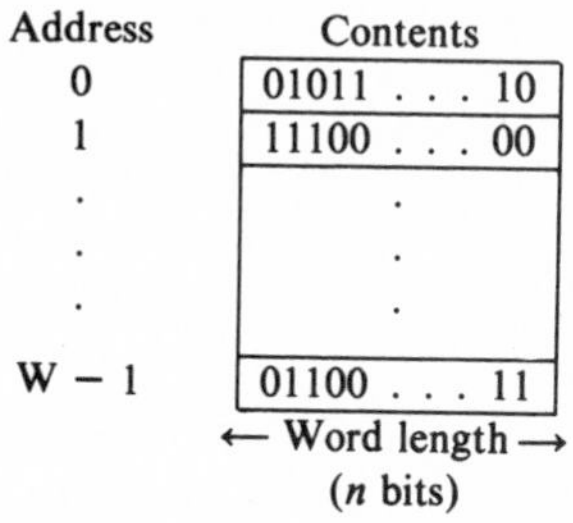

Address	Contents
0	01011 . . . 10
1	11100 . . . 00
.	.
.	.
.	.
$W - 1$	01100 . . . 11

$\leftarrow$ Word length $\rightarrow$
(n bits)

FIGURE 7–1. Logical view of the main memory, where W is memory capacity (total number of words)

Some computers, called *byte-addressable,* provide also a possibility to access a *byte,* a sequence of bits in which a single character may be stored. The representation of a character depends on the code adopted (see Appendix B); a byte usually consists of 8 bits. In a 32-bit computer, four 8-bit bytes are stored as a word. To provide byte addressability, it is necessary in this case to increase the *address space* (the number of available addresses) fourfold.

The registers and memory words (or bytes), where the operands reside, constitute the working space of an assembly language programmer.

B. MACHINE INSTRUCTIONS AND ASSEMBLY LANGUAGE

Programmers find it convenient to instruct the computer in a higher level language. Powerful statements of such a language lead to concise and readable programs. Each of these statements results in a number of consecutive actions taken by the computer. These actions are specified as instructions in the *machine language* of the computer by the software translator for the given higher level language.

The machine language, particular to a given computer model (or a series of models), consists of a set of binary instructions of a rigid format. Each instruction specifies:

(1) the operation to be performed;
(2) when applicable, the address of the operands. The number of operands depends on the type of the instruction and the design of the machine.

This specification is provided by the instruction *fields,* recognized by the control unit of the CPU. These fields are operation code (*op-code* for short) and address fields, with address modifiers (see Section E of this chapter) often present.

The following examples illustrate machine instructions and operands.

EXAMPLE 7-1

An example of a machine instruction† of a hypothetical computer is

| | 4 | |
| 8 bits | bits | 20 bits |

11000010 0111 01010010010010100101

| Op- | Register | Memory |
| code | number | address |

This is a register-to-memory instruction; if in our machine the binary code 11000010 signifies ADD, then the contents of the location with the specified memory address are added to the register 7 (i.e., 0111), and the result is left on that register.

Usually most or all of the machine instructions of a given computer occupy a single word.

The instruction shown above is therefore of a 32-bit computer. Since 8 bits are allocated to represent the op-code, the machine language of this computer may consist of up to $2^8 = 256$ different instructions. Similarly, the machine has $2^4 = 16$ general-purpose registers, numbered 0 through

---

† Understanding of the binary system is required for further reading of this chapter. A full discussion of this system is contained in Appendix A.

15, and $2^{20} = 1M$ memory locations may be directly addressed by the instruction (see Table A-1 of Appendix A for the values of powers of 2).

Note that if this computer were byte-addressable, with four 8-bit bytes stored to a word, four times as many addresses would have to be provided. Therefore, the memory address would be 2 bits larger (every additional bit, by allowing a selection between 2 alternatives, doubles the address space). This would significantly increase the cost of the computer.

Numerical data are represented in memory words in binary form as discussed in Appendix A.

EXAMPLE 7–2

An example of a fixed-point data item is

Sign bit

Magnitude

00000000000000000000000000011001 representing +25

In a complement representation of binary numbers, positive numbers have the sign bit of 0 and negative numbers have that of 1.

Alphanumerical data are usually encoded in a character code used in the given computer (see Appendix B).

EXAMPLE 7–3

Such a data item encoded in EBCDIC is

D   A   T   A

11000100 11000001 11100011 11000001 representing 'DATA'

We conclude that since a program contains at least several hundred instructions such as Example 7–1, programming in machine language is exceedingly tedious. Particularly difficult is providing absolute (binary) addresses of all the memory locations referenced by the instruction. If, after a program has been written, a data item or an instruction has to be removed or inserted, the address fields of many other instructions have to be modified.

EXAMPLE 7–4

It appears necessary to insert an additional data item into the location 05413_{16} of a program placed in memory as shown in Fig. 7–2. In this example, hexadecimal notation (see Appendix A–1) is used for shorthand.

Note that 5 hexadecimal digits provide a notation for 20 bits of address. Comparing Fig. 7–2(a) and 7–2(b), we can see that the address field of the sample instruction has been modified, since the corresponding data item was moved down. Similar modifications have to be made throughout the program.

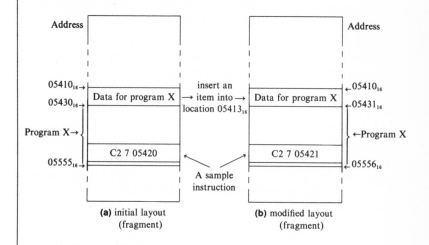

FIGURE 7–2. Illustration of the effects of a program modification

Barring exceptional cases, machine language is not used for programming. The need frequently arises, however, for a tighter control over the computer system resources (such as registers, memory locations, and CPU time) than that afforded by a higher level language. A programmer in such a language has no direct control over these resources; the control is exercised by the software translator, which, as a general-purpose program, cannot provide efficiencies possible in particular cases.

To realize these efficiencies, every computer model (or series) has its own *assembly language,* a low level programming language that permits the specification of machine operations with the use of *mnemonic op-codes* (easier to remember than their binary equivalents) and the specification of memory locations with *symbolic names (labels).*† A single assembly language instruction corresponds to a single machine instruction.

Programs written in assembly language are translated into the machine language by system programs called *assemblers,* which are significantly

† In assembly languages, both the names of locations holding operands (data) and holding instructions are called labels.

simpler and less time-consuming than higher level language translators. Program execution follows its *assembly*. The use of symbolic names afforded by assembly languages is particularly significant, since due to it the programmer does not, in general, specify absolute locations and the program may be placed anywhere in the main memory.

| EXAMPLE 7–5

The machine language instruction shown in Example 7–1, coded in the assembly language of our hypothetical computer, is here presented:

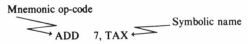

Mnemonic op-code

ADD   7, TAX   Symbolic name

It is assumed that the location with the address 01010010010010100101 has been called TAX in the program.

Therefore, in addition to mnemonic op-codes, assembly languages need to provide a set of so-called *pseudo-instructions*, instructions to the assembler program to assign a name to a location or to place a given data item into such a named location before the execution is started. Many pseudo-instructions functionally resemble declarations of higher level languages but are expressed in a greater detail.

C. INSTRUCTION SETS

An *instruction set* of a computer is the set of operations available in its machine language. From the programmer's point of view, this is also the set of instructions in the assembly language of the computer. Operation sets vary among computer models in dependence on their power and cost. A large and well-designed instruction set makes for an easy assembly language programming, resulting in efficient programs. Large sets require, however, extensive control unit circuitry and longer words to accommodate the increased length of the op-code field.

A typical instruction set is presented here for our hypothetical computer. While various machines have different instruction sets and formats, the concepts are the same.

Our computer has two essential kinds of instructions: *memory reference* (register-to-memory) instructions and *register-to-register* instructions. A memory reference instruction requires a memory access and therefore takes significantly longer to execute than a register-to-register instruction. In order to obtain an operand in a register in the first place, the main memory has to be accessed, however. The general formats of the two types of instructions are presented below.†

memory reference instruction	8 bits	4 bits	20 bits

register-to-register instruction	8 bits	4 bits	4 bits

In this case, a register-to-register instruction occupies only half a word. This fact is exploited in the design of the CPU hardware to save memory space.

The following instruction types constitute a complete instruction set.

1. DATA MOVEMENT

In order for an arithmetical or logical operation to be performed on a data item, the item has to be copied from the main memory into an ALU register.

Such an instruction, usually called "Load" has the general form

LOAD R, LOC

where

LOAD is the mnemonic op-code;
R is the register number;
LOC is the symbolic address of a memory location (in this case, the source of data).

To copy a data item from a register to the main memory, a "Store" instruction is used:

STR R, LOC

where LOC is the address of the location that receives the data.

To move a data item from a register R1 to another register R2, a register-to-register instruction is used:

MOVE R2, R1

† It should be noted that computers usually have a variety of instruction formats; in certain cases access to more than one operand in memory is possible with a single instruction.

2. ARITHMETIC

Four basic operations

ADD, SUB, MUL, DIV

are most often provided for fixed-point numbers (see Appendix A) and frequently also for floating-point numbers:

FADD, FSUB, FMUL, FDIV

Their general form, when a memory reference is required, is

op R, LOC

which means that after the operation op is performed on the contents of the register R and of the location LOC, the result is obtained in the register R, while the contents of LOC remain unchanged.

Since multiplication renders a result of double length with respect to the operands, the result is obtained in two registers, of which R is one. Conversely, before a division, the dividend is also placed in two registers.

If both operands are in the registers R1 and R2, a register-to-register instruction:

op R2, R1

is used. The result is obtained in R2. Operands of register-to-register instructions are the memory reference mnemonics with the prefix of R:

RADD, RSUB, RMUL, RDIV

3. LOGICAL OPERATIONS AND SHIFTS

Logical operations are carried out bitwise, i.e., the data item is treated as a string of bits with no dependence between them. Since the bits of a word are not addressable, the means of controlling the setting of particular bits in a word are the logical operations that implement the connectives of Boolean algebra (see Appendix C), such as

AND, OR, NOT

Their general form as a memory reference instruction is

op R, LOC

The AND operation places a 1 only in those positions of the result where *both* of the corresponding operand bits are 1's. The OR operation places a 1 in the result bit if *at least one* of the operands has a 1 in this position. The NOT applies to a single operand, which is transferred into the register R, and all its bits are inverted (see Table 3–1).

In the register-to-register form, we have

RAND, ROR, RNOT

Logical operations are aided by register shifts that allow the programmer to maneuver a particular bit into a desired position within the word. The most useful types of shifts are "Rotate" (a circular shift of the word) and "Logical Shift" (a part of the word is shifted out of the register, with 0's being shifted in at the other end). The direction of the shift is specified by the op-code:

RROT, LROT: rotate right/left;
RSH, LSH: shift right/left.

The number of shift positions is specified by the address parts in the memory reference format used for these instructions, which have the general form:

shift R, n

where n is the number of shift positions.

EXAMPLE 7-6

A 20-bit word is shown here for transparency
(a) The instruction

   RROT 5, 6

results in the manipulation

Register 5 (before)

| 11100101001111101001 |

Register 5 (after)

| 10100111100101001111 |

(b) The instruction

   LSH 2, 8

results in the manipulation

Register 2 (before)

| 10101110111110000101 |

Register 2 (after)

| 11111000010100000000 |

Note that the address field of these instructions is used for a different purpose. The central processor "knows" this from the op-code.

4. TRANSFER OF CONTROL

These instructions have a memory reference format; the address field specifies the target of transfer.

Three types of such instructions are needed at the assembly language level:

A. UNCONDITIONAL TRANSFER OF CONTROL

Usually called "Branch" or "Jump," this instruction has the following general form:

BR LOC

The next instruction to be executed is in the location named symbolically LOC.

B. CONDITIONAL TRANSFER OF CONTROL

These instructions differ widely among computer models. A partial set of such instructions is

BRZ R, LOC
BRL R, LOC
BRH R, LOC

These instructions cause the next instruction to be executed from the location LOC if, respectively, the contents of the register R are equal to 0, less than 0, and greater than 0. If the condition is not true, no transfer occurs and the next consecutive instruction is executed.

Since BRH and BRL instructions check the sign of the operand in the register, they may be used to check its leftmost bit irrespective of contents.

EXAMPLE 7–7

To implement a **while-do** loop:

while K ≠ L **do**
    begin
      .
      .
      .
    end

the following instructions may be used:

LOOP LOAD 1, K
    SUB 1, L
    BRZ 1, ON

        ⌈
        | body of the loop

    BR LOOP
ON . . .

where LOOP and ON are labels. Note that having more types of conditional transfer instructions would simplify the programming in a case such as a test for $K \geqslant L$, for example.

Since these transfer of control instructions usually follow the arithmetical or logical ones, some computers have hardware *flags* (i.e., single flip-flops used for a specific purpose), often called the *condition code*. These become automatically set or reset during an arithmetical or logical operation and are subsequently tested by conditional transfer instructions.

C. TRANSFER TO A SUBROUTINE

A special instruction is required to call a subroutine, since the return address (i.e., the address of the instruction immediately following the call) has to be saved in an established memory location or register.

The general form of this instruction, under the assumption that the return address is to be saved in the register R, is

JSR R, SUBR

where SUBR is the label of the first instruction in the subroutine, to which the control is presently transferred.

To provide for chain and recursive calls, more complex schemes for the saving of return address (and certain data), such as stack management, are available in some computers. In many computers an instruction causing the return from the subroutine to this address is also available, such as RET R where the register R holds the return address.

5. STOP OPERATION

This instruction stops the operation of the computer. It is *not* used to stop the execution of a program. We may call it

HLT

6. INPUT/OUTPUT

In this area, the greatest variance exists among computer models. The form of these instructions is correlated with the power of the computer (see Chapter 8-E for the discussion of the I/O function).

Due to the relative slowness of peripheral (I/O and secondary memory) devices in reading a single word, input/output is usually performed as a *block transfer*, i.e., the transfer of the contents of hundreds of consecutive memory words.

For some devices, the block is implicit in the nature of the device, such as the next card for a card reader or the next line in a line printer.

In this case the instruction has to specify:

$$\left.\begin{array}{l} \text{Input} \\ \text{Output} \end{array}\right\}\quad \text{device number, first location in main memory}$$

On the other hand, in the case of a secondary memory device, the following is needed:

$$\left.\begin{array}{l} \text{Input} \\ \text{Output} \end{array}\right\}\quad \begin{array}{l}\text{device number, first location in main memory,} \\ \text{first location on the device, number of words}\end{array}$$

There are also additional instructions required, such as "Start I/O," "Halt I/O," etc.; many of these are particular to the device.

D. INTRODUCTION TO ASSEMBLY LANGUAGE PROGRAMMING

The assembly language of our hypothetical computer is designed around the instruction set presented in the previous chapter. An assembly language instruction of this typical computer has one of the following two formats:

(a) memory reference instructions:

    label   op-code   register, symbolic address

(b) register-to-register instructions:

    label   op-code   register, register

The instruction fields are, therefore, the following.

label: optional, used when the transfer of control to this instruction is desired (consists of up to 6 alphanumerical characters, without blanks), starts in column 1;

op-code: one of the memonic instruction set, may not start in column 1;

register: one of 16 registers (0 through 15);

symbolic address: has to be defined as an instruction label or a data name in the given program.

An assembly language includes also a set of pseudo-instructions, directed at the assembler program. Their name derives from the fact that they do not belong to the machine instruction set and do not directly become a part of the assembled object code.

Our assembly language includes the following essential pseudo-instructions

(a) indicators of the beginning and end of a program:

    BEG, END

(b) a directive to the assembler to reserve a block of consecutive memory words:

label RES n

where n is the number of words to be set apart, and label is the symbolic address of the first of them. These words are used by the program to store results of the computation and do not contain meaningful data until they are stored in them;

(c) a directive to the assembler to store a constant in a memory location and associate the label with that location:

label CON N

Most assemblers have a number of such pseudo-instructions to store fixed- and floating-point binary and decimal constants. We assume that N is a fixed-point decimal number.

Assembly languages also allow for the use of comments, both as a separate line, and in-line, following the instruction. These are ignored by the assembler. In our case, a comment starts with an *.

The following programs illustrate the use of assembly language. Since the details of input/output are particular to a computer model, they are considered beyond the scope of this presentation; we will use

INP symbolic address
OUT symbolic address

to read or write the contents of a single memory word.

EXAMPLE 7-8

Problem

Determine the larger of the two integers X and Y, increment the result by 10, and output the answer.

Program

```
* A VERY SIMPLE PROGRAM
        BEG
X       RES 1
Y       RES 1
ANS   RES 1    * WILL HOLD THE ANSWER
TEN   CON 10
* OBTAIN AND COMPARE INTEGERS
*
        INP     X
        INP     Y
        LOAD    1, X
        SUB     1, Y
        BRL     1, YLAR
```

```
*
* X IS LARGER, OR INTEGERS ARE EQUAL
*
      LOAD    2, X
      BR      INCR
*
* Y IS LARGER
*
YLAR LOAD    2, Y
*
* OBTAIN RESULT
*
INCR ADD     2, TEN * REGISTER 2 HOLDS THE LARGER INTEGER
      STR     2, ANS
      OUT     ANS
      END
```

Notes

1. Any of the 16 registers that is not currently holding an otherwise needed value may be used instead of the given ones.
2. To move a value from one memory location to another, it has to be loaded into a register and subsequently stored (some machines have memory-to-memory instructions in their set while ours does not).
3. The needed constant 10 has to be stored in a memory location at the assembly time. Had we written

```
      ADD     2, 10
```

the contents of the location with the address (!) 10 would have been added to the contents of the register 2.
4. Study which programming decisions are necessary in this program and which are arbitrary.

EXAMPLE 7–9

This example, somewhat more complex, presents the application of assembly languages in logical processing (bit operations), the main strength of low level languages.

Problem

It is desired to count the number of bits whose value is 1 in a location PATTRN. (Remember that our machine has 32-bit words.)

Program

```
* COUNT NUMBER OF 1-BITS IN A WORD
         BEG
PATTRN  RES 1    * WORD TO BE ANALYZED
RESULT  RES 1    * NUMBER OF 1'S IN THE WORD
ZERO    CON 0
ONE     CON 1
LENGTH  CON 32   * TOTAL NUMBER OF BITS IN A WORD
*
```

```
*   INITIALIZE
*
        LOAD 3, LENGTH  * REGISTER 3 WILL HOLD THE
                        * NUMBER OF BITS REMAINING TO BE
                        * CHECKED
        LOAD 4, ZERO    * REGISTER 4 WILL HOLD THE
                        * CURRENT COUNT OF 1'S
        INP PATTRN
        LOAD 5, PATTRN  * REGISTER 5 HOLDS THE WORD; ITS
                        * RIGHTMOST BIT IS TO BE CHECKED
*
* NUMBER OF 1'S IN A WORD IS COUNTED BY CONSECUTIVELY
* SHIFTING ITS EVERY BIT INTO THE RIGHTMOST POSITION IN
* THE REGISTER WHERE IT IS "AND"-ED WITH "1" (SEE FOL-
* LOWING FIGURES)
  COUNT AND 5, ONE
* NOW REGISTER 5 HOLDS 1 IF THE RIGHTMOST BIT OF "PATTRN"
* IS 1
        RADD 4, 5   * ACCUMULATE THE COUNT OF 1'S
*
* CHECK FOR COMPLETION
*
        SUB 3, ONE
        BRZ 3, OUTPUT
*
* NOT COMPLETED YET—PREPARE NEXT ITERATION
*
        LOAD 5, PATTRN
        RROT 5, 1
        STR 5, PATTRN   * PRESERVE FOR NEXT ITERATION
        BR COUNT
*
* COMPLETED—OUTPUT RESULT
*
OUTPUT  STR 4, RESULT
        OUT RESULT
        END
```

The sequence below illustrates the execution of this program.

(a) initial contents of
    the location PATTRN: | 0110001010110001110010001110110 |

(b) during the first iteration of the loop COUNT:

Register 5

01100010101100011100100011101101

AND

Location ONE

00000000000000000000000000000001

Register 5

results in
00000000000000000000000000000001

(c) during the second iteration:

Register 5 (following rotation)

10110001010110001110010001110110

AND

Location ONE

00000000000000000000000000000001

Register 5

results in
00000000000000000000000000000000

(d) after the fifth iteration and rotation:

Register 5

10110101100010101100011100100011

shifted in from the right end

Register 4

00000000000000000000000000000011

holds the count of 3

Note

Execute the program by hand to count the number of 1's in the right-most byte (8 bits) of a word.

Two additional important facilities offered by the assemblers are literals and address arithmetic.

1. LITERALS

Literals constitute a facility whereby the programmer can use a constant directly, without declaring it with a pseudo-instruction (the assembler stores it automatically). A literal constant is simply placed by the programmer in the address field on an assembly language instruction, prefixed with a special symbol, such as =.

EXAMPLE 7–10

Instead of having defined in Example 7–9

    ONE CON 1

and used it as follows:

        AND 5, ONE

the programmer could simply use a literal constant:

        AND 5, =1

The special symbol = tells the assembler that the number 1 is meant, rather than the location whose address is 1.

2. ADDRESS ARITHMETIC

This allows the programmer to use an arithmetic expression to specify the address of the operand.

EXAMPLE 7–11

The programmer can write, for example,

        SUB 5, LOC + 3

to denote that the third location following the one called LOC is meant (and *not* that the contents of LOC are to be incremented by 3!).

E. OPERAND ADDRESSING

The specification of an operand address in main memory is the essential facility of low level languages. In assembly language such specification is provided symbolically; in a machine language instruction, binary address modifiers are used.

Several variations are offered to simplify this task. These are included in different combinations in various computer models.

1. ABSOLUTE ADDRESSING

The basic mode of addressing the operand stored in the main memory is to provide its full address in the instruction. This is called *absolute addressing* [see Fig. 7–3(a)].

2. IMMEDIATE ADDRESSING

Some computers allow the operand *itself* to be placed in the instruction; this is called *immediate addressing* [see Fig. 7–3(b)].

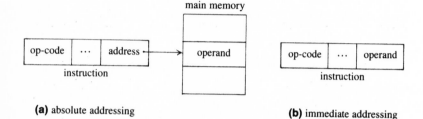

(a) absolute addressing

(b) immediate addressing

FIGURE 7–3. Absolute and immediate addressing.

There is only limited use for immediate addressing since, first, the operand has to be a constant known at the time the program is written, and second, the space available for an operand in the instruction format is limited.

3. ADDRESS MODIFICATION FOR LOOPING

The need for address modification stems from extensive use of loops as applied to data structures, such as tables. If, for example, the contents of a 100-word table starting with a location called TABLE

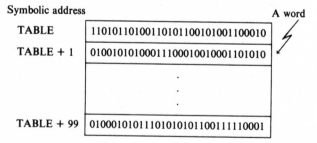

are to be added up in the register 3, the following instruction *cannot* be used within the loop to accomplish the task

ADD 3, TABLE   (*)

It is necessary to modify the address of the operand (TABLE) as the instruction is to be applied to consecutive data words.

Two alternative ways of achieving this are *indexing* and *indirection.*

A. INDEXED ADDRESSING

To provide *indexed addressing,* one or more *index registers* are necessary in the CPU hardware. When indexed addressing is used, the contents of the specified index register are automatically added by this hardware to the address field of the instruction. Thus the *effective address,* the actual address of the operand, is obtained.

This scheme of effective address computation is shown in Fig. 7–4.

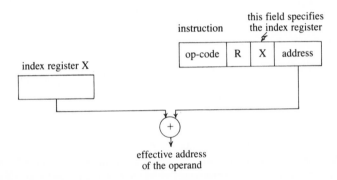

FIGURE 7–4. Address modification via indexing.

To indicate that the effective address is to be formed via indexing before the operand is accessed, the programmer modifies the instruction (*) as follows:

ADD 3, TABLE (1)

assuming that register 1 is the index register and contains the current offset from the beginning of the table.

Some machines have separate index registers, while in others general-purpose registers may be used for this task.

The following example presents the use of indexed addressing to total the contents of the 100-word table above.

EXAMPLE 7-12

```
*IN THIS CODE FRAGMENT IT IS ASSUMED THAT
*REGISTER 1 IS AN INDEX REGISTER
*NOTE USE OF LITERALS
        BEG
TABLE RES 100
            .
            .
            .


*INITIALIZE
        LOAD 1, =0    *INDEX REGISTER
        LOAD 2, =0    *REGISTER 2 WILL HOLD THE RESULT
        LOAD 3, =100 *NUMBER OF WORDS TO BE CONSIDERED
*ADDING LOOP
LOOP   ADD 2, TABLE(1)   *THE CRUCIAL INSTRUCTION
        ADD 1, =1
        SUB 3, =1
        BRH 3, LOOP
*RESULT IS NOW IN REGISTER 2
            .
            .
            .
```

B. INDIRECT ADDRESSING

In the case of *indirect addressing,* the address field of the instruction holds not the (direct) address of the operand, but the address of such an address. The effective address of the operand is obtained by the CPU treating the address field in the instruction as a pointer (see Fig. 7–5).

FIGURE 7-5.   Address modification via indirection.

To provide indirect addressing, the CPU has to be able to recognize indirection and fetch the effective address. An address modifier bit (D/I) in the instruction format indicates whether direct or indirect address is meant. In an assembly language, the programmer may denote indirection as follows:

    ADD 3, ANADDR,I

where ANADDR holds the address of another location.

In order to use indirection, the programmer needs a pseudo-instruction serving to place into a location the address of another one. Calling this pseu-do-instruction

DEF (for "Define address")

we have in our example of a table summation:

```
TABLE    RES 100
TABADR DEF TABLE
```

where TABADR is the pointer to the table. By consecutively "moving" the pointer through the table, we can use it to direct the loop as shown in the following example, where the same effect is achieved as in Example 7–12.

EXAMPLE 7–13

```
* THE CODE FRAGMENT EXEMPLIFIES THE USE OF
* INDIRECTION
            BEG
TABLE    RES 100
TABADR  DEF TABLE


            .
            .
            .

* INITIALIZE
            LOAD 2, =0        * RESULT REGISTER
            LOAD 3, =100      * NUMBER OF WORDS TO BE
                              * CONSIDERED
* ADDING LOOP
LOOP       ADD 2, TABADR,I   * THE CRUCIAL INSTRUCTION
* MOVE POINTER
            LOAD 4, TABADR
            ADD 4, =1
            STR 4, TABADR
* CHECK FOR COMPLETION
            SUB 3, =1
            BRH 3, LOOP
* RESULT IS NOW IN REGISTER 2

            .
            .
            .
```

Indirect addressing is also used in many computers to return from a sub-routine. Since a "Jump to Subroutine" instruction stores the return address in a register or in a special location, the return may be effected as follows:

BR BACK,I

assuming that the location BACK contains this return address.

4. ADDRESS MODIFICATION FOR EXTENSION OF THE ADDRESS SPACE

An instruction word has a limited space allotted for the operand address. If n bits are available for the purpose, only 2^n locations may be addressed. To circumvent this limitation, the following methods are used in computer design.

A. INDIRECT ADDRESSING

The instruction word provides only the least significant bits of the address of the pointer; the leading bits are implicit and provided by a CPU register. The pointer itself is of a full word length and constitutes the effective operand address.

B. BASE REGISTER ADDRESSING

A special register, called a *base register,* is specified among the address modifier bits. Its contents are added to the *displacement* (the part of the operand address contained in the instruction itself) to form the effective address.

If a machine uses both indexing and base register addressing, then

$$\text{effective address} = \text{displacement} + \text{contents of base register} + \text{contents of index register}$$

(This is the addressing scheme used in the IBM System/360–370 computers.)

F. USE OF ASSEMBLY LANGUAGE

A well-written assembly language program is usually more efficient (uses less computer system resources) than an equivalent program in a higher level language. This efficiency is due to the virtually direct access the programmer has to machine registers and memory words and to the direct use of the machine instruction set. Programming in assembly language is, however, a more demanding task: it requires specialized personnel and consumes more time. The resulting program is usually more difficult to understand and modify. Since an assembly language is indigenous to a particular computer model or a compatible series of models, such programs are not portable.

Assembly languages are used, therefore, when the nature of the task to be accomplished or the limitations of the given computer system mandate a particularly careful use of the system resources. Systems programming is one important area of this kind; programming of microcomputers is another.

G. ASSEMBLERS AND ASSEMBLY SYSTEMS

An assembler translates programs written in the assembly language of the given computer model into its machine language. Like any translator, an assembler is said to produce an object code from a source code.

Advanced assemblers produce *relocatable* object code that may be placed ("relocated") anywhere in the main memory for execution. The placement is performed by a systems program called a *loader*. Many assemblers provide macro facilities.

1. TASKS OF AN ASSEMBLER

The basic tasks of an assembler are, then:

(1) to "assemble" binary machine instructions from their assembly language equivalents, including
   (a) the translation of symbolic location names into binary memory addresses;
   (b) the translation of mnemonic operation codes into their binary equivalents;
   (c) assembly of address modifier bits;
(2) to provide the space for the data and to place required constants into their locations.
(3) to provide information for the loader.

The main task of an assembler is the translation of symbolic names referring to data items or instructions. Due to this function, the assemblers usually consist of two *passes*, i.e., two scans over the program to be translated. This strategy is brought about by the fact that programs contain *forward references*, i.e., references to a symbolic name before it is defined (in other words, before it appears as a label). In a single scan such references cannot be resolved without backtracking, which is sometimes used in one-pass assemblers.

EXAMPLE 7-14

Consider the following code fragment:

DATA   CON 10
.
.
.

BR   FRWRD
.
.
.

FRWRD ADD 5, DATA
.
.
.

To assemble the equivalent of the BR instruction, it is necessary to know the address of the location called FRWRD, which will not be known until the instruction ADD is reached during the scan by the assembler. (Note that the reference to the location DATA in ADD is a backward reference that may be resolved during a single scan.)

The two passes of common assemblers perform the following tasks:

2. PASS 1

All the symbolic names found in the label field of the source program are entered into the *symbol table*. A symbol table of an assembler (see Table 7-1) contains the symbolic names defined in the program with addresses of their locations relative to the beginning of the data and the program.

TABLE 7-1.   Symbol table of an assembler

Symbolic name	Relative location
DATA	0
.	.
.	.
.	.
FRWRD	5179
.	.
.	.

To keep track of the space that will be allocated to the data and instructions of the object program, a variable called the *location counter* is used. Initialized to a fixed value, usually 0, this location is incremented as the source program is scanned instruction by instruction. The increment equals the number of words (or bytes, if the machine is byte-addressable) needed to hold the given machine instruction or the data items described by a pseudo-instruction.

EXAMPLE 7-15

(a) If every machine instruction occupies a single word, the location counter is always incremented by 1.

(b) In our machine, when the pseudo-instruction RES is encountered, the location counter is incremented by the number of words being reserved.

In this fashion, the Pass 1 of an assembler creates a complete map of the memory placement for the object program, usually relative to the location 0.

3. PASS 2

The object code is created. The symbol table provides the substitutes for the symbolic names, and the fixed table of symbolic op-codes provides their binary equivalents.

If relocatable object code is produced, all the locations whose contents will depend on the program placement (these correspond to instructions and data with symbolic references) are marked.

Each program unit (i.e., the main program or a subroutine) is assembled separately. Some of the subroutines may be permanently stored in the secondary memory as relocatable object code.

4. LINKING AND LOADING

After the assembly has been completed, a system program called a *linker* resolves all *external references,* i.e., references to symbolic names that are not defined in a given program unit. The linker "appends," as it were, the subroutines to the main program and thus creates a *load module* (see Fig. 7–6), a relocatable unit of object code.

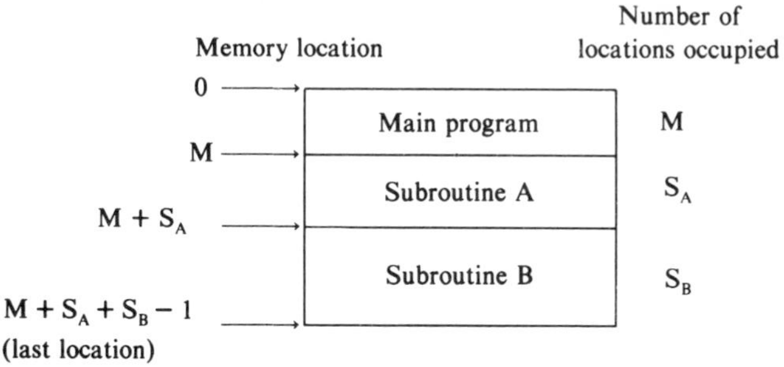

FIGURE 7–6. A load module (before loading)

Before the object code is executed, it has to be "loaded" in the actual memory locations selected for its placement. This task is performed by a *relocating loader,* a systems program that uses the relocation information provided by the assembler to substitute the actual memory addresses for the relative ones. A simple loader adds the address of the beginning location of the program in memory to all such addresses (since they were assembled relative to the location 0) and produces *absolute code.* The loader also transfers the program into the assigned space. Often the loader is combined with the linker into a *linking loader.*

The three system programs needed to translate and execute an assembly language program, i.e., assembler, linker, and loader, are often called an *assembly system.* Their action is illustrated in Fig. 7–7.

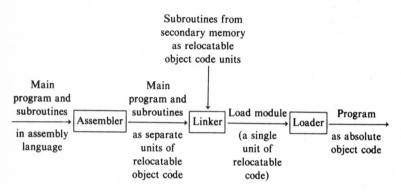

FIGURE 7–7. Assembly system

Linkers and loaders (or linking loaders) are also required to place in memory a higher level language program.

5. MACROASSEMBLERS

Some of the more sophisticated assemblers provide the so-called macro facility and are called *macroassemblers.* A *macro* is a sequence of statements with a name; once defined in a program, it may be used by simply writing its name and parameters. The macroassembler performs *macro expansion* by inserting the actual statements of the macro and substituting the parameters.

EXAMPLE 7–16
Assuming that our machine has a macroassembler, we will define a macro that adds the contents of any two memory locations X and Y and stores the result in the location X.

(a) Macro definition (by the programmer)

```
MACRO MEMADD(X, Y, REG)
LOAD REG, X
ADD REG, Y
STR REG, X
MEND
```

(b) Macro use (by the programmer)

.

.

.

```
SUB 1, Z
MEMADD TAX, INTER, 2
BRZ 1, BACK
```

.

.

.

(c) Macro expansion (by the assembler)

.

.

.

```
SUB 1, Z
LOAD 2, TAX
ADD 2, INTER
STR 2, TAX
BRZ 1, BACK
```

.

.

.

Note that MACRO and MEND are pseudo-instructions that serve as the delimiters of a macro. Note also that programmers find it convenient, when registers are needed by a macro, to have them specified as parameters.

The essential difference between macros and subroutines is that every macro use results in its code being actually copied into the program. A single subroutine copy exists, and a call to a subroutine results in a linkage, and not in a copy. Also, a subroutine is invoked during the program execution, whereas copies of macro code are inserted before the execution starts.

SUGGESTIONS FOR FURTHER READING

Peterson, J. L.: *Computer Organization and Assembly Language Programming,* Academic, New York, 1978.
A thorough general discussion of the assembly language programming and assembly systems, using a hypothetical, however typical, machine.

The following three texts introduce the assembly language programming of the most popular mainframe, mini- and microcomputer, respectively:

Struble, G. W.: *Assembler Language Programming: The IBM/360 and 370,* 2nd ed., Addison-Wesley, Reading, Mass., 1975.
Eckhouse, R. H., Jr., and Morris, L. R.: *Minicomputer Systems: Organization, Programming, and Applications (PDP-11),* 2nd ed., Prentice-Hall, Englewood Cliffs, N.J., 1979.
Leventhal, L. A.: *Introduction to Microprocessors: Software, Hardware, Programming,* Prentice-Hall, Englewood Cliffs, N.J., 1978.
Based on the Intel 8080 and Motorola 6800 micros.

8

ORGANIZATION OF
COMPUTER SYSTEMS

A computer system consists of a central processing unit, a main memory, a secondary memory, and input/output devices. The central processing unit (CPU) of a computer is composed of the control unit that executes machine instructions by activating all other facilities of the system and the arithmetic-logic unit (ALU) that performs data manipulation. The main, secondary, and, sometimes, archival memories are a part of memory hierarchy of a computer system that extends from the fast registers of the CPU through the much more capacious main memory to peripheral memory devices of large capacity and lower speed and cost. A system includes also a complement of peripheral input/output devices whose composition depends on need. In larger systems the control of peripherals is performed by dedicated processors, called channels. Components of a system are interconnected by groups of wires (with attendant circuitry), called buses.

In some cases, to increase the processing power, two or more CPU's sharing a single memory are employed in a configuration called multiprocessing system. Distant systems may be organized with the aid of telecommunication lines and hardware into computer networks.

The design of computer models and system configurations differ; the more general principles of computer organization are presented here.

The logic circuitry of which electronic components of computers are built is discussed in Appendix C.

A. CENTRAL PROCESSING UNIT
AND INSTRUCTION EXECUTION

The CPU, often called the heart of a computer, consists of two functional units. The control unit controls the execution of the program instructions expressed in the machine language of the given computer; the arithmetic-logic unit (ALU) manipulates data as mandated by these instructions.

A block diagram of the CPU with the essential interconnections is shown in Fig. 8–1 (no address modification hardware is included). In many computers these interconnections are organized into one or more collections of wires called *buses*. Each bus can be used for one data transfer at a time; thus the number of buses to an extent determines the speed of the CPU.

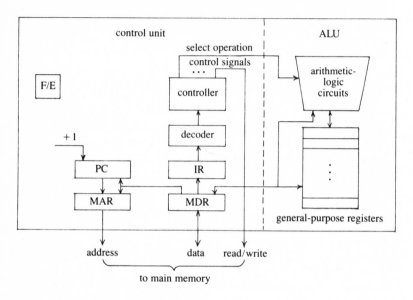

FIGURE 8–1. Central processing unit

The control unit *fetches* program instructions one by one from the main memory, decodes their op-codes, and sends control signals to other units of the computer system. The execution of a machine instruction consists, in turn, of a sequence of steps. These steps are carried out by the computer on orders from the controller.

The control unit consists essentially of the following elements:

- program counter (PC): register that holds the address of the next instruction to be executed;
- memory address register (MAR): holds the address of the memory location to be accessed;
- memory data register (MDR): holds the contents of a location that has been read or that is to be written into;
- instruction register (IR): holds the instruction while it is being executed;

- decoder: decodes the op-code of the current instruction (this circuit selects one of its 2^I output lines, based on the I bits of the op-code);
- controller: the essential circuit of the control unit, produces the sequence of control signals necessary to execute the instruction.

The control unit operates the computer by executing instructions of application and systems programs from the main memory of the computer. To execute some instructions, it is necessary to obtain also the data they require from the main memory. A single instruction is carried out during the so-called *instruction execution cycle* when it is obtained from the main memory and acted upon.

An example of a machine language instruction is shown in Example 7–1; examples of data used by such instruction are shown in Example 7–2.

Since both instruction and data are stored in the main memory as patterns of 0's and 1's, in order to distinguish between the MDR holding a data item and that holding an instruction, the F/E (fetch/execution) flag is located in the CPU. This flag indicates the current phase of the instruction execution cycle. There are two: the *fetch phase,* when the instruction is fetched from the main memory and its op-code is decoded ("understood"), and the *execution phase*, when the instruction is carried out, with the main memory being accessed, if necessary, to read or write data.

The instruction execution cycle consists of the following steps:

(1) fetch phase
  (a) Contents of PC are transferred to MAR (this is the address of the instruction to be fetched).
  (b) Main memory is accessed, and the current instruction is fetched into MDR.
  (c) The instruction is transferred from MDR to IR (since MDR may be needed for the data).
  (d) The op-code of the instruction is decoded.
  (e) To prepare for the execution of the next instruction, the contents of PC are incremented by 1 via the "hot 1" line shown. (It is assumed here that every instruction occupies a single word; if not, the increment to PC depends on the op-code decoded.)
  (f) The execution phase, specific to the given instruction, is initiated by changing the state of the F/E flag (flip-flop).
(2) execution phase

  Since every instruction has a different execution phase, three characteristic examples are presented:

(2–I) The machine language equivalent of ADD R, LOC
  (g) The operand address (symbolically called LOC) is transferred from MDR to MAR.

(h) The operand is read from the main memory into MDR.

(i) The contents of MDR are added by the ALU circuitry to the contents of the general-purpose register R.

(j) The fetch phase for the next instruction is initiated by changing the state of the F/E flag.

(2–II) The machine language equivalent of STR R, LOC

(g) The operand address is transferred from MDR to MAR.

(h) The contents of the general-purpose register R are transferred to MDR.

(i) The contents of MDR are written into the main memory location whose address is in MAR.

(j) The fetch phase is initiated by changing the state of the F/E flag.

(2–III) The machine language equivalent of BR LOC

(g) The address field of the instruction is transferred from MDR to PC.

(h) The fetch phase is initiated by changing the state of the F/E flag.

To minimize the instruction execution time, some of the above steps are performed simultaneously. The most time-consuming step is the memory access.

It may be observed that the instruction execution consists of a number of register transfers. The time required for such a transfer is called the *CPU cycle time* or *clock time* and is a function of the logic used in the CPU design. A typical instruction may require 8 to 16 such clock times. The CPU cycle time should not be confused with the main memory cycle time, usually a multiple of the CPU cycle time.

While the speed of computers differs vastly, it is convenient to think of a typical midscale-computer instruction as executed within 1–2 μsec.† Powerful processors execute tens of MIPS (millions of instructions per second).

To provide for indexing (see Chapter 7-E), CPU hardware has to include index registers and the circuitry needed to form the effective address. To provide for indirection, the third phase of instruction execution cycle, called the *indirect* (or *defer*) phase is required. The indirect phase comes between the fetch and execution phases and consists of the following:

(g) The address field is transferred from MDR to MAR.

(h) Main memory is accessed to read the effective address of the operand into MDR.

†1 msec (millisecond) = 10^{-3} sec   1K = $2^{10} \approx 1000$
 1 μsec (microsecond) = 10^{-6} sec   1M = $2^{20} \approx 1,000,000$
 1 nsec (nanosecond) = 10^{-9} sec

(i) The execute phase for this instruction is initiated.

The sequence of control signals necessary to execute an instruction is generated by the controller that actually implements the instruction set of the machine. The two techniques used to design the controller are hardwiring and microprogramming. *Hardwired control* is built as a network of logical gates and flip-flops to ensure execution of all instructions of the set. The recognition of the fact that the execution of every machine instruction constitutes a sequence of steps, micro-instructions as it were, led to the invention of *microprogramming*: placement of these micro-instructions in a special *control memory,* a part of the controller. A *microprogram* (called also *firmware*) is placed into the control memory (usually of a cheaper and faster *read-only* type, since its contents do not need to be modified) at the time the computer is designed. Microprogramming also offers broader possibilities in computer design.

The CPU executes the instructions of the system and application programs sequentially, with the consideration of transfers of control.

The CPU may switch from the execution of the current program when an *interrupt* occurs. This is a signal of a special condition requiring a fast action on the part of the CPU. The conditions causing an interrupt depend on the computer design; typically, these are exceptions arising during arithmetic (e.g., a division by 0, overflows, etc.), machine malfunctions and, very important, signals of completion of an input/output operation (see Section E-2 of this chapter).

When an interrupt occurs and is recognized, the execution of the current program is interrupted, with all the data necessary for its resumption being saved. The program counter (PC) receives the address of a system program *(interrupt handler)* designed to handle the particular type of interrupt. Subsequently, the interrupted program is resumed.

The arithmetic-logic unit of the CPU consists of circuitry required for data manipulation, such as fixed-point arithmetic, shifts, and logical operations. The amount of circuitry provided determines to a large extent the cost of the CPU. Floating-point arithmetic, for example, is often performed in software to cut down this cost. A set of general-purpose registers, in which operands are manipulated, is also located in the ALU.

The CPU of a large computer is often called a *mainframe,* to distinguish it from the minicomputers and microcomputers ("computers on a chip"). Most microcomputers actually consist of several integrated-circuit chips, of which one, called *microprocessor,* contains the complete CPU. Other chips of a microcomputer contain memory modules and input/output interfaces. Microprocessors are frequently embedded in a variety of equipment requiring extensive control, such as instrumentation devices, manufacturing machines, or intelligent terminals.

B. MEMORY HIERARCHY

At any point in time, there exist various technologies that may be employed to store information. Some of these offer high speed and are expensive; others, less costly, can be used as lower-speed high-capacity memories. Therefore, in a computer system, it is advantageous to hold the information in a hierarchy of memories. The higher elements of this hierarchy are fast, relatively expensive, memory units of small capacity. They hold the data and instructions that are either being currently processed by the CPU or will be required soon. The high-capacity units, standing lower in the hierarchy, hold the remaining information.

The memory hierarchy of the computer may include the following:

(1) Registers of the CPU hold the instruction currently being executed and the data being manipulated.

(2) A *buffer (cache) memory,* included in some machines, is also located in the CPU. It holds the data and instructions that will be needed by the CPU in short order; they are automatically brought into the cache from the main memory by special hardware.

(3) A main memory holds data and instructions directly accessible to the CPU (see Section C).

(4) A secondary memory, of large capacity, holds instructions and data that have to be brought into the main memory before processing.

   Fast secondary storage, such as drums and fixed-head disks (see Section D) are often configured with the main memory into a virtual memory system (see Chapter 9), automatically managed by software.

   Slower secondary storage devices of very large capacity hold the information managed by the input/output subsystem of the operating system.

(5) The *mass storage system* (or *archival storage*) is used to store even larger volumes of data than secondary storage at a much lower cost and with slower access. These are frequently automatic tape cartridge systems with capacities reaching 10^{12} bytes.

All machines have registers and main memories and almost all systems have slower secondary memories.

C. MAIN MEMORY

The main memory holds instructions and data that may be directly fetched for processing by the CPU during an instruction execution cycle. The essential unit of storage, a word, consists of a number of bits, fixed for a given computer. Each word has its own address (the main memory appears to a low level language programmer as shown in Fig. 7–1). In a byte-addressable computer, a word consists of a fixed number of bytes (typically, two or four 8-bit bytes), each having an address.

As shown in Fig. 8–1, in order to access a main memory location, its address is presented in the MAR, and the "write" or "read" signal is given; the contents of MDR are then copied into this location, or vice-versa.

Main memories are *random-access memories* (RAM); i.e., the time to access (read or write) any word is the same, independent of its address. The two common physical realizations of main memory are magnetic core memories and (now more frequent) semiconductor memories, both fully electronic. The time required to read the contents of a memory word is called the memory *access time;* the minimum time between two consecutive accesses is its *cycle time.* Memory cycle time is almost twice the access time in the case of magnetic memories; it is only somewhat larger in semiconductor memories. Main memory speeds differ; most frequently, memory access times are in the range of 0.5–0.75 μsec. The capacity of main memory ranges from about 16K words (or bytes) in small computers to tens of millions in very powerful ones.

Both the magnetic core and semiconductor memories have a *matrix organization,* a view of which is presented in Fig. 8–2.†

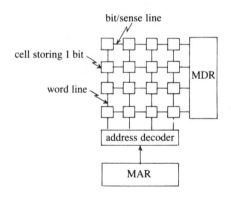

FIGURE 8–2. A main memory matrix

The memory matrix consists of a number of 1-bit cells (a core in the case of magnetics, a flip-flop for semiconductor memories).

†Alternative organizations, using the same principles, are also employed.

The word to be written into or read is selected (i.e., current is driven through its *word line*) after the decoding of its address contained in the MAR. When the memory is read, the *bit/sense lines,* through the sensing circuitry, copy the pattern of 0's and 1's contained in the word into the MDR. When memory writing from MDR occurs, the word line of the selected word and the bit/sense lines corresponding to the 1-bits in MDR together provide the current necessary to write 1's only in the corresponding bits of the selected word; the others are automatically cleared to 0. This is called the *coincident-current principle* of memory access.

The essential difference between the magnetic-core and semiconductor memories is the destructive readout in the magnetics. Due to their physical properties, while the state of a core is being ascertained, this state is destroyed and needs to be written back during the second half of the reading cycle. This write-back is performed automatically by the memory system, and the programmer is not aware of it.

While semiconductor memories are composed of flip-flops (see Appendix C), the magnetic ones consist of doughnut-shaped ferrite cores 0.02 to 0.05 in. in diameter (see Fig. 8–3), with the wires threaded through them.

FIGURE 8–3.   A magnetic core

The direction of current in the wires determines the direction of magnetism in the core; there are two stable magnetic states in such a core, one of which is considered a 0, and the other a 1.

Magnetic memory has the advantage of *nonvolatility:* when the current is removed, the information in the cores remains unchanged; semiconductor memories are volatile.

Certain semiconductor memory technologies (such as *bipolar semiconductors*) offer very high speeds; they are, however, costly and used mainly in CPU registers and cache memories. The access times offered by the so-called *MOS semiconductors* used predominantly as the main memories are close to those of magnetics, if somewhat faster.

D. SECONDARY MEMORY

The capacity of the main memory is limited by its cost. Alternative technologies provide the possibility to store less expensively high volumes of information not needing immediate accessibility to the CPU. This information is stored on secondary (also called auxiliary) memory devices and brought into the main memory for processing.

Since secondary memory devices are attached to the main memory in a fashion similar to the input/output devices (both classes are often called *peripherals*), the transfer of information between them and the main memory is managed similarly (see Section E).

The devices most frequently used for secondary storage are electromechanical with a magnetic storage medium: drum, disk, and tape. Due to the presence of mechanical components, such memories are inherently slower than the main memory. Drum and disk, relatively fast secondary memories, are *direct-access storage devices* (DASD): it is possible to bring their accessing mechanism in the area of the required data (on its track) and then reach the desired item by passing over the intervening ones. Tape, relatively inexpensive, is a *sequential-access device:* in order to access any item stored on it, all other items with lower addresses have to be passed over. This limits the application of tapes to cases when items have to be accessed in the sequence they are stored.

On all of these devices information is stored in a magnetic medium as a pattern of magnetic domains whose two alternative states are considered to be 0 and 1.

Newer secondary memory technologies, with no moving parts, are nonvolatile *magnetic bubble memories* (MBM) and volatile and faster *charge-coupled devices* (CCD).

Since all secondary memory devices are nonrandom access memories, the time needed to access a location is much longer than that subsequently required to access its physical successors. Therefore, information is accessed in the secondary memory as a *block,* a rather large sequence of words with consecutive addresses.

The speed of direct-access devices is characterized by two parameters: *access time* (to the first word or byte of the block) and *transfer rate* of the subsequent words or bytes. Sequential-access devices are usually not accessed in a direct mode, but sequential transfer of blocks is performed.

Typical capacities and speeds of secondary storage devices are presented in Table 8–1; the devices are further described below. The actual values of these parameters vary widely.

TABLE 8–1. Typical capacities and speeds of higher-performance secondary memory devices

	DRUM	DISK (moving-head) of larger capacity	TAPE
capacity (Mbytes)	4 for example, 800 tracks × 5000 bytes per track	per drive: 100 (more for large disks); for example, 20 surfaces × 400 tracks × 12,500 bytes per track	per 2400-ft reel: 50
access time (msec)	rotational delay: 8	rotational delay: 8 head motion: 30 total: 38	not applicable
transfer rate (Mbytes/sec)	1	1	0.2

1. MAGNETIC DRUM

A magnetic drum is a cylinder coated with magnetic material (see Fig. 8–4). Information is stored along circumferentially located *tracks,* with a *read/write head* fixed over each track. A drum rotates continuously, thus bringing the desired word under the appropriate head.

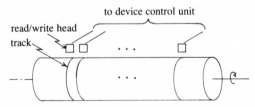

FIGURE 8–4. Magnetic drum

The drum access time consists of:

(a) negligible time needed by the drum circuitry to select the appropriate head;

(b) *latency time (rotational delay),* time needed for the given word to come under the head. The time needed for the half of a full drum rotation is taken as the average latency time.

A drum, used rather infrequently, is a fast device of limited capacity. The *volume* (physical carrier of information), in this case the cylinder itself, is not exchangeable.

2. MAGNETIC DISK

A magnetic disk is the most commonly used secondary storage device. Usually a *moving-head disk* (shown in Fig. 8–5) is employed.

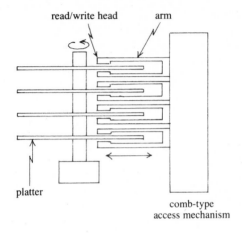

FIGURE 8–5. Moving-head disk

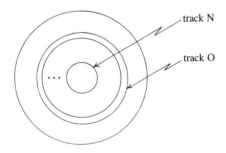

FIGURE 8–6. A disk surface

A disk consists of a set of platters resembling phonograph records. Each platter has two surfaces (see Fig. 8–6), with hundreds of concentric tracks, bearing the information, on each of them. The information is accessed by a comblike assembly of read/write heads on arms that can move laterally while the platters continuously rotate. In a moving-head disk, there is only one read/write head per surface. All heads move together; the set of tracks, one per surface, that may be accessed in a given position of access mechanism is called a *cylinder*. A cylinder thus consists of a single track on every surface, cutting through the surfaces, as it were.

Some disks are sector-addressable; i.e., in order to access a word/byte on a given track, the entire fixed *sector* (e.g., 512 bytes) has to be read.

The access time to a word consists of:

(1) negligible time for electronic head selection;
(2) *seek time* (head motion) needed to bring the head over the track desired, by moving the access mechanism;
(3) latency time (rotational delay), for the word to come under the head.

The seek time, considerably longer than the latency time (see Table 8–1), makes the moving-head disks slower than drums. These disks have, however, a large capacity and are often built with exchangeable *disk packs* (stacks of platters).

When a particularly high speed of access is needed, *fixed-head disks* with a single head per track are used. No seek time is present, since the head over the desired track is selected electronically. Such disks are expensive and have smaller capacity.

In smaller applications, such as mini- and microcomputer systems, *floppy disks* are often used. These very inexpensive devices resemble single flexible phonograph records placed in protective envelopes. They are easily exchangeable in a drive with a single head and store about 1 Mbyte of data.

3. MAGNETIC TAPE

Magnetic tape is the least expensive storage medium. Its use is limited due to the sequential nature of access.

The volume (reel) is exchangeable in the tape drive. Usually 7- and 9-track (the meaning of the word is different from that with disks and drums!) are used. A fragment of a 9-track tape is shown in Fig. 8–7.

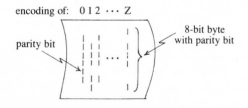

FIGURE 8–7. Fragment of magnetic tape

As the tape moves, the consecutive bytes come under the read/write heads (7 or 9 of these corresponds to the number of tape tracks) of the drive. The parity bit (added so that the number of 1's in a column is odd) serves error detection.

In minicomputers, magnetic tape is often used packaged in *cassettes* or larger *cartridges*.

E. INPUT/OUTPUT

The input/output sybsystem of a computer system transfers the information between the main memory and the outside world. It consists of the input/output devices whose nature and quantity depend on the configuration and the input/output control equipment responsible for controlling these as well as secondary memory devices.

1. INPUT/OUTPUT DEVICES

A multiplicity of input/output (I/O) devices is used in various systems. Some of them are designed for interaction with people; others interact with equipment outside the computer systems.

The most frequently encountered devices are discussed here.

(a) teletypewriters and display terminals: These devices are used for direct interaction with people They actually consist of two devices each: an input keyboard and a character printer in the case of *teletypewriters*, a keyboard and a cathode-ray tube display in the case of a *display terminal*.

Teletypewriters are rather slow (10–30 characters/sec) and provide a *hard-copy* (printed) output. Display terminals are capable of higher speeds and come in a great variety. *Alphanumeric displays* can display exclusively text, i.e., characters of their character set. *Graphic displays* are capable of representing various plots and pictures and are often able to accept input directly from the screen.

A clear trend is discernible toward so-called *intelligent terminals*, which have limited processing capabilities. They often contain built-in microprocessors.

(b) line printers: A line printer is essential for a hard-copy output. These devices print a line at a time and some are capable of speeds of 30,000 lines/min although speeds in the range 300–1000 lines/min are more typical. Only slower printers are of electromechanical construction; the faster ones use various electrostatic, thermal, ink-jet and other techniques to create a printed line and are thus called *nonimpact printers*.

(c) punched card readers and punches: The most widespread medium used by these devices is an 80-column card, where up to 80 alphanumerical characters may be represented. Fast readers process up to 2000, and punches up to 500, cards per minute.

(d) paper tape readers and punches: These are relatively slow devices, with fast readers operating at 500, and punches at 300, characters per second.

(e) consoles: These are used by system operators to monitor the operation of the computer and to communicate with it using panel switches and/or a keyboard.

2. INPUT/OUTPUT CONTROL

Input/output control is the means for transferring information between the main memory of the computer and a peripheral device (an I/O or a secondary storage unit).

The nature of this transfer is determined by the following factors in the peripheral operation:

(a) A single I/O transfer involves the transmission of many words (bytes), while usually a word at a time is being transferred.

(b) Due to the relative slowness of peripherals (particularly I/O devices), many instructions could be executed by the CPU while a single word is being transferred. However, only the CPU or a peripheral may access the main memory during a given memory cycle.

In general, an I/O transfer is identified as follows:

(a) device number;

(b) address of the first location in the main memory;

(c) in the case of a transfer involving a secondary storage device, the address of the first word (or byte) on this device, and the direction of the transfer.

(d) the number of words (bytes) to be transferred.

While the transfer is being performed word by word, elements (b) through (d) of this identification have to be updated after each word is transferred. The completion of the transfer has to be determined.

There are three methods of I/O control:

(a) wait loop I/O: The CPU itself controls the entire transfer process obeying the program instructions. In order not to miss a word, in good time before every word transfer is completed, the CPU enters a *wait loop* as instructed by the program, executing instructions that check for the completion. No other work is then done by the CPU.

This method is used only in rudimentary computers due to the long time spent by the CPU in the wait loop.

(b) interrupt I/O: In this case also the CPU itself controls the transfer. A hardware interrupt system is provided, however. This means that when the peripheral is ready after a word transfer, it generates an *I/O interrupt* signal to the CPU, making this fact known. Interrupts are processed by the CPU as described in the Section A of this chapter. They obviate the need for a wait loop.

(c) channel I/O: To free the CPU from most of the I/O chores, a separate I/O processor, called a *channel,* may be provided in larger computer systems. A channel receives a command (or set of commands) from the CPU that identifies the I/O operation. Subsequently, the channel initiates and controls the entire transfer process and sends an interrupt signal to the CPU following its completion.

Channels access main memory by *cycle-stealing:* when a channel needs a memory cycle, it is allotted to the channel, even though the CPU may require it too. This prevents the loss of information being transferred.

Channels are, to an extent, independent processors that execute a limited set of commands. In minicomputer systems, similar function is performed by much simpler *direct memory access* (DMA) controllers.

F. BUS ORGANIZATION OF A COMPUTER SYSTEM

Functional units of a computer system are interconnected in an organized manner to provide for necessary communication between them. Data are usually transferred between two units one word (or byte) at a time. Thus a collection of wires is needed for the interconnection; aside from data, these wires must also carry needed control information. Such a collection of wires, together with the circuitry needed to establish a connection through them, is called a *bus.* A single bus is usually shared by several units, only two of which may use it at a time. Various bus structures are used; two of the most popular ones are shown in Fig. 8–8. A single-bus structure [Fig. 8–8(a)] is typical for simpler mini- and microcomputers. While inexpensive, it provides for communication of only two units at a time, thus limiting the speed of the system.

In mainframe computers, multibus structures are employed. A typical two-bus structure is presented in Fig. 8–8(b). Simultaneous transfer of data between two units connected to each of the buses is possible. For example, while an instruction is being transferred from the main memory to the CPU, a transfer of information from a disk to the channel may also be taking place.

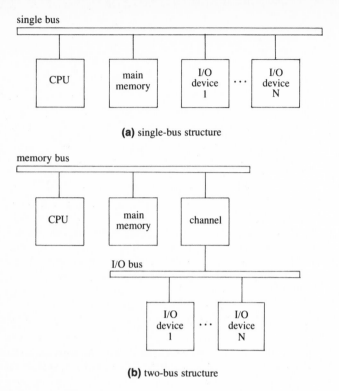

(a) single-bus structure

(b) two-bus structure

FIGURE 8–8. Bus structures

G. COMPUTER SYSTEMS WITH MULTIPLE CPU'S. COMPUTER NETWORKS

Computer systems with multiple CPU's include multiprocessors and computer networks that are actually interconnected multiple computer systems (some of which may, in turn, be multiprocessors).

1. MULTIPROCESSORS

To increase processing speed, it is possible to have several CPU's share the common main memory (see Fig. 8–9, where two CPU's are shown). The CPU's may execute different programs from this memory or cooperate in the execution of the same program.

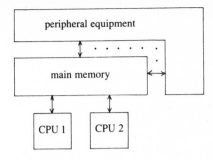

FIGURE 8–9. A multiprocessor

Multiprocessors offer also the benefit of increased reliability, since if one processor fails, others may take over.

The use of CPU's in such a multiprocessing system is directed by the operating system software.

2. COMPUTER NETWORKS AND DATA COMMUNICATION

A *computer network* is a collection of independent computer systems, usually located at distant sites, and remote terminals, all interconnected by a data communications network. Computer networks are created to share resources, such as special software and hardware facilities or databases that are available in various systems, and to distribute the processing load over these systems. They provide for *distributed processing* by bringing the computing power to the locations where it is needed.

For communication between their *nodes* (computer systems and remote terminals), networks of today use predominantly the existing telephone facilities. To interface with a telephone line suited only for low-frequency signals such as voice, *modems* (modulators-demodulators) are required. They transform digital signals into their voice-grade equivalents for the transmission over the line (modulation) and convert the modulated signal at the receiving end back to bits (demodulation).

In the simplest kind of network, a number of remote terminals, often with some processing capabilities of their own (so-called intelligent terminals), are connected to a computer system. As shown in Fig. 8–10, communication between a terminal and the computer is accomplished with a pair of modems and a telephone line. A special processor, usually a minicomputer, called a *front-end processor,* is frequently included to control the communication function for the CPU of the system.

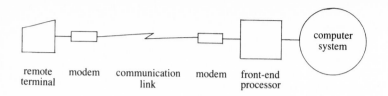

remote terminal   modem   communication link   modem   front-end processor   computer system

FIGURE 8-10. A simple data communication system

Computer networks have various topologies depending on the situation of the computer centers and remote terminal stations involved. Since network nodes communicate with one another only intermittently, not all of them have direct connections. Others are connected through intermediate nodes, some of which serve exclusively as switching centers through which messages flowing in the network are routed. These nodes have memory where the messages may be temporarily stored before they are forwarded. An example of a computer network is shown in Fig. 8–11.

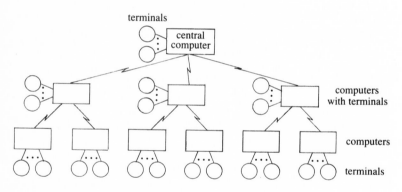

terminals — central computer

computers with terminals

computers

terminals

FIGURE 8-11. Computer network (hierarchichal organization)

In order to use the network more efficiently, messages in some networks are broken up into fixed-length *packets* (typically, 128–256 bytes) that are forwarded individually. Every packet consists of the actual information (part of a message), the identification of its destination, and the sequence code that specifies its position within the message. Thus, at its destination a message may be reassembled from its constituent packets. Networks of this type are called *packet-switching* networks and are an important alternative to *message-switching* networks, in which complete messages are transmitted, and *circuit-switching* networks, where a physical connection between sender and receiver is established for the entire transmission time.

Fixed procedures, called *protocols,* are followed in a network in order to establish a connection, use it, and ultimately break it.

Along with the networks relying on the existing telephone facilities, data networks have emerged in which the digital signal is transmitted directly (and thus no modems are needed). Digital communication offers much greater transmission rates and higher reliability. Coaxial cables or radio waves, the latter sometimes with the use of telecommunication satellites, may be employed to carry the digital data. As a matter of fact, in the not so distant future the telephone system itself will become all-digital, and the communication networks will be able to carry voice, images and data, all in the digital form.

SUGGESTIONS FOR FURTHER READING

Along with the books listed in the preceding chapter, the following general texts are recommended:

Sloan, M. E.: *Computer Hardware and Organization: An Introduction,* SRA, Chicago, 1976.
  Discusses the logic as well as the system level of computer design.
Tannenbaum, A. S.: *Structured Computer Organization,* Prentice-Hall, Englewood Cliffs, N.J., 1976.
Hamacher, V. C., Vranesic, Z. G., and Zaky, S. G.: *Computer Organization,* Prentice-Hall, Englewood Cliffs, N.J., 1978.
  Among other topics, introduces microcomputers and computer networks.
Hayes, J. P.: *Computer Architecture and Organization,* McGraw-Hill, New York, 1978.
  A more advanced text.

The following specialized books are also recommended:

Ogdin, C. A.: *Microcomputer Design,* Prentice-Hall, Englewood Cliffs, N.J., 1978.
Kraft, G. D., and Toy, W. N.: *Mini/Microcomputer Hardware Design,* Prentice-Hall, Englewood Cliffs, N.J., 1979.
Martin, J.: *Telecommunications and the Computer,* 2nd ed., Prentice-Hall, Englewood Cliffs, N.J., 1976.

COMPUTER SYSTEMS SOFTWARE. OPERATING SYSTEMS

The hardware of a computer system is capable of executing machine language instructions stored in the main memory.

For the fast automatic management of the computer system resources and for the programmer to be able to use a symbolic language rather than the binary language of the machine, extensive software facilities, systems programs, are required. Additional software utilities may also be provided to simplify the development of applications software (users' programs).

The most prominent developments in the computing industry are the decreasing costs of hardware as the result of technological progress and the increasing costs of professional labor directly related to software implementation. It is therefore increasingly important to provide an appropriate environment for the programmer's work.

Systems software, some of which is discussed elsewhere, is reviewed here. Operating systems, the software managers of hardware, are the main subject of this chapter.

A. OVERVIEW OF SYSTEMS SOFTWARE

A great variety of systems software exists. Its availability for a given computer model depends upon the size of the typical configuration and is greatly related to its popularity. Popular computer model series have several varieties of software products, with different performance parameters.

The following is a brief survey of the essential system software.

1. TRANSLATORS

A low level symbolic language native to a computer model, called assembly language, is translated into machine language by a relatively simple *assembler* (see Chapter 7–G).

Most higher level languages are translated by a *compiler* (see Chapter 6–

B) into a complete object program that may then be executed repeatedly. Some languages are translated by an *interpreter* (see Chapter 6–C), which translates and executes programs statement by statement. For several languages both compilers and interpreters are available.

2. LINKERS AND LOADERS

These two system programs serve to place translated code into the main memory locations from which it will be executed. If a program consists of a number of units (the main program and the subprograms), all the references between them are resolved by the *linker* (see Chapter 7–G). The entire program, with its data, is subsequently placed in the main memory locations by a *loader* (see again Chapter 7–G). A *relocating loader* has the capability to place a load module anywhere in the memory where the necessary number of consecutive locations is available.

3. OPERATING SYSTEMS

Operating systems manage the hardware resources of the computer system so as to establish the desirable mode of user–system interaction and provide for efficient utilization of the system resources. The complexity of operating systems varies greatly with the size of the computer system.

This sophisticated software is the main subject of the present chapter.

4. UTILITY PROGRAMS

Utilities are programs that simplify the use of the computer system by relieving the programmer of a particular task. These include the software aiding in the development of programs. Important examples are

- editors: text-processing software used to modify a program (or any other text) by deleting, inserting, or modifying lines, words, or characters
- debuggers: programs that execute a program under development step by step, output the values of its crucial variables, and produce its *memory dumps* (printouts of binary contents of selected memory areas), etc.
- sort/merge programs that may be used to process large files of data
- programs used to transcribe information from one device to another; for example, from a card deck in the card reader to a disk.

5. FILE AND DATABASE MANAGEMENT SYSTEMS

Most application programs, particularly in the business environment, are built around large volumes of data and organized into files (see Chapter 10). To maintain these files and obtain required data from them, *file management systems* are used.

In many cases it is beneficial, as discussed in Chapter 10, to unify the files concerning a particular aspect of the environment into a system, called a *database*. In this fashion, duplication of data is avoided, and all application programs access the data through a uniform software interface, called a *database management system* (DBMS). While complex, it affords flexible data management and the ability to answer sophisticated queries to the database.

6. TELECOMMUNICATION MONITORS

In a computer system with a number of remote terminals exchanging messages with the CPU, a special software package is often employed to provide for the communication between these terminals and the operating system. This package, called a *telecommunication monitor,* ensures terminal transparency: all application programs may be written without regard to the physical characteristics of the terminals, entirely managed by this monitor.

The relationship between the telecommunication monitor, the DBMS, and the operating system is suggested by Figure 9–1.

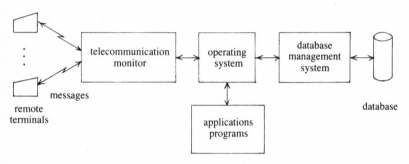

FIGURE 9–1.   Control software of an extensive computer system

B. FROM MANUAL CONTROL OF COMPUTERS
TO UNIPROGRAMMING

The functioning of an operating system is best appreciated when the operation of a rudimentary computer (such as an inexpensive microcomputer) without such a system is considered.

To run a single program, without subprograms, on a computer with an input and an output device and without an operating system of any kind, the following has to be done manually by the operator (in this case, usually the programmer).

(1) Since initially the main memory contains no instruction to be execut-

ed, the *initial program load* (IPL, also called *bootstrapping)* has to be performed. By setting switches on the operator console of the machine and pushing a button, a single instruction may be stored in memory. This instruction will read in the next one and so on, until the program loader (see Chapter 7–G) is stored in the main memory; it "pulls itself by its own bootstraps," as it were.

(2) The appropriate translator is loaded from an input device.

(3) The translator reads in the source program and produces the object program on the output device. If several passes of the translator are necessary, the operation is repeated several times with the intermediate forms of the program under translation.

(4) The object program is loaded (provided that the loader has remained in the main memory).

(5) The object program is executed, with the necessary data obtained through the input device.

If the program requires debugging, these steps have to be repeated for every run. The sequence becomes more complicated if subprograms are present.

As can be seen from the above, the job of executing a program written in a symbolic language consists of many *steps*. The sequencing between these steps, if performed by a human operator, is exceedingly slow as compared to the computer speed. During the *setup* of a step (providing for necessary inputs) the computer system is idle. Such processing is therefore not used for other than very small computer systems, dedicated to a specific application.

A software *operating system* manages the resources of a computer system by allocating them to the incoming jobs so as to provide a desirable environment for the users and efficiently utilize the system resources.

A simple operating system takes over the step-sequencing function of the operator and automatically performs the transitions between the jobs. A *batch* of programs is submitted by the computer operator (the user having been relieved of the duty), and the operating system allocates the needed resources and supervises their execution. In such a simple computer system there may be only a single program in execution at any given time; no job is started until the previous one has been completed. An operating system that manages the computer in this fashion is called a *uniprogramming* system. Depending on its complexity, it may provide many conveniences to the programmer (similar to the ones described below for a multiprogramming operating system), such as routines for handling input/output or a file system for storing programs and data on a secondary memory device. Most operating system routines are themselves stored on a disk or a tape and called into the main memory by the part of the operating system *resident* there, which is loaded following bootstrapping.

C. MULTIPROGRAMMING

A larger computer system consists of many different resources. A single program intermittently uses the CPU and performs input or output. Barring exceptional situations requiring considerable ingenuity on the part of the programmer, the program is unable to use the CPU while input or output is performed on its behalf. In a uniprogramming system, where only one program at a time may be executed by the system, much resource idleness results, while other jobs may be delayed. The lifetime in such system of two jobs of a very simple structure is shown in Fig. 9–2(a). Each of the two jobs is assumed to perform input, then require CPU processing, and subsequently perform output. No overlap is possible between the CPU use by one of the jobs and input or output by another in such a system, even though the hardware resources are idle.

To increase the resource utilization in the system and thereby to execute more jobs in a unit of time, *multiprogramming operating systems* have been designed. In such systems several programs may be in a state of execution at any time. Of course, in a system with a single CPU (i.e., without multiprocessing) only one program at a time can actually be using the CPU; "in a state of execution" means simply started but not yet completed.

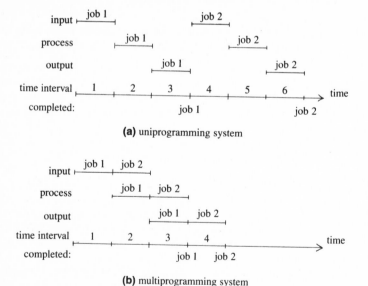

(a) uniprogramming system

(b) multiprogramming system

FIGURE 9–2. Nonoverlapped and overlapped job processing

From Fig. 9–2(b) it can be seen that the CPU-I/O overlap, the hallmark of multiprogramming, enables the same workload (two jobs) to be processed in a shorter time.

From the comparison of Fig. 9–2(a) and 9–2(b) it can be seen that multiprogramming increased the *throughput* of the system; i.e., the rate at which the jobs are being completed is increased. After the third time interval, in our idealized situation, one job will be completed per three intervals in the uniprogramming system, while in the multiprogramming system one job will be finished after every single interval. Increased throughput is due to the increased resource utilization.

Along with the throughput, an important measure of the system performance is job *turnaround time,* the time from the arrival of a job at the system to its completion. Part of the operating system responsibility is to ensure a short turnaround time to the jobs considered meritorious.

The essential conditions for multiprogramming are

(a) separate I/O processors, such as channels (see Chapter 8–E), have to be present in the system so that the CPU is available for processing and not involved in the supervision of input/output;

(b) a large main memory: necessary to hold the programs (or their parts) that currently belong to the so-called *multiprogramming mix,* i.e., they have been started and are competing for the system resources. Parts of this memory are also allocated as *buffers* to hold the information coming from the input device for a job that is not using the CPU or to hold the results of the CPU processing, ready for output.

Due to their capabilities, multiprogramming operating systems are relatively complex and use significant resources (memory space, CPU time, etc.) themselves. In other words, system *overhead,* the amount of resources consumed by the supervisory rather than application programs, is rather high.

D. BATCH VS. TIME-SHARING OPERATING SYSTEMS

Aside from the uniprogramming vs. multiprogramming distinction, an operating system may be classified with respect to the method of the CPU time allocation to the job being processed. This method is determined by the desired mode of user-system interaction.

In batch processing, the early and still predominant environment, the users submit the entire program to the system at one time with all the necessary data. In very simple systems, the computer operator collects these programs into a batch for processing; hence the name.

A *batch operating system* then causes the job to be processed so as to maximize the utilization of system resources and thus lower the computing cost. This often signifies that once the CPU is allocated to a job, it is being used until this job requires input or output, whereupon the CPU is allocated to another job. The operation of such a system is described further in Chapter 9–F. This is assuming the system is multiprogrammed, although in small computers uniprogramming usually is used.

The alternative is a *time-sharing operating system,* one designed to ensure a conversational use of computers (see the next section for the description of such processing). It attempts to provide a fast response—in seconds—to requests trivial in terms of processing time. A typical request would be to execute several instructions of a program. These requests are made by a number of users who are waiting at their terminals while the processing is taking place. Response time being of paramount importance, timesharing operating systems are distinguished mainly by their CPU scheduling method, called *time slicing*. The use of the CPU is allocated for a very short time (typically about 0.25 sec) consecutively to the programs of all of the users active at their terminals. The simplest of several schemes of such service is schematically exemplified in Fig. 9–3. In this *round-robin scheduling* scheme, each of the six users is given a *quantum* (slice) of the CPU time, following which the CPU is *preempted* and allocated to the next user (unless the request made by a given user is served in the time shorter than the quantum and no preemption is necessary).

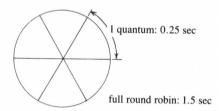

FIGURE 9–3. Time slicing

Remembering that about 250,000 machine instructions can be executed by a reasonably fast computer within a quantum time, we may conclude that most of the requests are completed within a single quantum. If not, the request will continue to be served after all others have received their quanta.

Due to their nature, time-sharing systems are usually multiprogrammed.

There also exist general-purpose operating systems that combine the time-sharing and batch capabilities. In such systems, the interactive requests receive a priority (are run in the *foreground*, as it is said), and the batch jobs are run in the *background*.

E. TYPES OF COMPUTER SYSTEMS

An operating system is used to manage the resources of the computer system in such a fashion as to make them easy to use. Since convenience depends upon users' needs, several types of systems exist. Some of these systems are created by making an appropriate application program running under the operating system a permanent part of the environment.

The essential modes of computer processing are discussed below. Among these, time-sharing, on-line, and real-time systems are often grouped together as *interactive systems*, since the response time, a few seconds or less, is of paramount importance in all of these. These are opposed to batch processing, which offers a relatively long job turnaround time, but aims at lowering computing costs. Many larger computer systems offer the users several processing modes.

1. BATCH PROCESSING

This most widely used type of processing relies on a batch operating system. The user submits a complete job: the program, the data, and the statements in the *job control language* of the system, requesting of it appropriate resources (CPU time, memory area, I/O devices, files). After a relatively long turnaround time (tens of minutes to hours), all the results are available.

In the business environment, application programming consists predominantly of generating summaries (reports) and obtaining specific information from permanently maintained collections of data stored on secondary memory devices. If batch processing is used to maintain these data and to obtain the reports, the input data are collected over a period of time in so-called *transaction files*. Periodically, a job (or a number of jobs) is run to update the permanently maintained *master file* and generate the necessary reports (see Fig. 9–4).

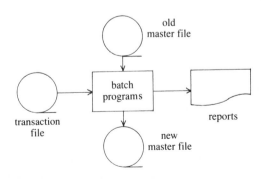

FIGURE 9–4. Batch processing

The main disadvantage of batch processing is the lack of current information from the data base, because information is out of date between runs, and the lack of easy access to the master files.

A variation of batch processing is a *remote job entry* (RJE) system, in which users submit their batch jobs via a remote terminal connected to the computer site by a cable or other telecommunication line. The output is most frequently obtained at the same terminal. In an RJE system, users often have access to a text editor and an extensive file system for storing their programs.

2. ON-LINE SYSTEMS

In an on-line system (also called a transaction-processing system), certain transactions, such as queries to data files or their updates are processed "immediately." In such a system the users have multiple (sometimes thousands of) access terminals from which they may introduce one or a few of the transactions exclusively (e.g., a bank teller may input the amount of a savings account deposit). The response of the system, such as an answer to a query, an acknowledgment of an update, or printing of a report, comes within seconds.

Usually such systems are permanent running application programs based on a multiprogramming batch operating system. This system, gaining an ever wider use in the business world, has the advantages over the batch system of wide accessibility to the users and of up-to-date data files. A schematic view of an on-line system is shown in Fig. 9–5.

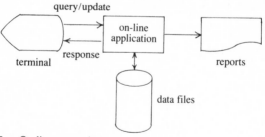

FIGURE 9–5. On-line processing

Examples of on-line systems include simpler applications, such as airline reservation systems or supermarket checkout systems with point of sale (POS) terminals, as well as more complex electronic fund transfer (EFT) systems and management information systems (MIS).

In larger organizations of today, multiple computer systems of various capabilities are installed. They are usually placed on individual sites, often remote, where the source data for a specific application are available or where the results of the computations are needed. If the application programs running on these computer systems share common data files or pass data to one another, this computing environment is defined as *distributed processing*. Usually both batch and interactive modes are available. More advanced distributed processing systems are organized into networks of computers and terminals with the use of telecommunication media (see Chapter 8–G–2).

3. TIME-SHARING SYSTEMS

Designed for fast service, the goal of such systems is to provide each user with an illusion of having the computer dedicated to himself/herself. General-purpose time-sharing service provides the user with a full complement of programming languages and facilities. At the heart of the system is a time-sharing operating system (see Section D of the chapter), which allocates to each user in turn the attention of the CPU.

A number of users (from 20 to 200, with the maximum number depending on the system) simultaneously interact with the computer. The time between the user's log-on and log-off is called a *session*.

During a typical session, the user:

(a) signs into the system by presenting a password;
(b) enters a program under the control of a text editor;
(c) usually saves this program in the file system under an assigned name;
(d) has the program translated (conceivably several times if there are errors discovered during the translation); the object code may also be saved;
(e) runs the program.

While the program is being run, the user may interact with it. For example, the program may be designed to request the data of the user or the result of partial execution may be reviewed by the user in order to then decide on further processing. Debuggers may be used to run the program and analyze its correctness.

A response to a trivial request, such as modifying the line of a program or executing several of its statements, usually takes a fraction of a second or a few seconds. Such a response appears instantaneous to a human.

In a system combining batch and time-sharing service, a job may be submitted from a time-sharing terminal to be run in a batch mode.

Along with the general-purpose time-sharing systems, there exist specialized time-sharing services offering a single programming language to the user. The language, such as BASIC or APL (see Chapter 6–A) is usually interpreted so that the programs may be translated and executed statement by statement.

Time-sharing systems are particularly well suited for program development hindered in the batch systems by long turnaround times. They are not used to run already developed production jobs due to the overhead related to switching the CPU from one program to another and the attendant need to swap programs in and out of the main memory.

4. REAL-TIME SYSTEMS

In *real-time systems*, a hard constraint is imposed upon the response time of the system. If the processing of the incoming data is not completed during the allotted interval, it becomes worthless and considerable harm may ensue.

Real-time systems are often designed as special-purpose operating systems in order to provide for fast management of the system hardware.

Such systems are often used for process control; for example, in an industrial plant or in a mission-control system supporting space flights. In this application a closed loop is formed, with the computer receiving the data about the state of the controlled entity through a set of sensors, processing it, and setting the control switches, valves, etc.

In an open-loop arrangement, real-time systems are used for data acquisition.

Response times required are often short (10 to 100 msec). Extensive data files are usually not needed, and the swapping of programs between main and secondary memories is avoided.

F. OPERATION OF A BATCH MULTIPROGRAMMING SYSTEM

In a multiprogramming system, more than one program is usually in a state of execution at any given time, while only one of these is actually using the CPU.

Programs gain control of the CPU only for a limited interval of time and lose it either due to their need for input/output or due to its preemption by the operating system in order for it to be allocated to a different program. The latter technique is employed rarely in batch systems and routinely, due to time slicing, in time-sharing systems. When a program loses control of the CPU, the operating system saves all the information needed to restore it (such as, for example, the address of the next instruction to be executed, the contents of all the general-purpose registers, etc.). The information that needs to be saved is often called the *context block* of the program, or *process status block*.

A program in execution, together with its context block, is often called a *process* or *task*. An operating system may create several processes to carry out a program step, but most frequently a single process is created.

Due to multiprogramming, a single job, or, more precisely, processes created on its behalf, undergo a number of transitions in the system. These are shown in Fig. 9–6.

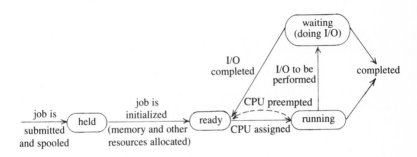

FIGURE 9–6. States of a job (process) in a batch multiprogramming system

A job (the job control information, program, and data) is submitted via an input device. For increased throughput, operating systems usually include so-called *spooling* routines. These routines read in the card deck of the job (or any other image of it, depending on the input device) and place all this information on a fast secondary memory device, such as a disk. Subsequently, the fast disk will play the role of the input device, which will speed up the processing of the job.

The job remains in held state until the operating system initializes it, by assigning to it the required main memory area and other resources specified in the job control information. An initialized job, having become a process, is now in the ready state where it is enqueued for the use of the CPU. When the CPU is assigned to it, the process is running. It has to relinquish the CPU when it needs to perform input or output (for example, to access a data file). The process is then waiting for the completion of the input/output operation, when it will become ready to use the CPU again. In exceptional cases, the CPU may be preempted from a process that is ready to use it. After many such bursts of CPU and I/O processing, the job is completed.

While the job is being processed, its results are placed in a secondary memory (e.g., on a disk) to be transferred after its completion by the spooling routine to the output device.

Programs run on behalf of a time-sharing user undergo similar changes of state. Due to time slicing, the user processes may be preempted and swapped out of the main memory.

G. FUNCTIONAL PARTS OF A MULTIPROGRAMMING OPERATING SYSTEM

The essential functions of a multiprogramming operating systems are

(a) allocation of computer system resources to jobs (strictly, processes) by maintaining queues of claimants and tables of available resources, such as CPU, memory, input/output devices, or files;

(b) accounting of resource use for billing purposes;

(c) protection of processes from each other and protection of the operating system from the user processes, as well as protection of files;

(d) provision for a proper interaction of *cooperating processes* (i.e., processes that carry out a certain program step together), available in many systems.

The main components of the operating system are responsible for resource allocation, which is performed in such a manner as to meet the remaining objectives.

The main resource allocation functions are discussed below.

1. CPU SCHEDULING

In the presence of several processes competing for its use, the CPU has to be assigned by the operating system in a fashion consistent with its performance objectives. Many scheduling strategies exist; the most frequently used are

- first-come–first-serve: to further fair play
- shortest-job first: to maximize throughput
- according to external priorities purchased by the users: to ensure a short turnaround time to the users who need it
- round-robin time slicing (or its variation) in a time-sharing environment.

The CPU scheduler maintains the queue of processes in the ready state, with the ordering according to the strategy (or strategies) selected.

In an operating system running both batch and interactive jobs, the latter are given preference.

2. MEMORY MANAGEMENT

The main memory of the multiprogrammed system is usually shared by several programs included in the multiprogramming mix (i.e., they are being run simultaneously). There exist many variations of such sharing; hardware support, such as special registers and data paths in the CPU, is usually required.

The relocating loader provides a degree of flexibility in program placement in the main memory. It permits placement of a translated program anywhere in the memory where the required number of consecutive locations is available.

A multiprogramming operating system frequently needs to remove a program or a part of a program from the main memory when the program is unable to use the CPU.

The loader provides only *static relocatability:* once a loaded and partially executed program is removed to a secondary memory, it has to be returned to its previous locations since all the address references in it are already *bound* to them.

To obtain *dynamic relocatability,* whereby the programs may be *swapped* between any sufficiently large area of the main memory and the secondary store, special *relocation registers* are required in the CPU. In their presence, all the memory references are formed by the hardware adding the contents of these registers to the address references contained in the program (see Fig. 9–7). This is similar to the use of base registers (see

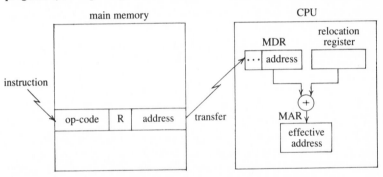

FIGURE 9–7.   Effective address formation with relocation register

Chapter 7–E), which are used for this purpose in some computers. The program may be *rolled out* from the main memory when not running, while the program to be run is *rolled in;* this scheme is called *swapping.*

A sophisticated memory management mechanism is a *virtual memory* system. This software mechanism unifies the main memory and a relatively fast secondary memory device (such as a drum or a fixed-head disk) to obtain the total with the advantageous characteristics of the two (see Fig. 9–8): a speed close to that of the main memory, a capacity of the secondary memory, and a price per word close to that of the secondary memory.

In a virtual memory system, the main memory holds only those parts of the programs in the multiprogramming mix that the CPU will most likely need immediately. Full copies of the programs are maintained in the secondary memory.

Since only such parts are brought in and out of the main memory during

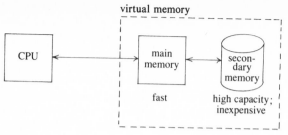

virtual memory

CPU ← → main memory ← → secondary memory

fast   high capacity; inexpensive

FIGURE 9–8.

swapping, the overhead due to it is significantly reduced. These parts are either fixed-sized (often 2K or 4K) chunks, called *pages,* or variable-sized *segments,* meaningful program units or data structures. There exist, therefore, paged and segmented virtual memory systems; in some systems segments are further subdivided into pages. The information concerning the residence of pages/segments is kept in tables, through which the translation of every memory reference is performed.

Virtual memory derives its name from the fact that every program may use more locations than physically available for it in the main memory.

3. MANAGEMENT OF INPUT/OUTPUT DEVICES AND OF INPUT/OUTPUT

The *input/output control system* (IOCS) was the early rationale for the emergence of operating systems. It is responsible for the input and output from the I/O and secondary memory devices. Channels, interrupts, and the use of buffer areas in the main memory make the CPU-I/O processing overlap possible. Since input/output is a complex function and since the operating system aims at overlapping the CPU processing of one program with the I/O of another, it is desirable for the operating system to be in full control of it. Therefore, input/output instructions (along with other instructions that may change the state of the entire system, such as the setting of the system clock) are protected from being executed by users' programs. To ensure this, many systems have two modes of operation: *program* (or *user*) *mode,* where only part of the machine instruction set may be executed, and *supervisor mode,* in which any instruction may be executed. The latter is accessible only to certain system programs.

An interrupt-driven IOCS usually includes the spooling feature and maintains the tables of I/O devices and queues of processes that need them. The system retains full control of device assignment: the user specifies only the type of the device needed in the job control information (e.g., a card-reader), and the system assigns the particular device out of the available pool.

4. FILE MANAGEMENT

To an operating system, *files* are named collections of information, stored in secondary memory. A file may be a program file containing, for example, a FORTRAN source program or a *binary file* with object code, or, on the other hand, a data file. Data files are organized in one of the ways described in Chapter 10.

An operating system contains a set of routines, called *access methods,* for every file organization method supported by it.

The file system precludes the necessity of reading programs in every time they are to be run and permits the storage of large volumes of data, a feature particularly important in the business environment. Sometimes, when a uniform treatment of data files is desired, a database management system (DBMS) is superimposed on the operating system.

To enable the authorized users to access files by specifying their name only, a *file directory* is kept by the operating system. A tree-like organization of such a directory is presented in Fig. 9–9.

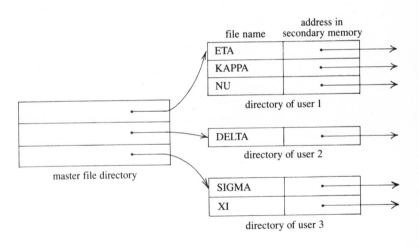

FIGURE 9–9. File directory

SUGGESTIONS FOR FURTHER READING

GENERAL DISCUSSIONS OF SYSTEMS SOFTWARE

Donovan, J. J.: *Systems Programming,* McGraw-Hill, New York, 1972.
  A design-oriented text.
Freeman, P.: *Software Systems Principles,* SRA, Chicago, 1976.
  A survey; includes several important papers on the subject.

OPERATING SYSTEMS ARE DISCUSSED IN

Haberman, A. N.: *Introduction to Operating Systems Design,* SRA, Chicago, 1976.
  Practical orientation, with solid theoretical underpinnings.
Brinch Hansen, P.: *Operating System Principles,* Prentice-Hall, Englewood Cliffs,
  N.J., 1973.
  Algorithmic orientation.
Katzan, H., Jr.: *Operating Systems,* Van Nostrand Reinhold, New York, 1973.
  Subtitled *A Pragmatic Approach,* this book contains a valuable detailed discussion
  of the IBM System/360–370 OS/MVT.
Madnick, S. E., and Donovan, J. J.: *Operating Systems,* McGraw-Hill, New York,
  1974.
  A thorough discussion with a view toward an implementation.

SPECIALIZED SYSTEMS ARE DISCUSSED IN

Watson, R. W.: *Timesharing System Design Concepts,* McGraw-Hill, New York,
  1970.
  An incisive analysis of software-hardware interaction, with excellent discussion of
  virtual memory techniques.
Davis, G. B.: *Management Information Systems: Conceptual Foundation, Structure
  and Development,* McGraw-Hill, New York, 1974.
Yourdon, E.: *Design of On-Line Computer Systems,* Prentice-Hall, Englewood
  Cliffs, N.J., 1972.
  This down-to-earth book may be used as a manual for the design of on-line sys-
  tems.

10

FILES AND DATABASES

Along with hardware and software, a major resource of many computer systems is data. This is particularly true in administration and business. In such systems there is a need permanently and securely to maintain large collections of data describing the environment of the application and to organize them for effective and efficient processing.

In the batch environment (see Chapter 9–E) these data are accessed during the periodic *production runs* of application programs oriented toward generation of reports. In the on-line environment the data have to be accessed in real time to provide the response to the incoming transactions.

Since the volume of data is large, they are stored on secondary memory devices (at this time, disks are used predominantly as on-line storage). To use such devices efficiently, an appropriate organization of the data stored on them is required. This physical organization of data, the actual storage method, may differ from the logical organization, the way the data are viewed by the application programs. The gap between the physical and logical organization is bridged by systems software.

Most frequently, data are stored as a set of separate files, each consisting of related records. Usually a given file consists of the same type of records. The logical organization of files is close to the actual physical placement of the data contained in them. These data are accessed through the access method routines of the operating system.

In more advanced applications, on the other hand, the data are organized into one or more databases. A database is a collection of records of various types with specified interrelationships between them. The relationships between the records reflect the dependencies between the real-world entities represented by the data. Since these cross-references are stored in an organized fashion in the database itself, complex queries to the database may be answered rapidly.

A database is accessed by the applications programs through an extensive system software program called a database management system (DBMS).

The overall logical structure of the database is defined by the data administrator with a model called a conceptual schema (or, simply, a schema). An application program that uses a part of these data and relationships may define its own view of the database, called an external schema, or subschema. The subschema is derived from the schema by the DBMS. A database provides the essential advantage of application program independence from the changes in the structure of the data.

A. FIELDS, RECORDS, FILES, AND DATABASES

Records were introduced in Chapter 5–E as one of the data structures used in computing. They are the essential structure for storing data residing in a secondary memory.

Data describe real-world *entities*. Some entities are tangible (e.g., an employee or a plane), others are intangible (e.g., a department of a firm or an airline flight). To describe an entity, the values of its *attributes* that are of interest to the application have to be stored as data (e.g., the name, address, and salary of an employee, or the number and time of departure of a flight).

An entity is described by a *record,* which consists of a number of *fields* (also called *data items*), each of which contains the value of an entity attribute. A collection of records related with respect to their use is called a *data file* or simply a *file* (compare Fig. 10–3). Usually files consist of the same type of records describing a set of entities.

As an example, in a payroll application a personnel file may be maintained that consists of one record per employee. Each record, in a very simple file, may consist of the following fields: employee number, name, address, weekly salary.

In order to access a record in a file, this record has to be identified by the contents of one or more of its fields. A field that uniquely identifies the record is called the *key* (or the *primary key*).

One or more databases are sometimes created for a given, usually large, application (such as, for example, a management information system or an airline reservation system). A *database* is an integrated collection of records of various types with the stored relationships between these records.

B. PHYSICAL VS. LOGICAL ORGANIZATION
OF DATA. BLOCKING

An important distinction exists between the logical and the physical organization of files and databases.

The *logical organization* of a file is the view that the application programs that use it have of it. Its *physical organization,* on the other hand, is its actual structure when stored on the secondary memory device. Frequently, this physical organization is simply called file organization.

Why the distinction? The logical structure of a file, apparent to the user, should be devoid of the details present in the actual storage method. In writing a program that employs a personnel file, for example, the user may be concerned with the composition of the records and the possibility of accessing them by the employee number on line. The user is not concerned, however, with the details of the actual file organization (for example, with the actual address of the record). Therefore, if the physical organization changes, the application programs remain unaffected. The physical structure of a file is dictated by the need to store it efficiently on a particular secondary memory device and to provide for the desired speed and mode of retrieval.

Thus, physical organization of data is the method adopted for its storage, while the logical organization is oriented toward the retrieval of data.

System software transforms the data demands expressed by the application program in logical terms (e.g. "What is the salary of employee number 55?") into the physical terms (record address). This is suggested by Fig. 10–1.

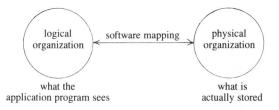

FIGURE 10–1.   Physical vs. logical organization

In many file systems, the access method routines of the operating system (see Chapter 9–G–4) are used to perform this transformation. The only logical relationship among the file records is usually the sequence of their keys. More complex logical relationships between the entities described by the data may be reflected in the databases managed by database management systems (DBMS).

An important technique in the physical file organization, leading to efficient use of secondary storage devices and often increased speed of access, is blocking: collection of several logical records into a single *physical record,* also called a *block.* It is the physical record that is read or written from/to the secondary storage device. Blocking technique is particularly effective when the records are stored in the order in which they are processed.

Since both a disk and a tape are nonrandom access devices (see Chapter 8–D), it takes much longer to access the first word (or byte) of a record stored in them than to access the succeeding ones. The larger the block accessed, therefore, shorter the access time per word. In the case of a disk, the size of the block is often determined by the hardware itself. Space saving due to blocking is most evident in tapes. The use of tape requires that *interrecord gaps* be left between physical records to allow for stopping the drive and then starting it again to access the next physical record. If logical records are not blocked, each is treated as a separate physical record, and therefore a gap has to be left between them [see Fig. 10–2(a)]. This may result in half of the tape reel being unused for data storage. Blocking diminishes the proportion of such space [see Fig. 10–2(b)].

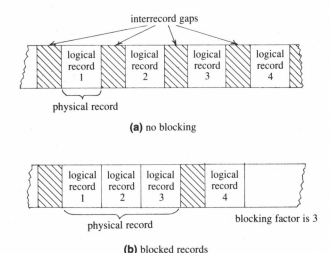

(a) no blocking

(b) blocked records

FIGURE 10–2. Blocking

The number of logical records aggregated into a single physical record (block) is called the *blocking factor*.

Blocking requires *buffering:* setting aside areas (called *buffers)* in the main memory to hold the physical record while the application program obtains logical records from it. The larger the blocks, the larger the buffers needed.

The system software, such as an access method, is responsible for recovering a logical record from the block. To provide the necessary information to this software regarding the composition of the file, the programmer has to "open" it before it is used. Afterwards, the file may be read from, written into, or both, depending on the access rights of the program.

Every time a file is read, a physical record is obtained in the input buffer. System software then deblocks it by selecting the needed logical record for the program. Thus, subsequent "read" operations by the application program may find the needed logical record already in the main memory buffer. During a "write" operation, the application program transfers logical records into the output buffer until a full physical record is accumulated and written into the file.

When the program no longer needs the file, it has to be "closed" in order to be prepared by the system software for reuse.

C. FILE ORGANIZATION

File organization is a method of placing records on the secondary storage device; it often includes the provision of additional information, such as tables, needed to access these records.

The aim of a given file organization is to ensure efficient storage of records and to provide for the desired type of access to them.

Access, i.e., reading or writing of a record, is the essential operation of a file. There are two different types of access: *sequential access,* which requires a search through the file, and *direct access,* which locates the record without such a search. In both cases, the record is identified by its key. As a consequence, sequential access is used to process records in the order in which they are stored; direct access does not impose such a limitation.

In the case of sequential access, the time required to locate a record depends on its position in the file; in direct access the dependence is very slight.

Sequential access as the main access mode is used exclusively in batch systems (see Chapter 9–E), where files are updated and summarized at regular, relatively distant, intervals. Between such updates the file contents do not reflect the changes in the environment (these are reflected in a transaction file being accumulated). In such a system, during a single processing run a number of file records are affected in the sequence in which they are stored. On-line processing (see again Chapter 9–E), which requires an immediate response to a transaction (a file update or a query), needs direct access.

Three methods of data file organization are predominantly used and supported by the operating system in the form of appropriate access methods: sequential, indexed sequential, and direct (also called random). These are discussed below and are compared in Table 10–1.

TABLE 10–1. Comparison of file organization methods

FILE ORGANIZATION	ENVIRONMENT OF APPLICATION	ADVANTAGES	DISADVANTAGES
Sequential	Batch	Simplicity of management; efficient use of storage; potential use of cheap storage device (tape); fast sequential processing from DASD	Insertions and updates practically impossible; general disadvantages of batch processing
Indexed sequential	Batch/on-line	No sorting of transactions required; both sequential and direct access possible	Space for index and time for its maintenance; slow direct access to large files
Direct (random)	On-line	No sorting of transactions required; fast access; direct access with little overhead	Additional space (about 30–40%) required to prevent excessive number of collisions; difficult to use when sequence is needed (e.g., to generate reports)

Other file organizations exist. An example is a *partitioned file*, consisting of named storage partitions (areas of consecutive locations), each holding many records stored sequentially. Partitioned organization is used to store program libraries rather than data.

1. SEQUENTIAL FILES

Sequential file organization is the simplest and most popular. The records are stored (sorted) in their key sequence. An example of a sequential file is shown in Fig. 10–3, the Social Security number, serving as a key, uniquely identifies the records that are stored in the ascending sequence of this key.

SS No. (Key)	Name	Weekly Salary	
010-55-7394	SMITH	300	
173-34-1010	JONES	500	← a field (data item)
231-35-8535	PETERS	250	← a record
⋮	⋮	⋮	

FIGURE 10–3. Sequential file

This is the file organization used in the tape- and card-oriented batch systems. All update transactions (deletions, insertions, or modifications of records) are accumulated over a period of time, on cards, for example, then transcribed onto a tape and sorted by key. Subsequently this sorted transaction tape is run against the master file and the new master file is created (see Fig. 9–4). Sequential file organization naturally may also be used with a direct access device such as a disk.

To access a record in such a file, it is necessary to search the file for the record with the given key. In a tape-oriented system there is no alternative to sequential search (looking at any intervening record and comparing the two keys). In a disk-oriented system, faster search methods may be utilized.

Efficient use of sequential files requires that a good proportion of records be accessed during each run. Insertions into such a file are impossible (barring special cases); *file reorganization*, generation of a new file from the existing one with the consideration of changes, is required instead.

2. INDEXED SEQUENTIAL FILES

In an *indexed sequential file,* the records are also stored in their key sequence. However, in order to provide for a fast, direct access to records, indexes are maintained. A file *index* is a table showing the placement of records on the secondary storage device in relation to their keys.

An indexed sequential file, therefore, may be accessed in the batch-oriented sequential fashion, as well as directly through the index in order to provide fast response. The index search, involved in direct access, is a much faster procedure than the file search in the case of sequential access. Binary search, discussed in 3–17, may be used for the purpose.

To store indexed sequential files, a direct-access device, such as a disk, is needed.

There are several ways to build the file indexes. These are automatically created by the software when the file is organized.

A popular method of indexing, closely related to the structure of disks (see Chapter 8–D), is shown in Fig. 10–4. The file records are placed on the disk in their key sequence cylinder after cylinder. They are located on consecutive tracks of a given cylinder, i.e., on consecutive disk surfaces. The index has, therefore, a hierarchical structure, with the highest value of the key on a given track or cylinder placed in the index.

When a large, many-cylindered disk is used, the cylinder index is often broken up into parts to speed up the file access. A master index is then added to these multiple cylinder indexes.

To access a record directly, first all the existing index levels are searched to find the track that holds it. Then the track itself is searched for this record. During sequential processing the index is not used.

If an insertion is to occur, the record is written into a special *overflow area,* with a pointer to it placed in the track where it logically belongs. Periodical reorganization is performed to merge the overflow area records with

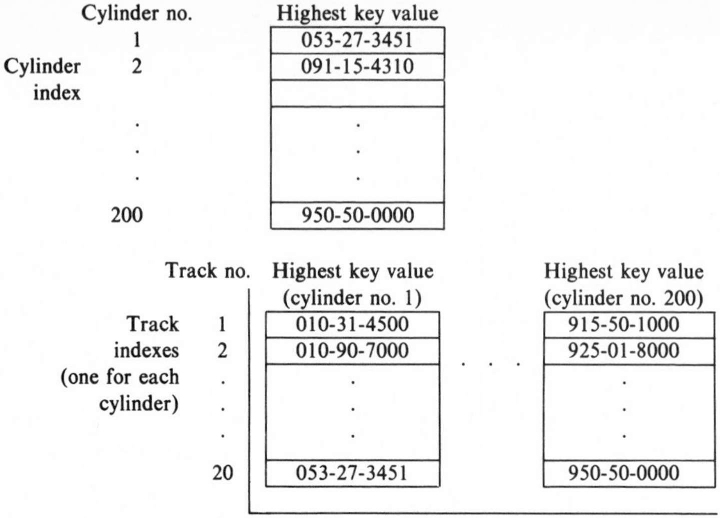

Cylinder no.	Highest key value
1	053-27-3451
2	091-15-4310
.	.
.	.
.	.
200	950-50-0000

Cylinder index

Track no.	Highest key value (cylinder no. 1)		Highest key value (cylinder no. 200)
1	010-31-4500		915-50-1000
2	010-90-7000	. . .	925-01-8000
.	.		.
.	.		.
.	.		.
20	053-27-3451		950-50-0000

Track indexes (one for each cylinder)

The disk has 200 cylinders and 20 surfaces (4000 tracks)

FIGURE 10–4. An index of an indexed-sequential file

those contained in the *prime area*. When a record is deleted, it is replaced by a special marker.

3. DIRECT FILES

Direct (also called *random*) *file* organization provides for fast direct access to records; however, the records are not maintained in a meaningful physical sequence. No index is needed.

Direct files are used for on-line applications. A direct-access device (e.g., a disk) is required. In a direct file, the record key is mapped (transformed) into the storage address of the record. A one-to-one functional transformation from the key to the address is rarely possible.

> **EXAMPLE 10–1**
> Consider the personnel file for a company with 1000 employees, to which direct access is desired, with the key being the Social Security number.
> If we wanted to equate the record key with its address, the size of the file would outgrow the realistic storage possibilities of the company, and the file would be almost empty.
> A solution would be to assign employee numbers and use these as the file key. This might, however, create difficulties in some applications where the access by such key is meaningless.

A set of methods, called *hashing* (or *randomizing*), is therefore used to spread the addresses generated from keys as uniformly as possible over the area allocated to the file. *Collision*, i.e., two keys being mapped into the same address, frequently occurs and has to be handled by the software.

Software routines (access methods) for the management of direct files have to include, therefore:

a hashing procedure;
a procedure for collision resolution to store and retrieve records with duplicate transformed keys.

Many hashing procedures exist. The *division-remainder method* is one of the most popular. The numerical key is divided by the prime number closest to, but smaller than, the number of physical sets of locations available for storage of the file records, and the remainder is taken as the address. This ensures a fairly uniform distribution of records over the available area. If the key is alphanumerical, a numerical value may be obtained for it through a manipulation of its representation in the given character code.

EXAMPLE 10-2

There are 100,000 words available for the small file, each record being 100 words long. The address of the first location is 5000.

The file is not blocked: a physical record consists of a single logical record. There are, therefore, 1000 physical record addresses.

The closest prime number is 997, which will serve as the divisor (for small files, the prime number of physical records should be allocated to begin with, for large files it does not matter).

To obtain the address of a record whose key is, for example, 5000, we divide and obtain the remainder:

$$\frac{5000}{997} = 5 \text{ with remainder of } 15$$

Hence, the address of the record is

$$5000 + 15 \times 100 = 6500$$

Note that the hashing of the following two keys will result in collision: 10000 and 14985.

The management software converts the address into the form required by the secondary storage device (e.g., cylinder number–track number).

Collision is handled either by placing the colliding record in the closest free space available, going consistently in one direction (so-called *open addressing* method), or by establishing a linked list of all colliding records. When a record is accessed, its key is verified and a search for the right record may issue. Sometimes, general overflow areas are used to place all colliding records.

To partially counteract the slowdown of access due to collision, the bucket method is used. A *bucket* is a block of words able to hold several logical records with duplicate transformed keys. The hashing procedure generates the address of the bucket rather than those of an individual record. A single "read" operation causes the entire bucket to be transformed to the main memory. Subsequently, the needed record is found by key comparison.

To limit the number of collisions, more space than is needed for the file has to be allocated to a direct file.

D. LOGICAL ORGANIZATION OF DATA IN DATABASES

In a file system, only the simplest logical relationship between the records in individual files is usually reflected. This is the sequence of the record keys, which is rarely meaningful in terms of the application program. In a database system, the records of several types that together describe the environment of the application are integrated into a whole by the information regarding their interrelationships, stored with the records themselves. Since a set of records of a given type may be considered a file, databases are often said to consist of several integrated files.

Database records contain, therefore, the fields in which the values of the attributes are stored, as well as the fields that contain structural information that establishes the relationship between the records.

The physical implementation methods such as:

- sequential storage of records
- device indexes and content indexes
- hashing (randomizing)
- construction of linked data structures (see Chapter 5), i.e., linked lists (in special cases, rings), trees, or networks

are utilized to store records in a database. The links (pointers) structure the collection of records so as to establish the essential logical organization of data. They may be considered cross-references between the records.

With the use of a file system (rather than a database) only simple accesses to the records is possible; they are limited to seeking information about the contents of a record field with the use of a key (e.g., "What is the weekly salary of employee number 1777?"). A database, with the relationships between the records being stored there, allows for complex queries (e.g., "What are the names of the employees who are involved in manufacturing the order of customer X?") which require that several files be consulted.

The following essential relationships between records may be reflected:

1. SEQUENCE

The records are ordered through a physical placement or linking into a list according to a key. The key may be unique (primary key) or not (*secondary key*). This technique is applied to the records of the same type (belonging to the same file, as it were).

With such a logical organization, a query of the type "Who is the next senior employee?" (if the key is "years of employment") or "Who are the employees earning more than $300 a week?" (if the file is ordered according to "weekly salary") may be answered without a full file search.

2. ASSOCIATIVE RELATIONSHIP

A number of records of the same type may be associated logically because the value of their selected field is the same. In other words, they belong to a common set, distinguished by this data item. Moreover, the file records may be classified according to several fields, this corresponding to classifying the entities they reflect according to several attributes. For example, the employees may be classified by their department, by their occupational skills, and by their salary brackets.

Queries such as "Who works in department *X*?" or "Who are the electricians?" can be answered.

Multiple-key access is then possible: i.e., the records may be retrieved based on the values of several attributes. Since these secondary keys serve to classify rather than identify the records, as the primary key does, they are, in general, not unique.

The following methods may be used to represent an associative relationship physically.

A. INVERTED FILES

Content indexes are added to the file, one for each classifying attribute. A *content index* of an *inverted file* lists the values of the attribute, with the pointers to all of the records which have the given value. In a fully inverted file, such index is provided for every field. An example of such an index is shown in Fig. 10–5. The use of content indexes ensures fast response to a query.

B. MULTILINKED LISTS

All the records with the equivalent value of the attribute are linked together to form a list. Every record is linked into as many lists as there are classifying attributes.

Occupation code	Addresses of records			
5	100	025	033	413
10	113			
12	007	715	114	
17	011	112		

FIGURE 10–5. Content index of an inverted file

To simplify manipulation, often doubly linked rings (see Chapter 5–F) are chosen as the list structure. An example is shown in Fig. 10–6.

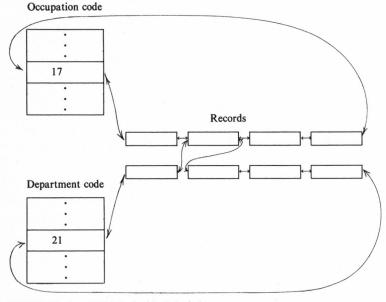

FIGURE 10–6. Multiple doubly linked rings

This structure helps to answer queries of the type "Who are all the members of the departments where our draftsmen work?"

3. HIERARCHY

The hierarchical relationship between the records is of subordination or ownership. Records of different types are involved; the records of one type may "own" or "be the superior of" the records of another type. Only strict hierarchy is allowed, and no record may be owned by more than one other record.

Examples of such a relationship are these between the department records and the employee records or between the customer records and the order records.

This relationship between the classes of records can be shown as in Fig. 10–7.

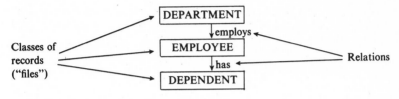

FIGURE 10-7. Hierarchical relationship

Trees (see Chapter 5–G) are the data structures used to represent hierarchical relationships.

4. GENERAL INTERRELATIONSHIP (NETWORK)

In the most general case, any type of relationship may exist between the classes of records. An example is shown in Fig. 10–8.

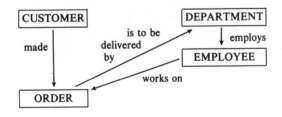

FIGURE 10-8. Network

In some database systems, such relationships are indirectly represented by trees or associations; in others, directly by network (plex) data structures.

E. DATABASE CONCEPTS

A *database* is an integrated set of files (i.e., records of the same type) related by their use and managed by a database management system (DBMS).

The essential purpose of integrating all or some of the data used by an application into a database is to render them into a single controlled resource whose structural changes are made transparent to the application programs by the DBMS.

The difference between the use of a file or a database system is illustrated by Fig. 10–9. As shown in that figure, many database systems allow the user to access data directly, without a necessity of writing a program for the purpose.

In a file-oriented system, the use of files is most often limited to the programs expressly designed for them, since the file formats differ. The relationships between the records in various files are not stored with the data; they are related when necessary by the applications programs themselves.

In a database system, the records contain the values of the attributes as well as the pointers and/or indexes that establish the relationships between the records. The format of the stored data is consistent. Databases are generally stored on direct-access devices such as disks.

The entire logical and physical structures of the database are centrally defined. The two are separated. A special *data description language* (DDL) is used to provide the description. The logical view of the database is described by the *conceptual schema* (or simply *schema*); the physical description is called the *internal schema*.

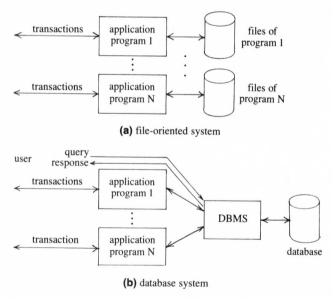

(a) file-oriented system

(b) database system

FIGURE 10–9.   File vs. database systems

A single application program most often uses only a fraction of data stored and only some of the relationships. Database users are therfore able to define in their application programs their own views of it, consistent with the overall schema. These descriptions are called *external schema,* or *subschema.* The program's use of the database is limited to the data so described. The dependencies between the three views of the database are illustrated in Fig. 10–10.

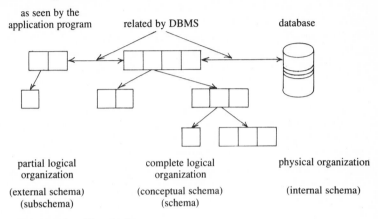

FIGURE 10–10. Use of schemas

The conversions of the program access requirements, stated in terms of its external schema, into the physical addresses are made by DBMS, often with the use of access methods.

EXAMPLE 10–3

Of the full database presented in Fig. 10–7, a program which prints invitations to the annual company picnic may take the view

Employee name	Dependents	Address

and define it by the external schema.

To process the data contained in the database, a *data manipulation language* (DML) is available to the programmer. This language allows the users to refer to the data in logical rather than physical terms which are unknown to them. This may be a self-contained language or an addition to a popular higher level language such as COBOL or FORTRAN. Many systems offer also a simple, English-like, *query language* for non-programmers who are thus able to interrogate the database directly on line, without having to write special programs.

Centralized data organization in a database system permits a single individual (or a special group) to have overall control over the data storage and use. This function is called *database administrator* (DBA) and consists primarily in the definition of the conceptual and internal schemas for the database. The database administrator also supervises the organization, maintenance, and documentation of the database and defines access authority to its elements and is responsible for its protection. In particular, the DBA provides for the *backup,* procedures for periodic duplication of data on another medium to protect them against destruction.

Database systems are often supported by a *data dictionary,* an orderly cross-referenced listing of all the data elements in the database, together with their description. Special software exists for maintaining this dictionary.

The basic advantage of the database is the program-data independence: application programs are not affected by structural changes in the database. These are "hidden" by the DBMS. Data redundancy, unavoidable in larger file systems, is avoided, which leads to increased consistency of data and storage economy. Better security and privacy safeguards are possible.

The cost of implementation and use of the DBMS is relatively high. These systems result in considerable overhead and require additional hardware resources.

SUGGESTIONS FOR FURTHER READING

File organization techniques are discussed on a practical level in the book by Yourdon referred to in the preceding chapter and, very thoroughly, in

London, K. R.: *Techniques for Direct Access,* Auerbach (now Petrocelli/Charter), Philadelphia, 1973.

Selected discussions of database systems

Kroenke, D.: *Database Processing,* SRA, Chicago, 1977.
   A fair amount of introductory material discussing data structures and file organization is included.
Martin, J.: *Computer Data-Base Organization,* Prentice-Hall, Englewood Cliffs, N.J., 1977.
   An eminently readable text.
Cardenas, A. F.: *Data Base Management Systems,* Allyn and Bacon, Boston, 1979.

COMPUTABILITY, TURING MACHINES, AND FORMAL LANGUAGES

This chapter introduces important theoretical areas of computer science with a minimal formalism.

The theory of computability outlines the limitations of computers, usually by establishing the classes of problems that cannot be solved by machines. Actual computers do not lend themselves well to a formal description that is to be manipulated by the tools of mathematics. Therefore, precise theoretical models whose capabilities are conjectured to be equivalent to those of computers have been used in the development of the theory. The models most often utilized for this purpose are Turing machines.

The study of language processing by computers led to the theory of formal languages. One of the practical aspects of this theory is the aid it provides in the translation of programming languages. Formal languages are sets of strings formed according to strict rules defined by their grammar. The theory of formal languages is closely related to the theory of automata that analyzes abstract information-processing machines. The most powerful of these machines, in terms of their computational capabilities, are again the Turing machines. A class of automata exists for each of the four classes of formal languages that recognizes the strings of the language by answering the question, is this string formed according to this grammar?

A. THEORY OF COMPUTABILITY

The *theory of computability* explores the limitations of computers by establishing what can and what cannot be computed by a machine. In such investigations the practical matters of the computation time and memory space required are of no concern.

Many important results in this field, proving the unsolvability of certain problem classes by computer, save much futile programming effort.

To formulate the theory, a mathematically precise model of computer and algorithm for it is necessary. Several such models have been developed, of which the best known is the Turing machine discussed in Section B. The basic approaches of the theory are presented here with the use of procedures, which are somewhat informal but close to those of the higher level programming languages.

To establish the capabilities of machines, the theory of computability analyzes what transformations of inputs into outputs they are able to perform or, in other words, what functions may be computed by them. It is not necessary to consider directly all possible functions with various numbers and types of arguments, since the universe of discourse may be narrowed with the use of an important tool known as Gödel numbering. This significantly simplifies the analysis needed to determine the limitations of automatic computation.

Gödel numbering makes it possible to consider, in the development of the theory, exclusively functions with single arguments that are nonnegative integers.

This device is subsequently used to prove that even in this limited area of consideration there are functions that are not computable; i.e., there are problems that cannot be solved with computers. The unsolvability of the important halting problem is further proven.

The argumentation of the proofs is as important as the results themselves, since it is typical for the theory of computability.

1. FUNCTIONS AND THEIR COMPUTABILITY

The theory of computability attempts to establish which functions† can be computed by machines.

A *function* (called also mapping) is a rule that associates with each element x of a set D (called the *domain* of the function) a single element y of a set R (called the *range* of the function). The element x is called the argument; and the element y, the value of the function for this argument. These notions are illustrated in Fig. 11–1.

---

† Note that the term "function" is used here with a meaning somewhat different from that used in programming languages.

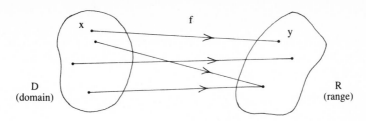

FIGURE 11-1. A function $y = f(x)$, where y is the value of f for the argument x

A function may be specified as a collection of ordered pairs (x, y) or as a procedure for the computation of the value for all arguments.

EXAMPLE 11-1

(a) The function

$$f(x) = 2x$$

has as its domain and range the set of all real numbers.

(b) The function

$$f(x) = x^2$$

has as its domain the set of all real numbers and as its range the set consisting of 0 and positive numbers.

A function is *computable* if and only if there exists an algorithm (see Chapter 1) that for any x belonging to the set D computes the value of $y = f(x)$. If a function is computable, a program that computes any such value may be implemented.

Related to the computability problem are the problems of enumerability and decidability, both of which may be reduced to computability. A set D of elements with a given property is *enumerable* if and only if there exists an algorithm that either determines that the set is empty or enumerates (lists) all the members of the set. A set D is *decidable* if and only if there exists an algorithm that can determine whether a given element belongs to the set or not. In other words, the problems consist in enumerating all the elements with a particular property (e.g., all even numbers) or deciding whether a given item has the given property.

2. GÖDEL NUMBERING

Through the device called *Gödel numbering* (after its inventor, Kurt Gödel), the considerations of the theory may be limited to the functions with a single argument, whose domain and range are nonnegative integers (also called *natural numbers*). A Gödel numbering is an encoding that converts multiple arguments as well as arguments of other types to a single nonnegative integer. This encoding may be used also to represent the inputs to the procedure that computes the function.

Several nonnegative integers $x_1, x_2, \ldots, x_n$ that are inputs to a procedure may be uniquely represented by a single integer z as follows:

$$z = 2^{x_1} \cdot 3^{x_2} \cdot 5^{x_3} \cdot \ldots \cdot p^{x_n}$$

where $2, 3, \ldots, p$ are the n first prime numbers.

The original numbers $x_1, x_2, \ldots, x_n$ may be recovered from the integer z since every integer has a unique decomposition into primes.

EXAMPLE 11–2

(a) The three inputs

$$x_1 = 4, \quad x_2 = 1, \quad x_3 = 2$$

may be encoded as follows:

$$2^4 \cdot 3^1 \cdot 5^2 = 1200$$

(b) From a Gödel number $z = 140$, the following inputs are uniquely recovered:

$$x_1 = 2, \quad x_2 = 0, \quad x_3 = 1, \quad x_4 = 1$$

since $140 = 2^2 \cdot 5 \cdot 7$

Inputs that are strings of any nature (e.g., real numbers or character data) may be individually encoded into their Gödel numbers with, for example, the use of their character code representations.

3. EXISTENCE OF UNCOMPUTABLE FUNCTIONS

The following argument proves the existence of functions that map nonnegative integers into nonnegative integers and that are not computable.

Let us assume that the set of all such functions over nonnegative integers is enumerable. This means that each function may be assigned a unique integer number: 1, 2, 3 . . . .

Let us then call these functions $F_1, F_2, F_3, \ldots$.

We will now construct another function:

$$H(k) = F_k(k) + 1 \quad \text{for} \quad k = 1, 2, 3, \ldots$$

This function also maps nonnegative integers into nonnegative integers. It is, however, neither one of the functions of the set $F_1, F_2, F_3, \ldots$, since for any k it is by 1 greater than $F_k(k)$.

We have therefore proven by contradiction that the set of all functions over nonnegative integers is not enumerable.

The set of algorithms that may be constructed to compute such functions is, however, enumerable. For example, each such algorithm (or procedure), treated as a string of symbols, may be assigned its unique Gödel number, which proves the point.

We conclude, therefore, that there are more functions over nonnegative integers than there are algorithms available to compute them. This proves the existence of functions that cannot be computed.

4. THE HALTING PROBLEM AS AN EXAMPLE OF AN UNSOLVABLE PROBLEM

The theory of computability has established many negative results, that is, has identified functions that cannot be computed or, in other words, problems that cannot be solved by machines.

A most important unsolvable problem (i.e., proven not to have automatic solution) is the halting problem.

The definition of the *halting problem* is contained in the following theorem: there does not exist an algorithm A that can decide for an arbitrary program P and input I whether the program P will stop when presented with this input.

The usefulness of such an (alas, impossible) algorithm in computing would be obvious.

The following argument proves the unsolvability of the halting problem. To represent algorithms, procedures resembling functions of programming languages are used; i.e., a value is assigned to the name of the procedure and is treated as a variable name in this respect.

Let us assume that we indeed have a procedure HALT that is the solution to the halting problem. The procedure, in pseudocode, looks as follows:†

```
Procedure HALT (<P, I>)
begin
        statements that determine whether P(I) halts;
        if P(I) halts then
                HALT←1
        else
                HALT←0
end
```

If such a procedure exists, we can also define the following procedure:

```
Procedure INVERT (Z)
begin
    while HALT (<Z, Z>) = 1 do
            INVERT←1; * OR ANOTHER ASSIGNMENT TO INVERT *
        INVERT←0; * ALSO ANY ASSIGNMENT TO INVERT WOULD DO *
end
```

†In further discussion, the angle brackets $<>$ stand for the Gödel encoding, e.g., $<P, I>$ is the Gödel number of P, I.

We may easily obtain the Gödel encoding of the procedure INVERT; let us assume it to be X.

Let us submit the Gödel number $<X, X>$ as the input to the procedure HALT. The result of the execution of the procedure HALT should be:

$$HALT (<X, X>) = \begin{cases} 1 \text{ if INVERT (X) halts} \\ \\ 0 \text{ if INVERT (X) does not halt} \end{cases}$$

However, considering the procedure INVERT, if HALT $(<X, X>) = 1$, then the **while-do** statement constitutes an infinite loop and the procedure INVERT does not halt!

Since we were able to find a procedure INVERT for which the halting problem cannot be solved, no general-purpose program that would decide on the termination of other programs for an arbitrary input is possible.

Another important example of an unsolvable problem is the so-called *equivalence problem,* namely, there is no program that can determine for two arbitrary other programs whether they are equivalent (i.e., whether they compute the same function). Like many other theorems on the theory of computability, this is proven by reduction to the halting problem. In other words, such proof amounts to establishing that if the given problem were solvable, the halting problem would also be solvable.

5. COMPUTATIONAL COMPLEXITY

The theory of computability is complemented by the study of *computational complexity,* the investigation of run time and memory space required for the solution of major classes of problems. This theory has established a number of bounds on such resource requirements and thus guides the programmer on the design of better algorithms.

An example of such a result is that the sorting of n items requires as a minimum on the order of $n\log_2 n$ comparison operations.

B. TURING MACHINES

In order to determine the computability of functions it is necessary to have a precise mathematical definition of algorithms. No such precision is possible with real computers (refer to Part One for the description of such algorithms, which is far from precise).

A number of theoretical constructs have been devised in which an exact definition of computation and of an algorithm is possible. The best known are the Turing machines; others include Markov algorithms, lambda calculus, and the theory of recursive functions.

A Turing machine is the most powerful of automata. An *automaton* is an idealized machine for information processing whose actions are specified in mathematical terms. What has become known as Turing machines was introduced by the British logician Alan Turing in 1936 and thus preceded the development of general-purpose electronic computers. A conjecture (as such it cannot be proved, but strong evidence exists in its favor), known as *Church's thesis* claims that a function is computable if and only if it can be computed by a Turing machine or a construct of an equivalent power. Thus, the power of these, as it would appear, "simple" machines is equivalent to the power of computers.

A Turing machine is an automaton that consists of a control unit, a tape, and a read/write head (see Fig. 11–2) together with the program designed for it.

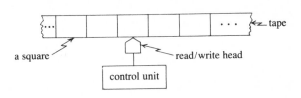

FIGURE 11–2. A Turing machine

The control unit of a Turing machine holds the information concerning the current state of the machine. A Turing machine can be in one of the finite number of states, determined by the algorithm, called a Turing machine program. A state reflects the past history of the computation due to the given program. The program is assumed to be "built into" the control unit.

The tape of a Turing machine serves as its memory and input/output device. It consists of an infinite number of squares, each containing a single symbol. Only a finite number of squares may contain the information needed by any computation; the rest of the squares are assumed to contain a special symbol, called a blank.

The machine is able to read and write information from a single square at a time, namely, the square pointed to by the read/write head. The read/write head moves from one square to the adjacent one as directed by the program and transmits the information between the tape and the control unit. The tape initially contains the input presented to the machine, is subsequently used as the working storage, and ultimately provides the output.

The algorithm to be followed by a Turing machine is called its program. This is a set of instructions ("rules") of a very restricted type. The machine carries out an instruction as a single step. Every instruction has the form of a quintuple; i.e., it consists of five ordered elements. Each quintuple specifies the action to be taken if the machine is in a given state, with the read/write head pointing to a given symbol. The action may consist of changing the symbol, moving one square left or right, changing the state, or a combination of these.

Quintuples have the following general form (although notational variations abound):

$$q_i, t_i, t_j, d_j, q_j$$

where

q_i is the present state of the machine;
t_i is the tape symbol read by the read/write head;
t_j is the tape symbol to replace the one being read
    (possibly, $t_i = t_j$, i.e., the read symbol is not replaced);
d_j is the prescribed direction of head movement
    (R for right, L for left, N for no move);
q_j is the state to be assumed next by the machine.

A quintuple should be interpreted as follows:

if $q_i, t_i,$ **then**
    t_j, d_j, q_j
else
        this quintuple does not presently apply

The flow of control within the program is accomplished by the machine selecting the quintuple that applies in the current state with the given symbol under its head.

The states are denoted as $q_0, q_1, \ldots, q_n$ and HALT. At least in one quintuple the next state symbol ought to be HALT to provide for the termination of the computation.

To describe a Turing machine, the following has to be specified:

the set of tape symbols, called the tape alphabet
    (it always includes the blank symbol);
the initial state of the machine;
the representation of the input data on the tape;
the initial position of the head;
the representation of the output(s) on the tape;
the program itself.

The following examples present two Turing machines.

EXAMPLE 11-3
    Problem
Design a Turing machine to increment any natural number (nonnegative integer) by 1.
    Solution
tape alphabet: b (blank), 1
initial state: q_0

input and output representation: an integer M is represented by M + 1 consecutive 1's (this is a typical representation, since it represents 0 as a single 1, to avoid having totally blank tape).

initial head position: anywhere to the left of the number.

The program	Comments
q_0, b, b, R, q_0	keep moving right while b under head
q_0, 1, 1, L, q_1	the number is reached
q_1, b, 1, N, HALT	in state q_1 the head is certainly pointing to b

Notes

1. Observe how the "transfer of control" from the first to the second quintuple occurs.
2. Note that when $q_i = q_j$, we may have a loop; in our case, the first quintuple is such a construct.
3. Note the necessity of having at least two states.
4. How would the program be modified, if the head were to start at the leftmost 1?

EXAMPLE 11-4

Problem

Design a Turing machine to add two natural numbers.

Solution

tape alphabet: b, 1

initial state: q_0

input representation: integers N and M are represented by N + 1 and M + 1 consecutive 1's respectively; the two integers are separated by a single b.

initial head position: at the leftmost 1 of the leftmost number

output representation: integer K, represented by K + 1 consecutive 1's.

Program

initial head position:

$$...bb111b11b...$$
$$\uparrow$$

head and tape after every step:

q_0, 1, 1, R, q_0	...bb111b11b...	move to reach separating b
	$\rightarrow\uparrow$	
q_0, b, 1, R, q_1	...bb111111b...	replace separating b by 1
	$\uparrow$	
q_1, 1, 1, R, q_1	...bb111111b...	
	$\rightarrow\uparrow$	reach the rightmost 1
q_1, b, b, L, q_2	...bb111111b...	
	$\uparrow$	
q_2, 1, b, L, q_3	...bb11111bb...	delete the rightmost 1
	$\uparrow$	
q_3, 1, b, N, HALT	...bb1111bbb...	delete the second rightmost 1
	$\uparrow$	

Notes

1. Note that the answer is K = 3, which indeed equals the original 2 + 1.
2. Check that the program works for special cases, for example, 0 + 0.
3. Which decisions in the writing of this program were necessary and which arbitrary?

While each computation requires a different Turing machine, a *universal Turing machine* exists that is able to simulate any other Turing machine. Thus, the tape of a universal Turing machine fulfills Church's thesis by being able to compute any computable function.

A given problem is solvable, that is, there exists an algorithm for its solution, if and only if, when this algorithm is presented as a program for a Turing machine, the machine halts. There is, of course, as shown above, no general algorithm that would establish this for an arbitrary program: the halting problem is undecidable.

C. FORMAL LANGUAGES

Languages are characterized by their syntax and semantics. Language syntax, which lends itself to a formal definition, permits the classification of the language as belonging to one of the four categories of the so-called Chomsky hierarchy of formal languages. The richness of natural languages surpasses, however, the possibility of such formal definition, while higher level programming languages can be approximated by the so-called context-free grammars of the hierarchy. A compiler for the language so defined may use this definition to parse programs.

1. SYNTAX AND SEMANTICS

Both natural and programming languages may be described by their two aspects: syntax and semantics. *Syntax* is the grammar of the language: it defines which strings of characters are valid constructs in the language. The syntax of a programming language determines which of the programs that are written in it are valid. *Semantics* defines the meaning of the language constructs. Even though a program may be syntactically correct, if its meaning is other than that intended by the programmer, the result of its execution will usually not be a solution to the problem.

EXAMPLE 11–5

In a natural language, English, the following two sentences have identical syntactic structure but certainly different meaning: A DOG BIT A MAN vs. A MAN BIT A DOG.

The syntax of artificial languages, such as programming languages, is restricted in comparison to natural languages, since all ambiguity is to be avoided.

To make computer processing of languages (programming languages today and, maybe, natural languages in the future) possible, a formal theory of languages has been constructed. The primary concern of these mathematical linguistics is language syntax, since no formal means of completely specifying semantics exists.

2. DESCRIPTION AND DERIVATION OF FORMAL LANGUAGES

A *formal language,* called below simply a language, is a set of strings formed by the concatenation (i.e., writing next to one another) of a finite number of symbols of the language in accordance with the rules specified for this language.

The set of all symbols that may appear in the strings of a language is the *alphabet* of the language.

According to these definitions, the following is considered a language:

$$L_1 = \left\{ x + y \mid y + x \right\}$$

over the alphabet x, y, +.

In the above notation:

L_1 is the name of the language;
braces: $\{$ and $\}$, contain the list of the strings of the language;
the symbol $\mid$ separates the individual strings and has the meaning of "or".

Thus this language L_1 consists of two strings only: $x + y$ and $y + x$.

An important distinction exists between the symbols of the language being described (in this case, the symbols x, y, +), and the symbols used to describe it ($\{$,$\}$, $\mid$). The latter set of symbols does not belong to the alphabet of the described language; it is said to belong to a *metalanguage* used for the description of other languages.

Such description specifies the rules according to which the strings of the language are formed. In order to be able to describe infinite languages (with an infinite number of strings, each of finite length) or, in general, languages with many strings, this notation has to be extended.

In the metalanguage used to specify the following language:

$$L_2 = \left\{ x^m + y^n \mid m \geqslant 1, n \geqslant 1 \right\}$$

the power symbols m and n signify that an arbitrary number of x and y symbols may appear in the strings of the language. Since m may differ from n, the numbers of x's in a string may differ from the number of y's. The symbol | is used here instead of the word "where"(and not "or"!) and the limitations on m and n following it specify that at least one x and one y are to appear in any valid string.

For example, according to the above specification, the following strings belong to the language L_2:

$$xxx + yy, x + y, x + yyyyy$$

while the following do not:

xy (+ has to separate x and y);
$x+$ ($n = 0$)

A fruitful alternative way to specify a language is by presenting its grammar. The grammar is built around the rules for generating all the strings of the language. These strings are obtained (generated) by a consecutive application of these rewriting rules (called also productions).

A *grammar* of a language consists of:

terminal symbols: the symbols that may appear in the strings of the language (i.e., belong to its alphabet);
nonterminal symbols: used only in the intermediate constructs during the generation of a string by the application of productions;
the *sentence symbol:* a selected nonterminal symbol, used to start the generation of all of the strings of the language;
productions (rewriting rules) of the general form:

$$\text{string-1} \rightarrow \text{string-2}$$

which means that the left-hand string may be replaced by the right-hand string.

Generation of a string of a language defined by the given grammar proceeds as follows:

(1) A production whose left-hand side is the sentence symbol (usually denoted S) is used first. Such a production (or several such productions) is always part of the grammar.
(2) A production may be applied to an intermediate string if the left-hand side of the production appears in this string. Such productions are applied, and thus a sequence of intermediate strings is obtained.
(3) The generation of the string is completed when no production can be applied to it. If this string contains only terminal symbols of the language, this is one of its strings.

Therefore, a string of a language is generated through a sequence of intermediate strings, called the *derivation* of this string. To connect the strings used in the derivation, the double arrow ($\rightarrow$) symbol is used.

EXAMPLE 11-6

Problem

Let us determine what language is defined by the following grammar.
terminal symbols: x, y, $+$
nonterminal symbols: S, T
the sentence symbol: S
productions:

$S \rightarrow x$
$S \rightarrow x + T$
$T \rightarrow x + y$

Solution

Either of the productions whose left-hand side is S may be applied initially.
The first of these results in the derivation

$S \Rightarrow x$

The second leads to the derivation

$S \Rightarrow x + T \Rightarrow x + x + y$

Therefore, the language is

$$L = \left\{ x \mid x + x + y \right\}$$

EXAMPLE 11-7

Problem

In the grammar of the Example 11-6, let us replace the productions by the following:

$S \rightarrow x$
$S \rightarrow S + y$

Let us determine the language so defined.

Solution

The first production generates the string x. If the second production is applied initially, we obtain:

$S \Rightarrow S + y \Rightarrow S + y + y \Rightarrow S + y + y + y \Rightarrow \ldots$

Then, by applying the first production we obtain any string of the following form:

$x + y + y + \ldots + y$

This infinite language may be described as:

$$L = \left\{ xZ^m \mid Z = + y, m \geqslant 0 \right\}$$

A production whose left-hand side string is contained in its right-hand side string is recursive: the substitution is "defined" partially in terms of itself. The second production in the Example 11–7 is of this kind.

3. CLASSIFICATION OF FORMAL LANGUAGES

A classification of formal languages based on the nature of the productions of their grammar was introduced by Noam Chomsky in 1959.

This classification established the hierarchy of formal languages, with these placed lower constituting a subset of the higher ones. Starting from the top, the following types of languages are distinguished:

(1) unrestricted languages, with any type of productions included in their grammar; even these fail to reflect the complexity of natural languages, although they most closely approximate them;

(2) context-sensitive languages, a model that encompasses programming languages but is rarely used due to the difficulty of manipulation;

(3) context-free languages, the most important category, since it closely approximates higher level programming languages and is rather easily manipulated; these are further discussed below;

(4) regular languages, as a very restricted type of formal languages.

This classification of languages applies also to their grammar.

Formal languages are related to automata (see Chapter 11–B) in that an automaton (a theoretical machine) of a particular complexity is needed to establish whether a string is a member of the language with a given grammar. Automata, analyzed from this point of view, are called acceptors for the strings of a language. Turing machines, as the most complex of automata, recognize the strings of unrestricted languages.

4. CONTEXT-FREE GRAMMARS AND THEIR ROLE IN COMPILERS

Context-free grammars are particularly important in the translation of higher level programming languages. Together with some additional rules, they may form the basis for the parser section of a compiler (see Chapter 6–B–2).

The productions of a context-free grammar are restricted to the form:

a single nonterminal symbol → a nonempty string

This means that in a derivation, symbols are never deleted from the previously generated intermediate string. The substitution of strings is performed without regard to the strings that surround it.

EXAMPLE 11-8

The following are the productions of a context-free grammar:

$S \rightarrow xY$
$Y \rightarrow xZv$
$Z \rightarrow x$

The programming language ALGOL, whose definition constituted an important step in the development of computer science, is almost completely defined by a context-free grammar presented in the so-called *Backus-Naur form* (or *BNF notation*). Since this metalanguage comes close to the full specification of ALGOL, this programming language comes close to being context-free.

In BNF notation, for economy of writing, several productions are often merged into one with the use of the symbol (|) that plays here the role of the connective "or."

The general form of BNF productions is

<N>:= string-1 | string-2 | ... | string-N

where

N is a nonterminal symbol;
string-I is a string, i.e., a concatenation of symbols, some of which may be terminal and some nonterminal;
angle brackets, < and >, serve to delimit the names of the language components (e.g., <expression>, or <logical constant>), i.e., nonterminal symbols.

Such a production presents, therefore, alternative strings that may replace the symbol N.

Consider, for example, the following productions of the BNF notation:

<digit>:= 0 | 1 | 2 | 3 | 4 | 5 | 6 | 7 | 8 | 9   (1)
<unsigned integer>:=<digit> | <unsigned integer> | <digit>   (2)
<integer>:=<unsigned integer> | +<unsigned integer> |
                                               −<unsigned integer>   (3)

The number −73 may be derived using these productions as follows (applicable productions are shown above the arrows):

$\langle integer \rangle \overset{(3)}{\Rightarrow} -\langle unsigned\ integer \rangle \overset{(2)}{\Rightarrow} -\langle unsigned\ integer \rangle$
$\langle digit \rangle \overset{(2)}{\Rightarrow} -\langle digit \rangle \langle digit \rangle \overset{(1)}{\Rightarrow} -7\langle digit \rangle \overset{(1)}{\Rightarrow} -73$

In a compiler the reverse process, that of identifying a program construct as valid, is important. During the syntactic analysis phase, the parse tree (form of a derivation) is produced as shown in Fig. 11–3.

A syntax-driven parser recognizes a string (e.g., a program or a particular statement) as a member of the language, i.e., a syntactically valid construct.

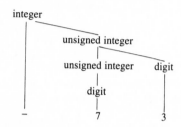

FIGURE 11–3. A parse tree

SUGGESTIONS FOR FURTHER READING

Denning, P. J., Dennis, J. B., and Qualitz, J. E.: *Machines, Languages, and Computation,* Prentice-Hall, Englewood Cliffs, N.J., 1978
An excellent and thorough textbook.

Kain, R. Y.: *Automata Theory: Machines and Languages,* McGraw-Hill, New York, 1972.
The author is striving for intuitive explanations.

Kurki-Suonio, R.: *A Programmer's Introduction to Computability and Formal Languages,* Auerbach, Princeton, N.J., 1971.
Terse and intuitive.

Hopcroft, J. E., and Ullman, J. D.: *Introduction to Automata Theory, Language, and Computation,* Addison-Wesley, Reading, Mass., 1979.
A widely recognized advanced text.

Aho, A. V., Hopcroft, J. E., and Ullman, J. D.: *The Design and Analysis of Computer Algorithms,* Addison-Wesley, Reading, Mass., 1974.
Analysis of algorithmic complexity.

Hantler, S. L., and King, J. C.: An Introduction to Proving the Correctness of Programs, in *ACM Computing Surveys,* Vol. 8, No. 3, September 1976.
Not discussed in the present book, this is an emerging area of theoretical computer science.

Appendix A
REPRESENTATION OF NUMERICAL DATA IN COMPUTER MEMORY

Numerical data are represented in the computer memory by finite numbers of bits. An integer or a real number is usually represented in a single word, usually from 8 to 64 bits long, depending on the computer model.

Since the numbers are stored in binary form, the knowledge of this radix system is useful to a higher level language programmer and necessary to an assembly language programmer. Conversions between the decimal system, used by humans, and the binary system, utilized in computers, are also of interest. As convenient shorthands for binary number representation, octal and hexadecimal systems are also used by programmers.

Two methods of binary number representation are employed in computers: fixed-point mode (predominantly to represent integers) and floating-point mode (to represent real numbers). As a floating-point number, a binary number is represented by two values: its mantissa and its exponent.

The obvious signed-magnitude representation of a binary value leads to cumbersome arithmetic algorithms (that are fully or partially implemented in the hardware of the computer). For this reason, the complement number representation is most frequently used; some machines utilize l's complement representation, others—2's complement.

1. RADIX NUMBER SYSTEMS

In *radix* (also called *positional*) number systems, the position of a digit in the number determines its contribution to the overall value.

If an unsigned mixed number N is represented by a string of digits

$$d_m d_{m-1} ... d_2 d_1 d_0 \; . \; d_{-1} d_{-2} ... d_{-n+1} \, d_{-n}$$

in a radix system with the *radix* (also called *base*) r, the value of this number is

$$N = d_m r^m + ... + d_2 r^2 + d_1 r^1 + d_0 r^0 + d_{-1} r^{-1} + d_{-2} r^{-2} + ... + d_{-n} r^{-n} \qquad (1)$$

and the value of digit d_i is $0 \leqslant d_i \leqslant r-1$

The point, placed between d_0 and d_{-1}, which divides the number N into its integral and fractional parts is called the *radix point*.

The digits

$$d_m d_{-m-1}...d_2 d_1 d_0$$

constitute the integral part of the mixed number N, and the digits

$$d_{-1} d_{-2}...d_{-n+1} d_{-n}$$

its fractional part.

EXAMPLE A-1

Our familiar decimal system is positional with the radix of 10.

A number that we write simply as 5713.171 is understood by us as

$$5 \times 10^3 + 7 \times 10^2 + 1 \times 10^1 + 3 \times 10^0 + 1 \times 10^{-1} + 7 \times 10^{-2} + 1 \times 10^{-3}$$

Note that digits at our disposal are

$$0 \leqslant d_i \leqslant 9$$

It is technologically convenient to use binary digits (bits) to represent numbers in computer memory. In the binary system, the radix is 2 and the values of bits are 0 or 1.

The binary representation of a number is rather long and therefore inconvenient for programmers to communicate or manipulate. There are two other radix systems that are used by humans as shorthands for the binary representation since the conversions between them and the binary system are very simple.

The first of these is the *octal system*, with the radix of 8 and digits 0, 1, 2, 3, 4, 5, 6, 7.

The other is the *hexadecimal system*, with the radix of 16 and digits: 0, 1, 2, 3, 4, 5, 6, 7, 8, 9, A, B, C, D, E, F. The first six letters of the Latin alphabet are used to represent the decimal values from 10 to 15, since in the hexadecimal system it is necessary to have

$$0 \leqslant d_i \leqslant 15_{10}$$

To avoid confusion, when various radix systems are used, it is customary to denote the radix of the number as its subscript, e.g., 47_{10}, 57_8, $2F_{16}$.

2. RADIX CONVERSION

A programmer often needs to convert a number from one radix system to another.

EXAMPLE A-2

Radix conversion is often required to "read" *memory dumps*, printouts of the contents of various registers and memory locations, helpful in program testing. Such contents are printed in octal representation in some computer systems and in hexadecimal in others.

The most convenient methods of conversion are presented here.

A. BINARY TO DECIMAL CONVERSION

To obtain the decimal value of a binary number, add the powers of 2 corresponding to those bits of the number being converted whose value is 1. This method follows from formula (1) above.

Table A–1 presents the values of 2^{-n} and 2^n for the values of n from 0 to 20. The most frequently used powers should be remembered (say, for $-3 \leqslant n \leqslant 10$).

TABLE A-1.   Values of 2^n and 2^{-n}

2^n	n	2^{-n}
1	0	1.0
2	1	0.5
4	2	0.25
8	3	0.125
16	4	0.062 5
32	5	0.031 25
64	6	0.015 625
128	7	0.007 812 5
256	8	0.003 906 25
512	9	0.001 953 125
1 024	10	0.000 976 562 5
2 048	11	0.000 488 281 25
4 096	12	0.000 244 140 625
8 192	13	0.000 122 070 312 5
16 384	14	0.000 061 035 156 25
32 768	15	0.000 030 517 578 125
65 536	16	0.000 015 258 789 062 5
131 072	17	0.000 007 629 394 531 25
262 144	18	0.000 003 814 697 265 625
524 288	19	0.000 001 907 348 632 812 5
1 048 576	20	0.000 000 953 674 316 406 25

EXAMPLE A-3

Binary number $N = 10110.101$ is to be converted to a decimal. Using Formula (1), we have

$$N = 1 \times 2^4 + 0 \times 2^3 + 1 \times 2^2 + 1 \times 2^1 + 0 \times 2^0 + 1 \times 2^{-1}$$
$$+ 0 \times 2^{-2} + 1 \times 2^{-3}$$
$$= 2^4 + 2^2 + 2^1 + 2^{-1} + 2^{-3}$$

This is the sum of powers of 2 corresponding to the 1-bits of the binary number N. Hence,
$$N = 22.625_{10}$$

B. DECIMAL TO BINARY CONVERSION

To convert a mixed decimal number to binary, the integral and fractional parts are converted separately, and the results are added.

CONVERSION OF AN INTEGER

A decimal integer I has the following binary representation according to Formula (1):

decimal number   binary representation of I

$$I = d_m 2^m + d_{m-1} 2^{m-1} + ... + d_2 2^2 + d_1 2 + d_0 \qquad (2)$$

To convert I to binary, we need to obtain the binary digits $d_m, ..., d_0$.

As can be seen from Formula (2), if a decimal integer I is divided by 2, the binary digit d_0 is the remainder (as a binary digit, it is smaller than 2). The quotient is, according to the right side of (2):

$$I/2 = d_m 2^{m-1} + ... + d_2 2 + d_1$$

The subsequent division by 2 will yield d_1 as the remainder, and so forth. The conversion procedure is then:

(1) Divide the decimal number by 2; the remainder is the rightmost bit of its binary representation.
(2) Keep dividing the quotient by 2 until it equals 0; the remainders are the bits of the binary representation, obtained in the order from right to left.

EXAMPLE A-4
Convert 22_{10} to binary.

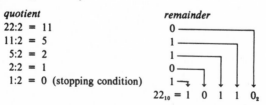

quotient	remainder
22:2 = 11	0
11:2 = 5	1
5:2 = 2	1
2:2 = 1	0
1:2 = 0 (stopping condition)	1

$$22_{10} = 1\ 0\ 1\ 1\ 0_2$$

CONVERSION OF A FRACTION

A decimal fraction F has the following binary representation according to formula (1):

decimal fraction   binary representation of F

$$F = \overbrace{d_{-1}2^{-1} + d_{-2}2^{-2} + ... + d_{-n+1}2^{-n+1} + d_{-n}2^{-n}} \tag{3}$$

To convert F to binary, we need to obtain the binary digits $d_{-1}, ..., d_{-n}$.

As can be seen from Formula (3), if a decimal fraction F is multiplied by 2, the bit d_{-1} is isolated as the only integral binary digit. It constitutes the leftmost bit of the binary representation of F. The procedure is continued until the number is exactly converted or the desired precision has been reached.

The conversion procedure is then: repeatedly multiply the decimal fraction by 2; the integral part of the product constitutes the current bit of the binary representation obtained in the order from left to right; this part is to be disregarded in the next multiplication.

If exact conversion is possible, the fractional part of the decimal number becomes 0 after a number of multiplications. The stopping condition is, therefore, that fractional part of the result be 0 or sufficiently close to 0, or that the desired number of bits be obtained.

EXAMPLE A-5

Convert numbers 0.625 and 0.317 to binary representation either exactly, or with four fractional bits.

(a)

	product		integral part
0.625 × 2 =	1.250		1
0.250 × 2 =	0.500		0
0.500 × 2 =	1.000		1

exact conversion; $0.625_{10} = 0.1 \quad 0 \quad 1_2$

(b)

0.317 × 2 =	0.634		0
0.634 × 2 =	1.268		1
0.268 × 2 =	0.536		0
0.536 × 2 =	1.072		1

four bits (stopping condition); $0.317_{10} = 0.0 \quad 1 \quad 0 \quad 1_2$

Note that the sum-of-powers-of-2 method provides a convenient checking procedure.

To convert a mixed number, add the results of the conversions of its integral and fractional parts.

EXAMPLE A-6

To convert 22.625_{10} to binary, we use the results of Examples A-4 and A-5 and obtain

$$22.625_{10} = 10110.101_2$$

C. CONVERSIONS BETWEEN BINARY AND OCTAL OR HEXADECIMAL SYSTEMS

Conversion of a number from its binary representation to the octal one can be performed by simply grouping bits by three, going in both directions from the radix point.

The last group in a fraction should be completed with 0's, if necessary. Each group of three bits constitutes an octal digit.

EXAMPLE A-7

$$\underbrace{11011}_{3\ \ 3} . \underbrace{1010111}_{5\ \ 3\ \ 4} \overset{00\ \ \text{(completion)}}{}$$

Hence, $11011.1010111_2 = 33.534_8$

Conversion of a binary number to its hexadecimal representation is performed by grouping bits by four going in both directions from the radix point.

The last group in a fraction should be completed with 0's. Each group of four bits constitutes a hexadecimal digit.

EXAMPLE A-8

$$\underbrace{11011}_{1\ \ B} . \underbrace{1010111}_{A\ \ E} \overset{0\ \ \text{(completion)}}{}$$

Hence, $11011.1010111_2 = 1B.AE_{16}$

To convert a number from its octal or hexadecimal representation to binary, octal digits should be written out as the equivalent three bits and hexadecimal digits as equivalent four bits, respectively.

Leading 0's in an integer, and trailing 0's in a fraction, due to conversion, may be subsequently dropped.

EXAMPLE A-9

Convert 346.174_8 to binary.

3	4	6		1	7	4_8
011	100	110		001	111	100

Hence, $346 . 174_8 = 11100110.0011111_2$

Convert $1A.FC_{16}$ to binary.

1	A	.	F	C_{16}
0001	1010		1111	1100

Hence, $1A.FC_{16} = 11010.111111_2$

D. CONVERSIONS BETWEEN DECIMAL AND OCTAL OR HEXADECIMAL SYSTEMS

To convert a number from its octal or hexadecimal representation to the decimal system, the general sum-of-powers-of-radix method based on Formula (1) may be used. The approach is similar to binary-to-decimal conversion.

The digits of the number represented in an octal or hexadecimal system are multiplied by the corresponding powers of the radix, and the results are added.

EXAMPLE A-10

Convert to decimal numbers 346.1_8 and $2A.F_{16}$

$$346.1_8 = 3 \times 8^2 + 4 \times 8 + 6 + 1 \times 8^{-1} = 230.125_{10}$$
$$2A.F_{16} = 2 \times 16 + 10 + 15 \times 16^{-1} = 42.9375_{10}$$

In order to convert a number from the decimal system to the octal or hexadecimal systems, it is convenient to convert it first to the binary system (see Section B above) and subsequently to the target representation by grouping (see Section C above).

3. BINARY ARITHMETIC ON UNSIGNED NUMBERS

Humans perform arithmetic in the binary system in the same way as in any radix system, including decimal. Here the "human way" with binary arithmetic is presented; the computers use more sophisticated representations of binary numbers as discussed later in this appendix.

Bit operations are performed as follows:

addition				subtraction			
0	0	1	1	0	0	1	1
+0	+1	+0	+1	−0	−1	−0	−1
0	1	1	0	0	1	1	0
			carry 1		borrow 1		

multiplication				division	
0	0	1	1	$1:1 = 1$	
×0	×1	×0	×1	$0:1 = 0$	
0	0	0	1		

EXAMPLE A–11

Four operations on binary numbers are presented in the manner they are carried out by humans:

```
  1100.01            1100.01
+ 1010.10          - 1010.10
 10110.11             1.11
```

```
                          101 1.001
      11.00        10.1 ⌐ 11011.1101
    × 10.10              -101
      0000               111
    + 1100              -101
      0000               101
    1100                -101
   111.1000               101
                         -101
```

Particular attention should be devoted to subtraction, which is relatively error-prone. Results may be checked by conversion of them and the operands to the decimal system.

4. FIXED-POINT REPRESENTATION. COMPLEMENTS

To represent integers in computer memory, *fixed-point representation* of binary numbers is usually employed. In such representation the position of the binary point is fixed with respect to the bits. So far as the programmer is concerned, the entire number is an integer although in some machines it is internally treated as a fraction.

The most obvious representation of a signed number in computer memory is the *signed-magnitude representation*. It consists of the bit standing for the sign, followed by the binary value of the number:

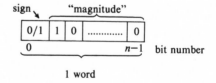

EXAMPLE A–12

In a machine with 8-bit words, the following are the word contents when the words hold fixed-point numbers in the signed-magnitude form:

		sign bit
-90_{10}		11011010
$+105_{10}$		01101001

Bit 0 of the word contains the sign bit; its value is by convention 1 when the number is negative, 0 when positive.

While this representation appears natural, it is not the most desirable one for computer arithmetic.

The addition of signed numbers being a very frequent elementary operation in computer processing, it is desirable to perform the addition of two numbers of opposite sign (or subtraction of two numbers of the same sign) using the same algorithm, which means the same hardware, as this for the addition of two numbers of the same sign.

The possibility of thus performing subtraction by addition is afforded if the numbers are represented in the complement form.

Complement arithmetic has validity throughout the radix number systems. In any such system we can perform the subtraction of a number as an addition of its inverse with respect to the largest number used (called a modulus).

EXAMPLE A–13

In decimal arithmetic, if we are limited to single-digit integers, the inverse with respect to 9 may be used as shown:

$$2 - 5 \equiv 2 + (9 - 5) = 2 + 4 = 6 \equiv 9 - 3$$

where $9 - 5$ is the inverse of 5 and 6 is the inverse of 3. Hence,

$$2 - 5 = -3$$

This example simply illustrates the use of complement arithmetic. A general algorithm for complement addition is presented below for the binary case.

Complement arithmetic has particular appeal in the case of the binary system since to obtain the inverse of a binary number no subtraction is required, only bit inversion. Such operation is simple and fast. Two types of complement arithmetic are in use in the case of the binary system. Some computers use 2's complement arithmetic to manipulate fixed-point numbers, and others use 1's complement.

An addition of two numbers of the same sign may cause *overflow,* with the result being larger than the maximum that can be held in a word of the particular machine. Such a result is invalid.

Multiplication and division of fixed-point numbers are performed by computers as a series of shifts and additions.

A. 1'S COMPLEMENT REPRESENTATION AND ADDITION

To obtain *1's complement* of a binary number the following is necessary:

(1) If the number is positive, its true magnitude is represented with the sign of 0.

(2) If the number is negative, every bit of the number is inverted (complemented) and the sign bit of 1 is appended.

To add two numbers in 1's complement representation:

(1) Add the numbers with the sign bits.

(2) The carry out of the sign bit (called *end-around carry*), if it occurs, should be subsequently added to the rightmost bit of the result.

(3) Overflow occurs if the sign of the result differs from the signs of the addends (which have to be the same for the overflow to take place). In the case of an overflow the result is meaningless.

In computer hardware the alternative method of checking the validity of the result is used: carries into and out of the sign bit are examined; if only one of these occurs, an overflow has taken place.

The result is obtained in its 1's complement representation. This means that if the result is negative (has the sign of 1), to establish its true value we have to invert all its bits. Naturally, in the machine memory the result remains in its 1's complement form.

EXAMPLE A–14

The computer memory has 8-bit-long words. The following operations are to be performed in 1's complement:

(a) $-124 + 67$

	magnitude (7 bits)	1's complements signs	
-124	1111100	1	0000011
67	1000011	+0	1000011
		1	1000110

Check of the result:

true magnitude is $-0111001_2 = -57$

(b) $-12 - 50$

	magnitude (7 bits)	1's complements signs	
-12	0001100	1	1110011
-50	0110010	+1	1001101
		1	1000000
		+	→1 end-around carry
		1	1000001

Check of the result:

true magnitude is $-0111110_2 = -62$

(c) $-55 - 73$

	magnitude (7 bits)		1's complements
		signs	
-55	0110111	1	1001000
-73	1001001	+1	0110110
		0	1111110

changed sign $\rightarrow$ the result is
meaningless due to overflow

B. TWO'S COMPLEMENT REPRESENTÀTION AND ADDITION

To obtain *2's complement* of a binary number the following is necessary:

(1) If the number is positive, its true magnitude is represented with the sign of 0.
(2) If the number is negative, it ought to be complemented (every bit of it inverted) and incremented (1 added to the rightmost bit). The sign bit of 1 is appended.

To add two numbers in 2's complement representation:

(1) Add the numbers with their sign bits; ignore the carry-out of the sign bit, if it occurs.
(2) Overflow occurs if the sign of the result differs from the signs of the addends, which are the same.

To establish the true value of a negative result (with the sign of 1) the simplest procedure is to:

(1) Invert all its bits.
(2) Add 1 to the rightmost bit of the result.

This is simpler than the obvious alternative of subtracting 1 from the result and complementing the difference.

EXAMPLE A-15

With a computer memory of 8-bit-long words, the following operations are to be performed in 2's complement:

(a) $-124 + 67$

	magnitude (7 bits)	2's complement
-124	1111100	0000011
	+	1
		0000100

67	1000011	1000011

addition:

signs	
1	0000100
+0	1000011
1	1000111

Check of the result:

true magnitude is

$$\begin{array}{r} 0111000 \\ +\quad\quad 1 \\ \hline 0111001_2 \end{array} = -57$$

(b) −12 − 50

	magnitude	*2's complement*
−12	0001100	1110011
		+ 1
		1110100
−50	0110010	1001101
		+ 1
		1001110

addition:

signs	
1	1110100
+1	1001110
1	1000010

1 (discard)

Check of the result:

true magnitude is

$$\begin{array}{r} 0111101 \\ +\quad\quad 1 \\ \hline 0111110_2 \end{array} = -62$$

5. FLOATING-POINT REPRESENTATION

Floating-point representation is used to store real numbers in computer memory. It expands the range and precision of the fixed-point representation. The manipulation of numbers so represented is, however, a more complex operation and consequently takes longer.

EXAMPLE A–16

The possibilities of the floating-point number representation may be illustrated by the fact that the IBM/360-370 computers with word length of 32 bits permit:

(1) in the fixed-point mode, to represent any number

$$M \leqslant 2^{31} - 1$$

(2) in the floating-point mode, to represent any number

$$M \leqslant 2^{252} \text{ (approximately)}$$

The floating-point representation of a number corresponds to the so-called scientific notation used sometimes to represent very large and very small numbers. For example,

$$1500 = 0.15 \times 10^4$$
$$0.00015 = 0.15 \times 10^{-3}$$

In this notation, assuming a known radix (10 in the examples above), a number is represented by two values: *mantissa* (also called *fraction*) and *exponent*.

Thus, a number is represented as

mantissa × radix ^{exponent}

In computers, a binary, octal or hexadecimal radix (depending on the machine) is implicit, while the values of the mantissa and exponent are stored. An example of the word format for such storage is shown as

exponent	mantissa
6 bits	10 bits

Both numbers are signed. The mantissa is usually represented in 2's complement.

Floating-point numbers are usually stored in the *normalized* form, with the mantissa being a fraction whose leftmost bit is different from 0 (i.e., in binary representation). Both numbers shown above are normalized.

The length of the mantissa in the number representation determines the precision of a floating-point representation in the given computer; the length of the exponent determines the range of numbers representable.

Overflow occurs during floating-point arithmetic when the value of the positive exponent is too large to be stored in its allotted space; underflow, when the absolute value of a negative exponent is too large (i.e., the number itself is too small to be representable). This is illustrated:

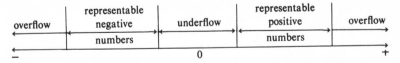

FIGURE A–1. Representability of floating-point numbers

To increase the precision of a floating-point representation, *double precision* (or, in general, multiple precision) floating-point numbers can be stored in some computer models. In this case, a number occupies two consecutive memory words, with the second word holding the extension of the mantissa.

SUGGESTIONS FOR FURTHER READING

Computer arithmetic is discussed in the general texts on computer organization listed in Chapter 8, as well as in:

Loomis, H. H., Jr.: Data Representation, in *Introduction to Computer Architecture*, ed. by H. S. Stone, SRA, Chicago, 1975.

Appendix B
CHARACTER CODES

Two character codes are employed commonly to represent alphanumerical data, special characters, and control characters: American Standard Code for Information Interchange (ASCII), a standard, 7-bit code, and the Extended Binary Coded Decimal Interchange Code (EBCDIC), an 8-bit code developed by IBM. There also exists a nonstandard 8-bit version of the ASCII code. Most computer models employ one of these codes.

1. AMERICAN STANDARD CODE FOR INFORMATION INTERCHANGE (ASCII)

The 7-bit ASCII code is shown in Table B–1. Thus, for example, the code for A is

b_7	b_6	b_5	b_4	b_3	b_2	b_1
1	0	0	0	0	0	1

and the code for blank space (b) is

b_7	b_6	b_5	b_4	b_3	b_2	b_1
0	1	0	0	0	0	0

TABLE B-1. ASCII Code

most significant bits

b4	b3	b2	b1	column→ row↓	0	1	2	3	4	5	6	7
				b7→	0	0	0	0	1	1	1	1
				b6→	0	0	1	1	0	0	1	1
				b5→	0	1	0	1	0	1	0	1
0	0	0	0	0	NUL	DLE	ƀ	0	@	P	`	p
0	0	0	1	1	SOH	DC1	!	1	A	Q	a	q
0	0	1	0	2	STX	DC2	"	2	B	R	b	r
0	0	1	1	3	ETX	DC3	#	3	C	S	c	s
0	1	0	0	4	EOT	DC4	$	4	D	T	d	t
0	1	0	1	5	ENQ	NAK	%	5	E	U	e	u
0	1	1	0	6	ACK	SYN	&	6	F	V	f	v
0	1	1	1	7	BEL	ETB	'	7	G	W	g	w
1	0	0	0	8	BS	CAN	(	8	H	X	h	x
1	0	0	1	9	HT	EM	)	9	I	Y	i	y
1	0	1	0	10	LF	SUB	★	:	J	Z	j	z
1	0	1	1	11	VT	ESC	+	;	K	[	k	{
1	1	0	0	12	FF	FS	,	<	L	\	l	¦
1	1	0	1	13	CR	GS	—	=	M	]	m	}
1	1	1	0	14	SO	RS	.	>	N	∧	n	~
1	1	1	1	15	SI	US	/	?	O	—	o	DEL

least significant bits

NUL Null	DLE Data Link Escape (CC)
SOH Start of Heading (CC)	DC1 Device Control 1
STX Start of Text (CC)	DC2 Device Control 2
ETX End of Text (CC)	DC3 Device Control 3
EOT End of Transmission (CC)	DC4 Device Control 4 (Stop)
ENQ Enquiry (CC)	NAK Negative Acknowledge (CC)
ACK Acknowledge (CC)	SYN Synchronous Idle (CC)
BEL Bell (audible or attention signal)	ETB End of Transmission Block (CC)
BS Backspace (FE)	CAN Cancel
HT Horizontal Tabulation (punched card skip) (FE)	EM End of Medium
	SUB Substitute
LF Line Feed (FE)	ESC Escape
VT Vertical Tabulation (FE)	FS File Separator (IS)
FF Form Feed (FE)	GS Group Separator (IS)
CR Carriage Return (FE)	RS Record Separator (IS)
SO Shift Out	US Unit Separator (IS)
SI Shift In	DEL Delete

CC: Communication control

FE: Format effector

IS: Information separator

2. EXTENDED BINARY CODED DECIMAL INTERCHANGE CODE (EBCDIC)

The 8-bit EBCDIC code is shown in Table B–2.

TABLE B–2. EBCDIC Code

least significant bits

most significant bits

	0000	0001	0010	0011	0100	0101	0110	0111	1000	1001	1010	1011	1100	1101	1110	1111
0000	NUL				PF	HT	LC	DEL	EOM							
0001				TM	RES	NL	BS	IDL			CC					
0010	DS	SOS	FS		BYP	LF	EOB	PRE			SM					
0011					PN	RS	UC	EOT								
0100	ƀ										¢	.	<	(	+	|
0101	&										!	$	*	)	;	¬
0110	–	/									,	%	_	>	?	
0111											:	#	@	'	=	"
1000		a	b	c	d	e	f	g	h	i						
1001		j	k	l	m	n	o	p	q	r						
1010			s	t	u	v	w	x	y	z						
1011																
1100		A	B	C	D	E	F	G	H	I						
1101		J	K	L	M	N	O	P	Q	R						
1110			S	T	U	V	W	X	Y	Z						
1111	0	1	2	3	4	5	6	7	8	9						

PF	Punch Off	LC	Lower Case	EM	End of Message
RES	Reader Stop	BS	Backspace	SM	Set Mode
BYP	Bypass	EOB	End of Block	DS	Digit Select
PN	Punch On	UC	Upper Case	SOS	Start of Significance
HT	Horizontal Tab	DEL	Delete	FS	Field Separator
NL	New Line	IDL	Idle	TM	Tape Mark
LF	Line Feed	PRE	Prefix	CC	Cursor Control
RS	Reader Stop	EOT	End of Transmission		

Thus, for example, the code for A is 11000001, and the code for a blank space (ƀ) is 01000000.

APPENDIX C
BOOLEAN ALGEBRA
AND COMPUTER LOGIC

Boolean algebra† is a calculus of binary variables. Its operations and the rules governing them serve to manipulate these variables in the same manner as "ordinary" algebra is used to operate on real numbers with their infinite set of values.

Extensive use of Boolean algebra in computing stems from the fact that the information transmitted in computer circuits and stored in them is represented by two values. These values may be variously interpreted: as 1 and 0, or **True** and **False**, or *on* and *off* switch positions.

Three essential interpretations of Boolean algebra are presented here, with particular consideration of its application in the computer logic design.

1. BASIC FUNCTIONS AND RULES OF BOOLEAN ALGEBRA

Boolean (also called *logical*) *variables* may assume one of two values. A variable may represent:

(a) a *proposition,* i.e., a statement that is either true or false; e.g., "the cover of this book is blue" or "this book has 300 pages" are propositions

(b) a *switching variable,* a signal in a digital circuit whose values are interpreted as either 0 or 1; e.g., a carry-out of a bit or an interrupt signal.

The most important operations of Boolean algebra, i.e., functions of logical variables, are presented in Table C–1.

Table C–1 is an example of a *truth table,* a tabular enumeration of all possible inputs (values of the operands) and their corresponding outputs (values of the function).

† Proposed by the English mathematician George Boole in the mid-19th century.

TABLE C–1. Essential functions of logical variables

OPERANDS		OPERATIONS AND SYMBOLIC OPERATORS					
		NOT	OR	AND	EXCLUSIVE OR	NOR	NAND
X	Y	$\bar{X}$	X+Y	X·Y or XY	X $\oplus$ Y	X ↓ Y	X ↑ Y
0	0	1	0	0	0	1	1
0	1	1	1	0	1	0	1
1	0	0	1	0	1	0	1
1	1	0	1	1	0	0	0

The only unary operation (i.e., acting on a single operand) is the negation NOT, which produces the complement of the operand.

The operations OR (called *logical addition* and denoted also $\vee$) and AND (called *logical multiplication* and denoted also $\wedge$) have the meanings familiar from everyday usage.

EXAMPLE C–1

Denoting the proposition "the cover of this book is blue" as X, and the proposition "this book has 300 pages" as Y, the proposition "this book has 300 pages and a blue cover" is true *only* if both X and Y are true; on the other hand, for the proposition "this book has 300 pages or a blue cover" to be true, it is sufficient that either X or Y be true.

The EXCLUSIVE OR function of the variables is true when the values of the variables differ. The NAND function may be thought of as AND followed by NOT; NOR, as OR followed by NOT.

Using Boolean variables and operators, *Boolean expressions* may be formed. These express more complex logical propositions or conditions.

The following order of precedence (unless modified with parentheses) applies, starting with the highest:

(1) NOT
(2) AND, NAND
(3) OR, EXCLUSIVE OR, NOR.

To manipulate these expressions, some properties of Boolean algebra have been postulated and others derived from them. The essential properties have been brought together in Table C–2.

TABLE C-2. Essential properties of Boolean algebra

Name of Property	IDENTITY	
	expressed with OR, NOT	expressed with AND, NOT
Commutative	$X + Y = Y + X$	$X \cdot Y = Y \cdot X$
Associative	$\cdot (X + Y) + Z = X + (Y + Z)$	$(X \cdot Y) \cdot Z = X \cdot (Y \cdot Z)$
Distributive	$X \cdot (Y + Z) = X \cdot Y + X \cdot Z$	$X + (Y \cdot Z) = (X + Y) \cdot (X + Z)$
Involution		$\overline{(\bar{X})} = X$
Idempotency	$X + X = X$	$X \cdot X = X$
Complement	$X + \bar{X} = 1$	$X \cdot \bar{X} = 0$
Absorption	$X + X \cdot Y = X$	$X \cdot (X + Y) = X$
De Morgan's	$\overline{(X + Y)} = \bar{X} \, \bar{Y}$	$\overline{(X \cdot Y)} = \bar{X} + \bar{Y}$
Zero element	$X + 0 = X$	$X \cdot 0 = 0$
One element	$X + 1 = 1$	$X \cdot 1 = X$

2. USE OF BOOLEAN ALGEBRA IN COMPUTING

Boolean algebra is used in computing in three following guises:

A. PROPOSITIONAL ALGEBRA

Logical variables are used to represent propositions encountered in algorithm design. Both higher and low level programming languages offer logical operations that manipulate such variables.

The following examples show two characteristic applications of logical variables and expressions. (We will use **not, and, or** to denote the functions.)

> **EXAMPLE C-2**
>
> (a) Use of logical expressions to control the program execution flows is exemplified by the following statement:
>
> **if** AGE $>$ 50 **and** PAY $>$ 500 **or** AGE $>$ 55 **then**
>
> .
> .
> .
>
> **else**
>
> .
> .
> .
>
> (b) If the language offers the data of **Logical** type, the use of such data in assignment statements is possible.
>
> Only one bit is needed to store a logical variable (**True** corresponds to 1, **False** to 0). This results in significant memory savings in some cases.

```
* DATA REPRESENT 1000 EMPLOYEES, SOME OF WHOM
* SUBSCRIBE TO THE COMPANY ORGAN
* SEX — 1 FOR FEMALES, 0 FOR MALES
* SUBSCR — 1 FOR SUBSCRIBERS
* SELECT — 1 FOR SELECTED EMPLOYEES
Logical SEX(1000), SUBSCR(1000), SELECT(1000)
Integer AGE(1000), PAY(1000)
        .
        .
        .


* SELECT FEMALE SUBSCRIBERS EARNING OVER $500 AND
* MALE SUBSCRIBERS OVER 25
I ← 1;
while      I ≤ 1000 do
     begin
          SELECT(I)← SUBSCR(I) and (SEX(I) and
               PAY(I) > 500 or not SEX(I) and AGE(I) > 25);
          I ← I + 1
     end
```

B. ALGEBRA OF CLASSES

Logical variables are used to represent the belonging (1) or not belonging (0) of an object to a particular set (class). This interpretation is often used in theoretical computer science.

C. SWITCHING ALGEBRA

Presence or absence of a signal (corresponding to the "signal" of 1 or 0) in a circuit, or a "stored" bit of 0 or 1 in a memory cell may be represented as a logical variable, in this case, called a switching variable. The general properties of Boolean algebra may therefore be applied to the design of such circuits.

3. COMPUTER LOGIC

Computer logic, the circuitry that processes and stores binary information, is designed with the aid of switching algebra.

Basic logic circuits, called *gates,* implement Boolean functions. A gate is an electronic switch or a combination of switches equal to the number of inputs. A "closed" switch transmits the signal whose presence corresponds to 1; and "open" switch leads to the absence of signal, a logical 0.

EXAMPLE C-3

The OR gate may be considered a parallel connection of switches [see Fig. C–1(a)], while the AND gate corresponds to a series connection [see Fig. C–1(b)].

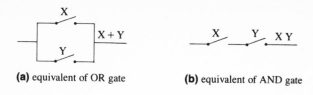

(a) equivalent of OR gate   **(b)** equivalent of AND gate

FIGURE C–1.   Action of gates

The standard representations of gates are shown in Fig. C–1. All gates but NOT may have more than two inputs; the actual number of inputs, called *fan-in,* is limited by the consideration of actual electronic circuitry.

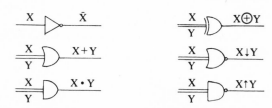

FIGURE C–2.   Gate symbols

Some gates, or combinations of gates, form a *functionally complete set.* This means that any logical function may be designed with the exclusive use of such gates. Such sets are

(1) OR, NOT
(2) AND, NOT } usually OR, AND, NOT are used for better design
(3) NAND
(4) NOR

Combinational switching circuits are logical circuits without memory elements: their outputs depend only on the present inputs. They are built exclusively of gates such as in Fig. C–2, without closed loops.

Their design is carried out in the following steps:

(1) The circuit input/output behavior is specified in the truth table.
(2) An optimization procedure, based on the properties of Boolean algebra, is used to optimize the design. The criteria of optimality depend on the limitations imposed by the actual electronics.
(3) The circuit is specified.

The use of a truth table to obtain the circuit specification is illustrated by the following example.

EXAMPLE C-4

Problem

Design a *half-adder*: a circuit that accepts as inputs 2 bits and produces their sum and the carry, if necessary. (Such a circuit may be used to add the least significant bits of two numbers.)

Solution

The truth table for the 2 output bits, S (sum) and C (carry) is shown below. X and Y are input bits.

X	Y	C	S
0	0	0	0
0	1	0	1
1	0	0	1
1	1	1	0

Circuit optimization is beyond the scope of this book (this circuit cannot be optimized, anyhow).

To derive the logical expression for the circuit directly from the truth table, the following procedure is used.

For every output bit:

(1) consider only the rows where the output has the value of 1; this output will be 1 if *either* (OR gate if more than one 1 is present) of the combinations expressed by these rows will occur;

(2) for a combination expressed by any row to occur, *all* (AND gate) of these imputs must have specified values; i.e., the inputs whose value is 0 have to be inverted.

This procedure leads to the so-called sum-of-products, two-level (AND-OR) representation of the circuit.

In our example,

$$S = \bar{X}Y + X\bar{Y}$$
$$C = XY$$

The circuit is specified as shown in Fig. C-3.

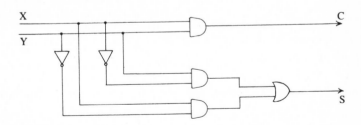

FIGURE C-3. Half-adder

Sequential switching circuits include memory elements, and their output at any time is determined not only by the present inputs but also by the contents of the memory, i.e., by past inputs.

The basic memory unit is a flip-flop, capable of storing a single bit. The contents of the memory determine the state of the circuit, since its reaction (outputs) to given inputs depends on these contents. Therefore, the contents of a flip-flop are referred to in switching theory as a *state variable*.

There exist several flip-flop designs, all of them consisting of two gates with a feedback. Flip-flops retain their state (0 or 1), remembering it, indefinitely, until an input signal changes this state.

For example, a *trigger* flip-flop with its block-diagram and *transition table*, showing input/output relationships, is presented in Fig. C–4.

INPUT T	CURRENT STATE Q ("stored value")	NEXT STATE Q′	
0	0	0	no change
0	1	1	of state
1	0	1	change
1	1	0	of state

FIGURE C–4. Trigger and its transition table

Note that both the state variable Q and its complement Q̄ are available as outputs.

The transition table confirms that the trigger may serve as a memory cell, since:

(1) when the input is 0, the state is preserved ("remembered");
(2) the state may be changed by presenting the input of 1.

Examples of sequential switching circuits are registers, counters, and the CPU itself.

In general, a sequential switching circuit may be represented as shown in Fig. C–5.

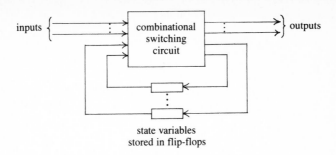

inputs combinational switching circuit outputs

state variables
stored in flip-flops

FIGURE C-5. General representation of a sequential switching circuit

The physical implementation of computer logic changes with technological progress. A typical gate has about half a dozen electronic components, such as transistors, diodes, resistors, etc. Today, most logic circuits are manufactured in the form of *integrated circuits* combining, in the case of large-scale integration over 100 gates (and sometimes hundreds of thousands) on a semiconductor chip of 0.15 in².

SUGGESTIONS FOR FURTHER READING

Dietmeyer, D. L.: *Logic Design of Digital Systems,* 2nd ed., Allyn and Bacon, Boston, 1978.
Kohavi, Z.: *Switching and Finite Automata Theory,* 2nd ed., McGraw-Hill, New York, 1978.

Index

Abacus, 4
Absolute addressing, 140, 154
Absolute code, 162
Acceptor, 230
Access:
  methods, 199, 203–5, 215
  time, 171, 173–74, 176
Activation record, 87
Ada, 127
Address, 10, 138, 171
  arithmetic, 153
  space, 138, 158
Addressing, operand, 140, 153–58,
  168–69
ALGOL, 31, 68, 70, 72, 77, 79–81, 83,
  85, 87, 124, 127, 231
ALGOL 68, 69, 124
Algorithm, 8, 15, 17–21, 69, 94, 99,
  219
Alphabet of formal language, 227
Alphanumeric characters, 27
and, 39–40, 251
APL, 124, 125, 193
Architecture, computer, 137
Argument, *see* Parameter
Arithmetic-logic unit (ALU), 9, 138,
  165, 168–69
Array, 26, 29–30, 94, 100, 102–3, 104,
  125
  dimensions, 29
  element (subscripted variable), 29
  subscript (index), 29, 30
Artificial intelligence, 7, 127
ASCII, 99, 247–48
Assembler, 129, 141, 159–63
Assembly languages, 3, 121, 129, 137–
  58

Assignment statement, 32–34, 50
Associative relationship, 211
Atanasoff, John V., 5
Attribute, 104, 202, 214
Automata, 222, 230
Available space, 102

Babbage, Charles, 4, 127
Backup, 216
Backus-Naur form, 124, 231
Base, *see* Radix
Base register, 158, 197
BASIC, 124, 125, 193
Batch, 187
  processing, 189, 191–92, 194–95, 205
begin-end (compound statement), 37,
  49–50
Binary arithmetic, 239–44
Binary search, 64–66
Binary system, 139, 233–34
Binary tree, 111–12
Binding, 197
Bipolar memory, 172
Bit, 10, 26, 95, 98–99, 101, 137, 171,
  234
Bit/sense line, 172
Blank, 98, 114, 116
Block (in programming languages), 84
Block (in secondary storage), 173,
  203–4
  transfer, 147
Blocking, 203–5
  factor, 204
Block-structured languages, 83–85
BNF notation (Backus-Naur form),
  124, 231
Boole, George, 250

Boolean algebra, 39, 250–53
Boolean (logical) data, 27, 98, 250, 252
Bootstrapping, 187
Bubble sort, 55–58
Bucket, 210
Buffering, 189, 204–5
Bus, 166, 179
Business data processing, 191–92
Byte, 99, 138, 171
Byte-addressable computer, 138, 140

Cache memory, 170, 172
Call (invocation), 68–70, 72–74, 76
  by name, 80–82
  by reference (address), 78–79, 82
  by value, 79–82
  by value-result, 80, 82
Card reader/punch, 10, 178
Cartridge, tape, 177
case (multiple choice) statement, 37, 59, 62–63
Cassette, tape, 177
Central processing unit (CPU), 2, 5, 9–10, 165–69, 180–81, 194–95
Channel, 179, 189
Character, 98, 138
  codes, 99, 114, 116, 138, 140, 220, 247–49
  sets, 98, 177
  strings, 27, 94, 103, 114–17
Characteristic (exponent), 96, 98, 245
Charge-coupled devices, 173
Chess by computer, 110
Chip, 5, 257
Chomsky, Noam, 230
Chomsky hierarchy, 226
Church's thesis, 223, 226
Circuit switching, 182
Clock time, 168
COBOL, 31, 72, 74, 77, 78, 85, 87, 104, 124, 125–26, 215
Coincident-current principle, 172
Collating sequence, 99, 116
Collision, 209
Column-major order, 103
Comments, in programming, 35
Common (global) data, 68, 78, 83–84
Communication, computer, 181–83
Compiler, 129–34, 230, 232
Complement arithmetic, 241
Complement representation, 140, 241–44

Complex data, 95, 98
Compound statement (begin-end), 37, 49–50
Computability, 219, 222–23
Computability theory, 217
Computational complexity, 222
Computer(s):
  graphics, 7, 177
  logic, 253–57
  science, 121–22
  system, 2, 121–22, 165
  types of, described, 1, 2, 5
Concatenation, 115
Conceptual schema, 202, 214
Condition, in statements, 37–41
Condition code, 147
Console, operator, 178, 187
Constant, 27, 32
Content index, 211–12
Context (status) block, 194
Context-free languages, 230–32
Context-sensitive languages, 230
Controller, in CPU, 166–67, 169
Control memory, 169
Control unit, 9, 165–69
Cooperating processes, 196
Copy rule, 81
Core, magnetic, 172
Counting loop, see Loop—indexed
CSMP, 124, 129
Cycle-stealing, 179
Cycle time:
  CPU, 168
  main memory, 168, 171
Cylinder, 176

DASD, see Direct-access storage devices
Data, 1, 26, 94–117, 201
  acquisition, 194
  complex, 95, 98
  description language, 214
  dictionary, 216
  double-precision, 95, 98, 245–46
  integer, 27, 95–96
  item (simple data) 25, 26, 27, 94; See also Field—record
  logical (Boolean), 27, 98, 250, 252
  manipulation language, 215
  numerical, 27, 94–98, 233–46
  structures, 7, 15, 25, 26, 30, 94, 99–102
  type, 26–27, 31, 94, 127

FORTRAN *(cont'd)*
127, 215
FORTRAN 77, 74, 127
Forward reference, 159
Front-end processor, 181
Function (in mathematical logic), 218
Function (in programming), 68, 75–77
   intrinsic (built-in), 77, 116
Function reference, 75–76

Gate, 253–54
Generations of computers, 5
Global data, 68, 78, 83–84
Gödel, Kurt, 219
Gödel numbering, 218–19, 221
goto statement, 37, 51–52, 63
GPSS, 124, 129
Grammar, 228, 230
Graph (network; plex), 112–14, 213
   directed (digraph), 113

Half-adder, 225
Halting problem, 221–22
Hard-copy devices, 177
Hardware, 2, 17
Hardwired control, 169
Hashing, (randomizing), 209–10
Head, read/write, 174, 175
Hexadecimal system, 140, 234–35, 238–39
Hierarchical computer network, 182
Hierarchical relationship, 212
Higher level programming languages, 3, 6, 16, 18, 26, 31, 35, 66–67, 84, 94, 116, 121, 123–29, 141, 162, 230
Hollerith, Herman, 4

Identifier, 52, 69, 126, 130
if-then-else (decision statement), 37, 42–45, 51
Immediate addressing, 154
Indexed addressing, 155–56, 168
Indexed loop, *see* Loop statement
Indexed sequential file, 206, 207–8
Index of indexed sequential file, 207
Index register, 155
Indirect addressing, 156, 158, 168–69
Indirect (defer) phase, 168
Infix notation, 132
Information, 1
Initialization of job, 195

Initial program load (IPL), 187
Input/output:
   control system (IOCS), 198–99
   devices, 2, 9, 10, 31–32, 177–78
   See also Terminal
Inputs of program, 20, 21, 26
Input statement, 31–32, 50
Instruction, 1, 2, 9–10, 17, 21, 137
   counter, 166–69
   execution cycle, 167–68
   memory reference, 142
   register, 166–68
   register-to-register, 142
   set, 3, 137, 142
Integer data, 27, 95–96
Integer division, 33, 95
Integrated circuit, 257
Intelligent terminal, 177, 181
Interactive computing, 124, 190
Interface:
   between modules, 72, 93
   table, 90, 93
Internal schema, 214
Interpreted languages, 125, 127, 128, 135
Interpreter, 134–35
Interrecord gap, 204
Interrupt, 169, 179
   handler, 169
   input/output, 179
Inverted file, 211
Invocation, *see* Call
Iteration, 48, 89
   See also Loop statement

Jacquard, Joseph, 4
Job, 194–95
   control language, 191

Key, 64, 90, 104, 107, 202, 206, 209, 211
   secondary, 211
Keyword, 130

Label, 52, 64, 67, 99, 141
Lambda calculus, 222
Large scale integration (LSI), 5
Last-in–first-out list (LIFO; stack), 87, 90, 109, 147
Latency time (rotational delay) 174, 176
Leibniz, Gottfried, 4

State variable, 256
Step, 187
Stepwise refinement, 15, 37, 52, 90
  See also Top-down design
String (in formal languages), 228
String (in programming), *see* Character—strings
Structure chart, 90, 92
Structured programming, 37, 66, 127
Subprogram (procedure), 15, 68–69
  internal, 83
  See also Module
Subroutine, 68, 69–75, 163
Subschema (external schema), 202, 215
Subscripted variable (array element), 49
Substring, 115
Supervisor mode, 198
Supervisor system, *see* Operating system
Switching circuit, 253–56
  combinational 254–55
  sequential, 256
Switching in computer networks, 182–83
Switching variable, 250
Swapping, 194–95, 197
Symbolic addressing, 28
Symbolic processing, *see* Word processing
Symbol table, 130, 160–61
Syntactic analysis, 130–32
Syntax, 226–27
System, of programs, 68, 90
Systems programming, 158

Table, 105
Task (process), 194–95
  status (context) block, 194
Telecommunication monitor, 186
Teletypewriter, 177
Terminal, 10, 177, 181–82, 190, 192
Terminal symbol, 228
Three-address code, 131, 133
Throughput, 189
Thunk, 81
Time-sharing, 190, 193–94
Time slicing 190
Token, 130
Top-down design, 23, 52–58, 90
  See also Stepwise refinement
Track, 174–76

Transaction, 205
  file, 90, 191
  processing system, *see* On-line systems
Transfer of control, 26, 145–47
  unconditional (**goto** statement), 37, 51–52, 63
Transfer rate, 173
Transition table, 256
Translators, 3, 9, 18, 26, 28, 30, 31, 77, 97, 101, 123, 141, 184, 187
  See also Assembler; Compiler; Interpreter
Traversal (of tree), 112
Tree, 110–12, 213
  binary, 111–12
Trigger, 256
Truncation, 97
Truth table, 39, 250–51, 254–55
Turing, Alan, 4, 223
Turing machine, 218, 222–26
Turnaround time, 189, 191, 194
Two's complement, 241, 243–45

Underflow, 97, 245
Uniprogramming, 187–88
UNIVAC I, 5
Universal Turing machine, 226
Unsolvable problems, 221–22
User mode, 198
Utility programs, 3, 185

Variable, 27–29, 32
  initialization of, 95
  name, 28, 31–32, 52, 67
  scope of, 83–84
Virtual memory, 170, 197–98
Volatility of memory, 172
Volume, 175
Von Neumann, John, 5

WATFIV, 127
WATFOR, 127
Wait loop, 178–79
while-do, *see* Loop statement
Word (in memory), 10, 95, 98, 99, 101, 138, 171, 173, 179
  length, 138
  line, 172
Word (symbolic; text) processing, 7, 27, 94, 114–17, 124, 127, 128
Write into memory, 10, 34, 171–72